欢迎：中学汉语课本

HUANYING

An Invitation to Chinese

JIAYING HOWARD AND LANTING XU

VOLUME 4

Cheng & Tsui Company
Boston

18 17 16 15 14 13 12 11 1 2 3 4 5 6 7 8 9 10

Published by
Cheng & Tsui Company, Inc.
25 West Street
Boston, MA 02111-1213 USA
Fax (617) 426-3669
www.cheng-tsui.com
"Bringing Asia to the World"™

Hardcover edition:
ISBN 978-0-88727-738-2

Paperback edition:
ISBN 978-0-88727-786-3

Library of Congress Cataloging-in-Publication Data

Howard, Jiaying.
Huanying : an invitation to Chinese = [Huan ying : Zhong xue Han yu ke ben] / by Jiaying Howard and Lanting Xu.
p. cm.
Chinese and English.
Includes index.
Parallel title in Chinese characters.
ISBN 978-0-88727-662-0 (v. 1) -- ISBN 978-0-88727-615-6 (v. 1 : pbk.) 1. Chinese language--Textbooks for foreign speakers--English. I. Xu, Lanting, 1963 Jan. 28- II. Title. III. Title: An invitation to Chinese. IV. Title: Huan ying : Zhong xue Han yu ke ben.

PL1129.E5H67 2008
495.1'82421--dc22

2008062314

Illustrations: Murray Thomas, Landong Xu, Qiguang Xu and Augstine Liu
Photos: Pezhi Bai, Lanting Xu, Jiaying Howard, and Chuan Zhuang
Textbook design: Linda Robertson
Chinese text editing: Irene Liu

Printed in Canada

PUBLISHER'S NOTE

Demand for Chinese curricular materials at the secondary school level has never been greater. In response, Cheng & Tsui is pleased to offer *Huanying*—the first comprehensive secondary-school series written by experienced Chinese teachers in North American schools and based on ACTFL National Content Standards for Foreign Language Learning. Designed specifically for the North American classroom, *Huanying* offers a learner-centered communicative approach, a great variety of engaging activities, contemporary topics that appeal to secondary school students, a full-color textbook design, and additional resources that will reduce teacher preparation time and allow teachers to focus on teaching.

The Cheng & Tsui Chinese Language Series is designed to publish and widely distribute quality language learning materials created by leading instructors from around the world. We welcome readers' comments and suggestions concerning the publications in this series. Please contact the following members of our Editorial Board, in care of our Editorial Department (e-mail: **editor@cheng-tsui.com**).

ONLINE RESOURCES

Audio Downloads

Users of this textbook have access to free, downloadable audio files that correspond to both the textbook and workbook for *Huanying*, Volume 4. The sections in your textbook and workbook that have corresponding audio files are marked with an audio CD icon: . To download the audio files, you simply need to register your product key on our website.

Your Product Key: 7UNE-RANU

Instructions for Downloading Audio Files:

1. Visit the Cheng & Tsui Download Center at **http://www.cheng-tsui.com/downloads**
2. Enter your product key.
3. Download the audio files.
4. For technical support, please contact support@cheng-tsui.com or call 1-800-554-1963.

Textbook Audio Content:

- Dialogues
- New Words

Workbook Audio Content:

- Listening Practice

peerSource

Teachers and students of all Asian languages can find and share resources, ideas, classroom activities, and more at Cheng & Tsui's free online community, PeerSource (my.cheng-tsui.com).

CONTENTS

UNIT 4 往前看 Looking Forward

PREFACE

Huanying: An Invitation to Chinese (欢迎：中学汉语课本) is a series designed for secondary school students who are non-native speakers of Chinese with minimal or no background in Mandarin Chinese. Following the *Standards for Foreign Language Learning* developed by the American Council on the Teaching of Foreign Languages (ACTFL), *Huanying* offers four volumes covering four years of study at the secondary school level and taking students to an intermediate-high level of language proficiency, or the equivalent of two years of college Chinese.

Huanying is organized around thematic units that are essential to everyday communication. All material in each unit—vocabulary, grammar, idiomatic expressions, and culture—is carefully developed with learners' interests and real-life uses in mind. *Huanying* intends to develop language proficiency by taking students gradually from their immediate surroundings to the bigger world. The topic domain is similar throughout the series—self, family, school, daily life, and the larger community—with each subsequent volume building more complexity and depth into the themes and calling for more complex language use. Throughout the series, students learn vocabulary related to each theme, grammar and idiomatic expressions needed to communicate about the theme, and cultural information that helps to contextualize the language use. Language practice focuses on authentic communicative tasks that integrate several modalities of language skills and are intellectually engaging. Individual, pair, and group activities are rooted in meaningful contexts that appeal to students' interests and allow them to present, interpret, and negotiate meanings through active communication.

Each volume of *Huanying* is designed for an entire school year, based on one instructional hour (50 minutes) of language class per day. With language use gaining more depth and complexity, the length of material grows as well. Six units comprise Volumes 1 and 2 and four units Volumes 3 and 4. Each unit includes five lessons and one unit review lesson. Teachers may plan to use five hours to study one lesson for Volumes 1 and 2, and seven to eight hours per lesson in Volumes 3 and 4. After the unit review lesson, a unit test can be given to students to assess their learning; pre-prepared unit tests appear in the *Huanying Teacher's Book.*

What Is the Pedagogical Philosophy Behind *Huanying*?

Our Goal: Communication and Self-Awareness

Huanying was developed based on a belief that the purpose of learning Chinese is not only to communicate in Chinese accurately and appropriately, but also to develop competence in shaping the content of interactions by understanding speakers of other languages. *Huanying* is designed to help students achieve this goal through monitored language input via sequenced and organized instruction; vigorous language practice via performance-based communicative tasks and constant reinforcement of language skills; systematic evaluation via quizzes, unit tests, and student self-assessment; and in-depth experience of the rich and varied social and cultural contexts in which language practice is embedded. All of the above serve the purpose of helping students communicate in Chinese from the very first day of class and gradually develop the knowledge and ability not only to understand but also to reflect.

Our Content: Incorporating the "5 C's"

Huanying reflects the philosophy outlined by the *Standards for Foreign Language Learning* developed by the American Council on the Teaching of Foreign Languages (ACTFL). Incorporating the principles of "5 C's" (Communication, Culture, Connections, Comparisons, Communities), it strives to provide students with the necessary knowledge and skills that will enable them to be "linguistically and culturally equipped to communicate successfully in a pluralistic American society and abroad." *Huanying*'s primary focus is on meaningfulness, which is the core of communication. By embedding language input and output in communicative tasks set in a broader socio-cultural context, *Huanying* requires students to draw from other academic disciplines and the knowledge of their own cultures to facilitate their understanding of Chinese language and culture. *Huanying* also provides students with opportunities to extend their knowledge in Chinese by exploring the Chinese-speaking communities around them. The ultimate goal of *Huanying* is for students to become more aware of themselves, as well as their own language and culture, through the study of Chinese.

Our Approach: Teaching for Understanding

Huanying differs from traditional Chinese language instructional approaches by adopting an integrated approach that promotes teaching for understanding. Instead of teaching discrete bits and pieces of language (vocabulary, sentence structures, and idiomatic expressions) through repetitive drills without any meaningful context, *Huanying* takes real-life communication tasks as its starting point. This holistic approach allows *Huanying* to teach vocabulary, grammar, and cultural information not in isolation, but rather in context. In order to enhance accuracy in language use, language points are practiced in context. Practice of form, meaning, and function are always interwoven in the communication tasks. Through varied forms of learning tasks, students learn to comprehend, use, and analyze the Chinese language. In brief, *Huanying's* approach affords students opportunities to construct their own understanding of new concepts and, therefore, to become more effective learners. Based on our belief in teaching for understanding, *Huanying* pays particular attention to topics and situations that are both authentic and appealing to students. Authenticity and relevance are motivational tools that produce life-long learners.

Our Strategy for Success: Negotiate Meaning in Context

Successful language learners know how to negotiate meaning by relying on their previous knowledge and by analyzing and discovering cues from the communicative context. To help students become successful language learners, the activities in *Huanying* are designed to stimulate students' schemata, or schemes of how one perceives the world, to aid students in comprehension—understanding both the main ideas and specific information—and to guide students step-by-step through challenging tasks. *Huanying* also tries to convey the idea that language proficiency cannot be achieved from word-by-word translation. Effective learners approach language learning by looking at context and structure, not by putting together dictionary definitions.

Huanying involves students in every step of the learning process. Students not only actively participate in learning activities, but also make decisions about using appropriate strategies to accomplish tasks. To help students build a tolerance for some ambiguity and risk as they explore a new language, we have purposefully made certain pedagogical decisions: 1) In general, we do not provide English translations for dialogues and texts in the textbook and workbook. In Book 4, a cultural segment is added. Because its content is quite different from the dialogues and texts students have learned so far, a loose English translation is provided to facilitate students' understanding. 2) In the texts and activities we include some new words that are not glossed yet but they do not interfere with students' overall comprehension of the text/task. 3) We gradually decrease the use of pinyin as learning progresses 4) Starting from Volume 3, we gradually increase the use of Chinese in language explanation and culture information. 5) We ask students to periodically assess their own learning.

How Is *Huanying* Structured?

The structure of *Huanying* can be best described by using the "3 P's" (Presentation, Practice, Production) language instruction model as an analogy. The textbook focuses on presentation, and the student workbook focuses on practice and production.

As many teachers still rely on textbooks as the starting point for class organization and planning, we want to assist teachers to achieve success in their teaching. The textbook and workbook are derived from a carefully planned communicative curriculum, with corresponding goals and tasks. The teacher's book is intended to make lesson preparation more efficient for busy teachers; it contains workbook activities, answer keys, suggestions on how to facilitate a learner-centered classroom, plus quizzes and unit tests.

Textbook

Volume 4 of *Huanying* includes four units, each focusing on one theme. There are five lessons and a review lesson in each unit, so that two units are typically covered per semester. Learning goals are clearly stated at the beginning of each unit, and students can check their progress by taking a self-assessment questionnaire at the end of the unit. A typical lesson consists of two dialogues or texts (with new vocabulary highlighted in color), a new word list (with simplified and traditional characters, pinyin, parts of speech, and English explanations), language notes, some knowledge-related language activities ("Extend Your Knowledge"), a brief review of learned materials ("Gain New Insight through Review"), and information about Chinese proverbs, idioms, legends, stories, and culture.

At the end of the textbook four indexes are provided: vocabulary (Chinese-English and English-Chinese), proper nouns, and language notes. There is also an appendix of dialogues and texts in traditional characters, designed for students who would like to learn traditional Chinese characters alongside simplified ones.

Workbooks

The workbook component contains a wealth of communicative, ready-to-use language activities and is divided into two parts: Volume 4 Part 1 for the first semester, and Volume 4 Part 2 for the second semester. For each lesson, the workbook has three types of language practice: Listening Practice, Integrated Language Practice, and Writing Practice. Listening Practice involves two or more skills—usually listening/reading, listening/writing, listening/speaking, etc. It is distinct from Integrated Language Practice because students will need the accompanying audio files to complete these activities. Integrated Language Practice includes a variety of communicative activities such as interviews, bingo, board games, role-play, email correspondence, oral reports, and more. Students will benefit from this hands-on format that lets them use different language skills simultaneously (for example, interviewing a classmate while taking notes and filling out a chart in the workbook). Teachers will benefit because all of the activities are presented in a convenient, ready-to-use format—students can do all activities directly in their workbooks and photocopying other materials is not necessary. Writing Practice (in place of Chinese Character Practice in Volumes 1 and 2) focuses on helping students master the new words and sentence structures while improving language accuracy. It can also be used for homework assignments.

Audio Files

Huanying's accompanying audio files contain recordings of the dialogues, texts, and vocabulary in the textbook, along with audio clips to be used for Listening Practice in the workbook. Audio files can be downloaded free of charge from the publisher's website: http://www.cheng-tsui.com/downloads/huanying.

Teacher's Books

The teacher's book includes copies of all student workbook activities with answer keys, together with "Notes to the Teacher" (in both simplified Chinese and English) that help teachers effectively conduct the activities and facilitate a communicative classroom environment. Additional information at the front of the book includes general tips on lesson planning and classroom management, and an overview chart of content covered in the course. The appendix contains quizzes and unit tests, with answer keys. Two quizzes are provided for every lesson: one is a vocabulary quiz that can be given at the beginning of the lesson or after the vocabulary is learned, and the other is a general quiz that can be given at the end of the lesson. Preparing for quizzes and tests is made simple for teachers—just a matter of photocopying.

Acknowledgments

First of all, we would like to thank Ron and Ken for their support and understanding when we spent more time with *Huanying* than with them. Without them, *Huanying* would be impossible.

We wish to thank our illustrators Dr. Murray R. Thomas, Qiguang Xu, Landong Xu, and Augustine Liu for creating wonderful line art to suit our special instructional needs. Many thanks also go to Chuan Zhuang and Peizhi Bai for giving us permission to use their photographs. We would also like to thank the many Chinese language teachers whom we met at professional conferences and workshops. Their professional support and encouragement are invaluable to the compilation of this textbook series. Our gratitude also goes to the Chinese language students at Bellarmine College Preparatory and La Jolla Country Day

School. Their unique perspectives and insightful comments serve as a constant reminder that this textbook series is designed for them and that the successful implementation of the curriculum relies, by and large, on their involvement.

Last, but not least, we would like to thank the editors at Cheng & Tsui for their meticulous reading of our manuscripts and their suggestions and comments to make *Huanying* a better series.

We hope that *Huanying* will introduce secondary school students to Chinese language and culture in a practical and engaging way. Learning a foreign language opens up a new world for exploration, and the new world welcomes (*huanying*) young adventurers.

ABBREVIATIONS OF PARTS OF SPEECH

Abbreviation	*Part of Speech*
abbr.	abbreviation
adj.	adjective
adv.	adverb
aux.w.	auxiliary word
conj.	conjunction
excl.	exclamation
m.w.	measure word
n.	noun
num.	number
ono.	onomatopoeias
o.v.	optative verb
part.	particle word
p.n.	proper noun
prep.	preposition
pron.	pronoun
s.p.	set phrase
v.	verb
v.c.	verb plus complement
v.o.	verb plus object

第一单元：世界在变化

UNIT 1 The World Is Changing

LEARNING GOALS OF UNIT 1

By the end of this unit, you will learn how to:

- Give detailed descriptions of travel
- Give detailed descriptions of everyday objects
- Give detailed descriptions of various places
- Give detailed descriptions of facilities
- Give detailed descriptions of common practices
- Describe, in some detail, computer technology
- Narrate, in some detail, a present event in logical sequence
- Narrate, in some detail, a past event in logical sequence
- Summarize the major characteristics of a phenomenon

1.1 交通越来越方便了
Transportation Has Become More Convenient

对话一

大卫：汤姆，暑假你去哪儿玩了？

汤姆：我先去北京看了爷爷奶奶，然后跟他们一起参加了一个"东北五日游"的旅行团。你呢？

大卫：我回了一次香港，还去法国看了我爷爷奶奶。

汤姆：你在法国住了多久？

大卫：三个星期。我原来打算在爷爷奶奶家住两个星期，然后坐火车从法国去意大利玩一个星期，最后从意大利回香港。可是我在法国的那三个星期，差不多天天下大雨，铁路交通受到了影响，结果我没去成意大利。

汤姆：从法国坐火车去意大利要很长时间吗？

大卫：不，十多个小时，晚上上火车，第二天上午就到了。

汤姆：那跟从上海坐火车去北京差不多。这次，我和杰米就是坐动车去北京的。路上才用了十个小时。我们早上出发，晚上就到了。要是去的地方不太远，我觉得坐火车旅行比坐飞机有意思。在火车上，可以看到许多不同的风景。

大卫：我同意，所以我本来打算坐火车去意大利，可惜最后没去成。在去北京的路上，你看到什么？

汤姆：很多城市和乡村，还有许多自然景色。在上海住久了，我特别喜欢农村的景色。

大卫：那你去东北的时候，有没有机会去农村参观一下？

汤姆：那个旅行团安排我们去参观了两个村子。为了让我们了解以前中国的农民是怎么生活的，我们坐了一个多小时的马车，从第一个村子到第二个村子去。

大卫：那两个村子离得挺远的吧？

汤姆：不太远，要是坐汽车大概十五分钟。

大卫：马车走得那么慢？坐飞机从香港到上海也只需要一个多小时。

汤姆：我觉得坐坐马车也不错，让我知道以前大家是怎么旅行的。导游说，以前，那个地方没有公路，也没有汽车。要去别的地方，大家只能坐马车或者走路。

大卫：现在大不一样了，交通越来越方便，世界也变得越来越小了。

对话二

凯丽：　上个周末你做什么了？

玛丽娅：星期六在家做作业，星期天我去看张爷爷了。

凯丽：　张爷爷现在身体怎么样？

玛丽娅：从找到优盘以来，他一直在写小说，精神很好，身体也比以前好了。那天我去他家的时候，他的一个高中同学从美国来看他。他们在一起谈得很高兴。

凯丽：　高中同学？张爷爷是什么时候上高中的？

玛丽娅：大概是四十年代吧。他的老同学林爷爷是一九四七年去美国上大学的。对了，你知道林爷爷从上海去旧金山花了多长时间吗？

凯丽：　一两天吗？

玛丽娅：不。他说花了差不多一个月。先从上海坐船去香港，这样就花了五六天。然后再从香港坐船去旧金山，又用了三个星期。

凯丽：　这么长时间啊？

玛丽娅：对，我听了也吓了一跳。好在那是六十多年以前的情况。林爷爷说，现在他住在旧金山附近，这次他从离开家到上海，一共才用了十几个小时。他先坐轻轨去旧金山机场，在旧金山上飞机，过了十多个小时就到上海了。下飞机以后，他坐机场专线车直接就到了旅店。林爷爷一再说，现在的交通真是太方便了。

凯丽：　从一个月减少到十几个小时。再过六十年，大概一两个小时就能从中国到美国了吧？

玛丽娅：谁知道呢？那时候也不知道我们住在哪儿。可是只要有机会，我一定会去看你的。

凯丽：　好，一言为定。

生词

	Simplified	*Traditional*	*Pinyin*	*Part of Speech*	*English*
1.	游	遊	yóu	*v.*	tour
2.	铁路	鐵路	tiělù	*n.*	railway, railroad
3.	可惜		kěxī	*adj.*	it's a pity, it's too bad, unfortunate
4.	自然		zìrán	*adj./n.*	natural, nature
5.	景色		jǐngsè	*n.*	scenery, scene
6.	村子		cūnzi	*n.*	village
7.	农民	農民	nóngmín	*n.*	farmer
8.	马车	馬車	mǎchē	*n.*	horse cart, horse-drawn carriage
9.	大概	大概	dàgài	*adj./adv.*	about, approximately, probably
10.	公路		gōnglù	*n.*	highway
11.	轻轨	輕軌	qīngguǐ	*n.*	light rail
12.	一再		yīzài	*adv.*	repeatedly, time and again
13.	减少		jiǎnshǎo	*v.*	decrease, reduce
14.	一言为定	一言為定	yī yán wéi dìng	*s.p.*	it's a deal, a promise is a promise

专名

15.	东北	東北	dōngběi		Northeast

语言注释

1. 可惜 (It's a pity..., it's too bad ..., unfortunate)

When something didn't happen as you had expected or planned, you can use 可惜 to express disappointment or regret. 可惜 is an adjective, which can be used as a comment to begin a sentence, or as a predicate.

Used at the beginning of a sentence

可惜今天汤姆没有来。要不然我们的晚会会更热闹。
It's a pity that Tom didn't come today. Otherwise, our party would have been livelier.

可惜我帮不了你的忙。
It is unfortunate that I won't be able to help you.

Used as a predicate

昨天你没有去听讲座很可惜。那个讲座有意思极了。
That you didn't go to the lecture yesterday is a shame. That lecture was extremely interesting.

他不去上大学很可惜。
That he didn't attend college is unfortunate.

2. 大概 (About, approximately, probably)

大概 can be used either as an adjective or an adverb. When it is an adjective, it is usually placed before a number, with the meaning of 差不多 or 左右 (about, approximately).

从上海飞到北京大概两小时。
It took about two hours to fly from Shanghai to Beijing.

这台电脑大概五千元。
This computer costs around 5000 yuan.

大概 can also be used as an adverb, with the meaning of 可能 or 也许 (perhaps, probably).

今天下午大概要下雨。
Perhaps it will rain this afternoon.

他大概太忙了，所以没有来玩滑板。
He was probably too busy, so he didn't come skateboarding.

3. 从···以来 (Since...)

从···以来 is a time phrase that indicates a period of time — from a point of time in the past up to now. This time phrase is usually placed at the beginning of a sentence.

从去年三月以来，他就住在北京。
Since last March, he has been living in Beijing.

从新超市开门以来，每天去那儿买东西的人都很多。
Since the new supermarket opened, every day there are a lot of people who go there to shop.

4. 一再 (Repeatedly, time and again)

一再 is an adverb, usually used before a verb to indicate a repeated action.

我一再请他来，可是他总是没空。
I have repeatedly invited him to come, but he is always busy.

老师一再说，做完了作业应该再检查一遍。
The teacher said time and again that we should check our finished homework.

学无止境

Now you have learned some words about tours, travel, and transportation. Here are a few more words related to tours. Pinyin is provided for new characters only.

特价游 *tour special*	旅游网 *tourism website*	一日游 *one-day tour*
豪 (háo) 华游 *luxurious tour*	自助游 *self-guided tour*	旅游线路 *tour route*
出发城市 *starting city*	出行天数 *number of days on tour*	出发日期 *starting date*
景区 *scenic area*	全程导游 *tour guide throughout the trip*	导游服务 *tour guide services*
门票自理 *entrance ticket not included*	午餐自理 *lunch not included*	空调旅游车 *air-conditioned coach*

YOUR TURN:

See if you understand the following two advertisements on a tourism website.

北京长城一日游 *¥130*

 长城	定金: ¥50 出发城市：北京 出行天数：1天 出发日期：天天发团 门票：长城门票 午餐：中餐，十人一桌，八菜一汤，酒水自理 欢迎在线预定或者电话预订：4000-9797

Based on the above advertisement, briefly describe the tour. Your description needs to include when, where, and what.

特价美西旅游“北美假期”为您提供美国西部7日游 ***$588***

 旧金山	主要景点：洛杉矶 (Luòshānjī, Los Angeles)、旧金山、优山美地(Yosemite)国家公园等美国西部有名的景点 出发日期：周一、二、四、五、六 特价：买二送一

线路行程 第一天：到达洛杉矶 第二天：洛杉矶一日游 第三天：洛杉矶→旧金山 第四天：旧金山一日游 第五天：优山美地国家公园一日游 第六天：圣地亚哥 (San Diego) 一日游 第七天：洛杉矶自由游 第八天：离开洛杉矶	 优山美地国家公园

Summarize the above tour according to the advertisement. Describe how the tour cost can be discounted.

温故知新 GAIN NEW INSIGHT THROUGH REVIEW

“温故知新”是中国的一个成语，意思是：在复习学过的知识的时候，我们会有一些新的想法，而且可以学到一些新的知识。

Now let's review some words. Place the following words into four categories.

公交	轻轨	船	自行车	飞机	码头
出租车	火车	马车	航班	汽车	游船
马路	航空公司	地铁	起飞	跑道	铁路
火车站	动车	机场专线车	公路	地铁站	机场

轨道 (rail) 交通	空中交通	地面交通	水上交通

中国文化一瞥

Chinese proverbs

The following proverbs can be used to describe transportation and travel. Pinyin is provided only for those phrases with new characters.

1. 四 通 八 达

lead in all directions; accessible from all directions; reach out in all directions

IN USE:

中国的铁路四通八达。

China's railways are accessible everywhere.

在一些大城市里，公共交通四通八达。

In some large cities, public transportation reaches out in all directions.

YOUR TURN:

Can you use 四通八达 to describe the following situations?

1. 如果你想去那个城市，可以坐飞机、火车、汽车和船。	可以	不可以
2. 这个地方有公路，可是没有公交车。所以如果你要去那儿，可以开车，或者骑自行车。	可以	不可以
3. 这儿是一个铁路中心，每天有许多从各地来的火车经过这儿。	可以	不可以
4. 浦东国际机场每天有许多国际航班，飞往世界各国。	可以	不可以

2. 四 面 八 方

four sides and eight directions; all around; all directions; on all sides

IN USE:

上海火车站总是人山人海的。每天从四面八方来到上海的旅客有一百多万。

The Shanghai Railway Station is always extremely crowded. Every day, more than a million people arrive in Shanghai from all over.

那个风景区四面八方都很美丽。

The scenic area is beautiful all around.

YOUR TURN:

Based on your own situation, answer the following questions:

1. 在你住的地方，要去四面八方容易吗？
2. 在你住的地方，居民是从四面八方来的吗？
3. 在你住的地方，能不能买到从四面八方来的东西？

3. xīng luó qí bù
星 罗 棋 布

scattered all over like stars in the sky or pieces on a chessboard; spread out, scattered everywhere

IN USE:

这个城市里公交车站星罗棋布，要去哪儿都非常方便。

Bus stops are scattered everywhere in the city. Going everywhere is convenient.

这个地区的风景点星罗棋布，随便你往哪儿走，都可以到达一个景点。

This area's scenic spots are scattered everywhere. Whichever way you walk, you will reach a scenic spot.

YOUR TURN:

Select one word from the list and make a sentence with 星罗棋布.

超市	快餐店	咖啡馆	银行	饭店	礼品店

Chinese Legends

Introduction:

In Unit 1 you will be discussing the dramatic modernization that Chinese people have experienced since the early 1980s. While learning about the modern trends in people's daily lives, you may be wondering if the traditional Chinese worldview still has a hold on the Chinese imagination. To help you better understand the traditional Chinese beliefs, we have included some popular Chinese legends in this unit. Perhaps after reading these stories you will be able to tell whether the traditional values and beliefs still have a role in contemporary China.

Since the content is quite different from the texts you have learned so far, a loose English translation is provided to facilitate your understanding.

盘古开天地

中国人相信 (xiāngxìn, believe)，很久很久以前，天和地是合在一起的，没有被分开。那个时候，宇宙 (yǔzhòu, the universe) 就像一个大鸡蛋，里面一片混沌 (hùndùn, chaos)，也没有光亮。在这个鸡蛋里面住着一个人，叫盘古。他在这个"大鸡蛋"里睡了差不多十万八千年。睡醒 (shuìxǐng, wake up) 以后，看到周围 (zhōuwéi, around) 黑黑的，盘古就举 (jǔ, lift) 起手来一挥 (huī, wave)，一下子就把"大鸡蛋"打碎 (suì, broken) 了。鸡蛋里面又轻又清的东西慢慢地升 (shēng, rise) 起来，变成蓝色的天；那些又重又浊 (zhuó, muddy) 的东西就变成了地。盘古站在天地的中间，用手举着蓝天，脚踩 (cǎi, step on) 着大地，这样过了十万八千年，盘古把天和地永远 (yǒngyuǎn, forever) 分开了。

Pan Gu Creates the World

Many Chinese believe that, in the beginning heaven and the earth were not separated. The universe was formless chaos, much like a large egg. Inside this egg there lived a man whose name was Pan Gu. He slept in this "large egg" for roughly 180,000 years. When he woke up, he saw only darkness and chaos. He raised his arms and with a single wave, he broke the egg. Suddenly, the weightless and clear elements in the egg rose to become the blue sky, while the heavy and muddy elements formed the earth. Pan Gu stood between heaven and earth, holding the sky above him. After 18,000 years Pan Gu permanently separated heaven and earth.

YOUR TURN:

Does your culture have a creation myth? How is it similar to or different from the Chinese myth? Prepare an oral presentation in Chinese on a creation myth from your own culture.

你知道吗？

从1876年中国建造了第一条铁路以来，铁路交通已经成为中国人最常用的交通工具之一。中国的铁路四通八达，火车站星罗棋布，每天有三万多次列 (liè) 车 (scheduled trains) 开往中国的四面八方。

因为坐火车旅行的人非常多，所以如果你打算出去旅行，最好提前 (beforehand) 买好火车票，特别是如果你打算假日坐火车去外地旅行。中国铁路交通最忙的时候是春节以前的一两个星期。因为住在四面八方的人都要回家过年，所以火车非常挤。有时候，要买到火车票不太容易。春节前的一个月，不少人就开始忙着买火车票。

现在你可以上网去买火车票。中国的火车站也都卖火车票。城市里还有一些火车售 (shòu, sell) 票处 (Railways Ticket Office)。另外，如果你愿意付一点儿服务费，一些旅行社和旅店也能为你买火车票。根据季节，火车票的价格 (jiàgé, price) 会改变。春节以前，火车票的价格最贵。

1.2 卡的世界 A World of Cards

逛商店

对话一

凯丽： 今天晚上，我打算去东方百货公司逛一逛，你想去吗？

大卫： 我好像不需要买什么东西。不过，反正晚上没什么事，陪你去逛逛也行。你为什么非要去东方百货公司呢？那儿离学校挺远的。

凯丽： 哦，我过生日的时候，姥姥送给我一张东方百货公司的礼品卡，所以我想去那儿看看。

大卫：　听你一说，我想起来了，我需要买一个新钱包。我现在的钱包太小了。

凯丽：　哇，你发财了吗？需要大钱包放很多钱？

大卫：　不是，我是需要一个大钱包放很多卡。我的钱包只放得下五六张卡，可是我有差不多二十张卡，所以我得去买一个能放得下二十张卡的钱包。

凯丽：　你怎么会有那么多卡呢？

大卫：　你看，这是我的学生证、学校图书馆的借书证、上海图书馆的借书证、这里有交通卡、电话卡、信用卡、现金卡、银行卡、学生食堂的饭卡、超市的会员卡…

凯丽：　等一等，那张是什么卡？

大卫：　那是健身房的会员卡。

凯丽：　要放下这么多卡，的确需要一个大钱包。其实，我的卡也挺多的。除了那个健身房的会员卡以外，你有的卡我都有。看来，我也应该去东方百货公司买一个大一点儿的钱包。

大卫：　那好吧，晚上我们就去买钱包。

对话二

大卫：　你看，这是我昨天买的钱包，现在我的卡都有地方放了。

玛丽娅：你怎么有三张上海银行的卡呢？

大卫：　哦，这张是银行取款卡；这张是现金卡；这张是信用卡。

玛丽娅：去商店买东西的时候，这些卡都能用吧？

大卫：　不能用取款卡，但是可以用现金卡和信用卡。买完了东西，只要刷一下就行了。

玛丽娅：现金卡和信用卡有什么不同？

大卫：　现金卡需要你把钱先放到卡的账户里才能用。信用卡是你从银行借钱花，花完了以后，银行会告诉你一共借了多少钱，然后你再把钱还给银行。其实我平时不用信用卡。这是父母给我的，他们说只有在紧急情况下，我才能用。

玛丽娅：你说你需要把钱先放在现金卡里，这是什么意思？

大卫： 其实，我们用的很多卡都是一种现金卡。比如，你去买电话卡、交通卡、礼品卡什么的，都需要先付钱。你买了50元的电话卡，就可以打50元的电话。买了一个商店50元的礼品卡，就可以在那个商店买50元的东西。有些现金卡是银行发的，银行会根据你银行账户里有多少钱，来决定你可以花多少钱。如果你的账户里有50元，那么你可以用现金卡买50元的东西。

玛丽娅：这么说，现金卡就跟现金一样。那你带钱不就行了吗？

大卫： 带卡比带钱方便啊，一张卡又小又轻。

玛丽娅：听上去方便，其实也不一定。你想，我们去借书，要带借书证；去坐车，要带交通卡；去医务所，要带学生证；去买东西，要带现金卡；去超市，要带超市会员卡；去锻炼身体，要带健身房会员卡；去银行拿钱，要带取款卡。这个卡那个卡的，忘了带，或者带错了卡，就不能办事了。

大卫： 你说得对，所以我买了一个大钱包，把所有的卡都放在一起，这样去哪儿办事都没有问题了。

玛丽娅：也有问题，万一你的钱包丢了，你不就什么事都办不成了吗？

生词

	Simplified	Traditional	Pinyin	Part of Speech	English
1.	礼品卡	禮品卡	lǐpǐn kǎ	*n.*	gift card
2.	钱包	錢包	qiánbāo	*n.*	wallet
3.	学生证	學生証	xuéshēng zhèng	*n.*	student ID card
4.	借书证	借書証	jièshū zhèng	*n.*	library card
5.	信用		xìnyòng	*n.*	credit
6.	现金	現金	xiànjīn	*n.*	cash
7.	会员	會員	huìyuán	*n.*	membership, member
8.	的确		díquè	*adv.*	indeed, really
9.	取款		qǔkuǎn	*v.o.*	withdraw money
10.	刷（卡）		shuā (kǎ)	*v.(o.)*	swipe the card
11.	账户	賬戶	zhànghù	*n.*	account
12.	办	辦	bàn	*v.*	do, handle
13.	万一	萬一	wànyī	*conj.*	in case, if by any chance

专名

14.	东方	東方	Dōngfāng		East

语言注释

1. Directional complement to indicate results

In Lesson 1.2 of *Huanying*, Volume 2, we learned "directional complements," such as 过来、回去、起来 etc. These words tell us whether an action moves towards or away from the speaker. The same structure, however, can also be used to indicate the result of an action. For example, in Dialogue 1 of this lesson, David said, "我想起来了，我需要买一个新钱包。" (It occurred to me that I need to buy a new wallet.)

Note: This structure is used with a limited number of verbs. It may be more helpful, at this stage of learning, to remember 想起来 as a set phrase rather than figuring out if this structure will or will not go with a certain verb.

我想起来我把手机放在书包里了。
I remembered that I put my cell phone in my backpack.

这些问题我都回答出来了。
I have answered all the questions.

我们把那么多的东西都吃下去了。
We have eaten so much food.

你把大家说的记下来了吗?
Did you write down what everyone said?

2. 的确 (Indeed)

的确 is an adverb and is used before a verb or an adjective.

他的确来听讲座了吗? 我怎么没看见他?
Did he really come to the lecture? How come I didn't see him?

用交通卡的确很方便。
It is indeed convenient to use the mass transit card.

3. 来 (To indicate a "means to an end" relationship)

Sometimes, 来 is placed between two verbal phrases to indicate a relationship of "means" and "end." The 1st verbal phrase indicates the means and the 2nd verbal phrase shows the end.

老师根据什么来决定学生的学习成绩?
On what basis does a teacher decide a student's grade?

你能用什么方法来做这个数学难题呢?
What ways can you use to solve this difficult math problem?

你可以打电话来预定音乐会票。
You can call to reserve the concert tickets.

4. 这个Noun那个Noun的 (Too much of the same thing)

This is a colloquial expression, usually placed at the beginning of a sentence to draw people's attention to the topic. Then a comment is made about the topic. The two nouns after 这个 and 那个 can be the same. If you use two different nouns, their meanings should be related.

这个卡那个卡的，太麻烦了。
There are too many cards. It is inconvenient.

这个舅舅那个阿姨的，我妈妈的亲戚非常多。
There are so many uncles and aunts. My mother has many relatives.

购物中心里有这个店那个店的，昨天他逛了一天也没逛完。
The shopping center has too many stores. Yesterday he spent the day looking around, but still didn't look at every store.

5. 办（事）(Handle business/procedures/paperwork)

As in English, Chinese use different verbs for "doing things." 办 is usually used when we want to talk about taking care of business transactions, paperwork, procedural work, and office business.

下课以后我要去银行办事。
After class I will go to the bank to run an errand.

你知道我应该去哪儿办驾照吗？
Do you know where I should go to get a driver's license?

6. 万一 (In case)

万一 is a conjunction that forms a conditional clause. It means "just in case," or "if by any chance."

万一你忘了带借书证，就不能借书了。
If by any chance you happen to forget your library card, you won't be able to check books out.

万一有紧急情况，我可以用父母的银行卡。
In case there is an emergency, I can use my parents' bank card.

学无止境

We have learned about many types of cards. Here are some additional cards that are used in China. Pinyin is provided for new characters only.

Card	English	Notes
工作证	employee ID card	issued by the employer
身份 (fèn) 证	ID card	issued by the government
军 (jūn) 人证	military ID	issued by the military
居留证	resident card	issued by the local government, showing the resident is authorized to live and work in an area
工资卡	salary card (Similar to an ATM card)	Chinese employers directly deposit employees' salary to a bank. Employees use a 工资卡 to withdraw money from the bank
上网卡	Internet card	purchased to access the Internet via phone or cable services
无线上网卡	wireless card	purchased to access the Internet via wireless services
公费 医疗证	medical care ID card	this card is issued by the government and covers all medical costs for certain procedures and treatments
医保卡 or 保险卡 (in Taiwan)	medical insurance card	Chinese employees are insured through a government-sponsored plan. The card is also used as an ID card. It records the card-bearer's payment and balance data
会员证	membership card	usually issued by a professional, non-commercial organization

YOUR TURN:

Do you have some ideas about the differences between 证 and 卡? Tell your classmates what you think.

温故知新 GAIN NEW INSIGHT THROUGH REVIEW

We have learned quite a few proverbs and idioms about business and money. From the following list, choose five that are related to business and money.

不怕不识货，就怕货比货	五光十色
一寸光阴一寸金	挥金如土
酒肉朋友	一分钱一分货
十全十美	马到成功
视财如命	好货不便宜，便宜没好货

中国文化一瞥

Chinese proverbs

The following proverbs are used to describe a large quantity. Pinyin is provided only for those phrases with new characters.

1. bǐ bǐ jiē shì
比 比 皆 是
in abundance; be seen everywhere

IN USE:

在这条美食街上，小吃店比比皆是。
On this food street, snack shops can be seen everywhere.

去国外旅行，常常会觉得有趣的人和事比比皆是。
When traveling abroad, you often feel that interesting people and things are everywhere.

YOUR TURN:

Based on the description, name that place.

在这里，你看到	这是什么地方？
旅客比比皆是。	
汽车行人比比皆是	
各国食品比比皆是	
月饼比比皆是	

2. 不 计 其 数

countless

IN USE:

这本汉语词典非常好。不计其数的学生在用这本词典。

This Chinese dictionary is very good. Countless students are using it.

现代科学给我们的生活带来了不计其数的变化。

Modern science has brought countless changes to our life.

YOUR TURN:

The following are things you can find online. Circle those you think are countless and compare notes with a fellow student.

网页	博客	电子邮件	照片
新闻	音乐	电视剧	电影
商业网站	黑客	聊天室	网上电话

3. pū tiān gài dì

铺 天 盖 地

cover up the sky and the earth; overwhelm

IN USE:

科学的发展带来了铺天盖地的新词汇。
Scientific development has brought an overwhelming amount of new words.

你看外边的风雪铺天盖地。今天不用去学校吧？
Look, the blizzard blotted out everything. We don't need to go to school today, do we?

YOUR TURN:

Use 铺天盖地 to describe one phenomenon that you feel is overspreading. (Hints: new products, advertisements, homework, junk email…)

Chinese Legends

女娲 (Wā, a surname) 造人

女娲是中国传统故事里的一个女神 (nǚshén, goddess)。盘古把天地分开以后，女娲看着蓝色的天和绿色的地，心里很高兴。可是，因为在绿色的大地上没有人，只有动物，女娲觉得很寂寞 (jìmò, lonely)，所以她决定照着自己的样子，用黄土 (huángtǔ, loess) 和水，造出了一个个小泥人 (nírén, clay figurine)。她把这些小泥人一放到地上，小泥人就活了。他们跳啊，笑啊，非常高兴。慢慢地，女娲觉得这样一个一个地造泥人太慢了，于是她就用一根绳子 (shéngzi, string)，沾 (zhān, be stained with) 了黄泥，用力一挥，一点一点的黄泥洒 (sǎ, sprinkle) 在地上，都变成了人。中国人相信他们都是女娲的后代。

Nü Wa Creates Humans

Nü Wa is a goddess in Chinese mythology. After Pan Gu separated heaven and earth, Nü Wa enjoyed looking at the blue sky and green earth. However, after a while she felt lonely as there were no humans, only animals, living on earth. Using her own figure as a model, she took loess and water to mold small clay figurines. As soon as she placed each clay figurine onto the earth, it came to life. They danced and laughed and were very happy. Slowly, Nü Wa came to feel that molding each figure individually was too time consuming. She dipped a rope in clay and flicked it so blobs of clay landed everywhere; each of these blobs became a person. Many Chinese people still believe that they are the descendants of Nü Wa.

YOUR TURN:

Is there a myth about the origin of life in your own culture? How is your myth similar to or different from the Chinese myth? Prepare an oral presentation in Chinese on the creation myth or myths in your own culture.

你知道吗？

虽然在中国的城市里，用银行卡、现金卡、信用卡的人越来越多，但是多数的中国人还是用现金。在中国，除了一些大超市、大百货公司、大饭店、航空公司等等接受银行卡以外，许多小商店都只收现金。没有现金，在中国生活会很不方便。早上你去小吃店买早饭，中午去饭店吃午饭，晚上去菜场买点儿菜回家做饭，吃完了饭去看电影，在你家旁边的小店买点儿用的东西，这时候你都得用现金。

可是最近几年来，用卡的地方也一年比一年多了。发工资的时候，公司把员工的工资放到银行里。要用现金的时候，大家就拿着工资卡去银行拿钱。坐公交车的时候，不少人都用交通卡。这样你上了车只要刷一下卡，不用带很多零钱 (pocket change) 了。去超市买东西，那里用会员卡，有了会员卡，可以买到特价的东西。用手机可以买电话卡，卡里的钱打完了，可以再买一张，这样打电话比较便宜，不用每个月付电话服务费。想上网可以买上网卡，这样在什么地方都可以上网。中国人的生活也越来越离不开卡了。

小吃店

在公共汽车上

1.3 日新月异 Rapid Changes

课文一

Send	Reply	Reply All	Forward	Print	Delete

明英：你好！

自从你离开上海以后，两三个星期过去了。一直没有收到你的电邮，我们都非常想念你。

开学以后，我们都忙着学习。这是我们在高中的最后一年，老师怕我们考不上大学，所以给的作业比较多。我每天一下课就做作业，有时候要做四五个小时。大家都觉得学习压力挺大的。

这个学期我搬到新的宿舍楼去了，新楼生活很方便，不出宿舍楼，就能上网。楼里还有自动售货机，可以买到饮料和点心。幸亏新楼有这些服务，要不然，我得走十五分钟去天天超市才能买到吃的东西。学校旁边的那个小店关门了，因为那里要建设一个非常大的居民社区。现在工人每天24小时都在学校外边修路，要把只有两个车道的马路修成有四个车道的。听说，除了居民住房以外，还要盖学校、医院、社区图书馆、社区健身房、商业服务中心、科技服务中心等等。建设这个社区会用两三年的时间。也就是说，在我们毕业以前，我们每天都要经过建设工地。

自动售货机

虽然上海不是一个新城市，但是常常让人感觉到这是一个新城市，因为每天都有新的发展和新的变化。大理呢？那儿跟上海不太一样吧？

等着你的电邮！

凯丽

上海

课文二

Send	Reply	Reply All	Forward	Print	Delete

凯丽，你好！

很高兴收到你的电邮。请别怪我到今天才回信。我没有忘了你，也没有忘了大家，可是自从我们搬家到大理以后，一直上不了网。我们住的房子非常旧，没有电话，更没有宽带了，所以就没跟你联系。你可能会问，为什么不发短信给你。我到大理的第二天，就去大理旁边的一个大湖游泳，结果把手机放在湖边，忘了带回来了。因为手机丢了，又不能上网，所以就跟外边联系不上了。

我父母也希望我们家可以装宽带，这样上网会比较快。可是在这儿装宽带非常麻烦。昨天，他们找到了一个公司，那个公司建议我们装一个无线上网的设备。今天，终于又可以上网了。我马上就给你写信。请告诉玛丽娅、汤姆和大卫，我也会马上给他们写信的。

我父母这次来云南，是要研究中国少数民族的历史。他们觉得大理是一个非常理想的地方，因为有许多少数民族住在这儿。大理被分成古城和新城。我们现在住在古城。古城不太大，可是有六七百年的历史。虽然古城的房子比较旧，但是我们都很喜欢这里的文化历史。

大理的风景非常美丽，附近有一个大湖，还有一些山。这里的气候也很好，一年四季都很暖和。来大理非常方便，可以坐飞机、火车和汽车。如果放寒假的时候你有空，请一定到大理来。我可以做你的导游，带你走一走，看一看。

请问大家好！

明英

大理古城

生词

	Simplified	Traditional	Pinyin	Part of Speech	English
1.	日新月异	日新月異	rì xīn yuè yì	*s.p.*	change rapidly, change day by day
2.	自从	自從	zìcóng	*prep.*	since
3.	想念		xiǎngniàn	*v.*	miss, think about
4.	自动	自動	zìdòng	*adj.*	automatic
5.	售货机	售貨機	shòuhuòjī	*n.*	vending machine
6.	幸亏	幸虧	xìngkuī	*adv.*	fortunately, luckily
7.	关	關	guān	*v.*	close, shut, turn off
8.	车道	車道	chēdào	*n.*	(driving) lane
9.	住房		zhùfáng	*n.*	housing, house

10. 盖	蓋	gài	*v.*	build
11. 经过	經過	jīngguò	*v.*	pass, go by
12. 工地		gōngdì	*n.*	construction site
13. 装		zhuāng	*v.*	install
14. 无线	無線	wúxiàn	*adj.*	wireless
15. 设备	設備	shèbèi	*n.*	device, equipment
16. 终于	終於	zhōngyú	*adv.*	finally, in the end, at last
17. 理想		lǐxiǎng	*adj./n.*	ideal
18. 古		gǔ	*adj.*	ancient
19. 城		chéng	*n.*	city

专名

20. 大理	Dàlǐ	Dali (a city in Yunnan)

语言注释

1. 自从…以后 (From… on, since)

自从…以后 introduces a time phrase or a time clause. A past action or a point of time in the past is placed between 自从 and 以后.

自从他开始学习中文以后，他每天看中文电视节目。
Since he started to learn Chinese, he has been watching Chinese TV programs every day.

自从一九九一年以后，他们就住在这个社区。
Since 1991, they have lived in this community.

2. 幸亏 (Fortunately, luckily)

今天幸亏不下雨了，我们可以去打网球。
Fortunately, it has stopped raining today and we can go play tennis.

幸亏那个咖啡馆可以无线上网。
Fortunately, the café has wireless service.

3. 也就是说 (In other words)

After you say something, you can use 也就是说 to further clarify the meaning and implication of what was said.

汤姆喜欢独立生活。也就是说，他希望能离开父母自己一个人出去住。
Tom likes to live independently. In other words, he hopes he can leave his parents' place and live by himself.

常常有人说，中国的变化日新月异。也就是说，每天都有变化。
People often say that China is changing rapidly. In other words, every day, there is change.

4. 终于 (Finally, at last)

工人每天工作二十四个小时，终于在三天里把路修好了。
The workers worked 24 hours a day and finally had the road repaired in three days.

我找了很多地方，终于在房子后面找到了小猫。
I looked in many places and finally found the kitten behind the house.

学无止境

We have learned some words about infrastructure. Here are some additional words that are related to a city's infrastructure. Pinyin is provided for new characters only.

通信网络 (luò) *communication network*	供水系统 (tǒng) *water supply system*	供煤 (méi) 气系统 *gas supply system*
下水道 *sewer*	供电系统 *electricity supply system*	消防 (xiāofáng) *fire fighting*
医疗 (liáo) *medical care*	应急系统 *emergency system*	道路 *road*
邮电 *postal service*	城市建筑 *city building*	绿化地带 *green area*

YOUR TURN:

1. Try to find out how to say "infrastructure" in Chinese.
2. In the space provided below, write down six words that are related to your school's infrastructure. Compare notes with your classmates, and see if you can fill all the cells.

温故知新 GAIN NEW INSIGHT THROUGH REVIEW

We have learned many words about buildings and houses. See if you remember how to say the following in Chinese:

house		window	
architecture		bedroom	
the second floor		residential area	
a large building		student dormitory	
room		dining room	
front door		kitchen	
living room		historical building	

中国文化一瞥

Chinese proverbs

These proverbs are about change. Pinyin is provided only for those phrases with new characters.

1. wù huàn xīng yí
物 换 星 移
Things change and stars move; things change

IN USE:

虽然物换星移，但是我们永远是朋友。
Although things change, we will be friends forever.

物换星移，我的老家跟十年以前不一样了。
Things change. My hometown is different from ten years ago.

YOUR TURN:

Which of the two opinions do you support? Try to elaborate on it with some examples.

1. 物换星移，我觉得世界上每件事都会变化。
2. 虽然物换星移，可是我觉得世界上有些事是不会变化的。

2. 改 天 换 地
transform heaven and earth; change the world

IN USE:

最近五年，这里有了改天换地的变化。
In the last five years, great changes have taken place here.

中国一百年来的历史是改天换地的历史。
China's history in the last century is a history of great changes.

YOUR TURN:

Can you use 改天换地 to describe the following situations?

以前这儿是农村，现在这儿是城市。	可以	不可以
以前考试，她在前六名，现在她在前三名。	可以	不可以
以前小弟考试总是不及格，现在是全班第一。	可以	不可以
五十年前坐船去美国要二十多天，现在坐飞机去美国只要十二个小时。	可以	不可以

3. tiān fān dì fù
天 翻 地 覆

heaven and earth are overturned; the whole world is turned upside down

IN USE:

爸爸一出门，家里就天翻地覆了，我吃完了所有的饼干，小妹爬上了树，猫到冰箱里把鱼都吃完了。

As soon as Dad left, our house was turned upside down. I ate all the cookies, Little Sister climbed up a tree, and our cat went into the refrigerator and ate all the fish.

这个小村子有了天翻地覆的变化。以前农民去外地都坐马车，现在都开汽车了。

The small village had gone through great upheavals. In the past, farmers travelled by horse carts and now they drive cars.

YOUR TURN:

Tell a short story about how the world (big or small) was turned outside down. Be sure to use the proverb 天翻地覆.

Chinese Legends

夸父 (Kuā Fù, a proper name) 逐日 (zhúrì, chase the Sun)

传说夸父是古代的一个巨人 (jùrén, giant)，住在北方的高山上。他的耳朵上挂着两条黄蛇 (shé, snake)、手里拿着两条黄蛇。有一年，天气非常热，夸父去跟太阳赛跑。他跟着太阳从东边跑到西边，太阳总是比他跑得快。夸父跑啊跑啊，跑得很渴 (kě, thirsty) 的时候，就停下来，到黄河和渭河 (Wèihé, the Wei River) 去喝水。就在夸父马上就要追上太阳的时候，黄河和渭河的水都被他喝干了。他渴得不得了，所以想去喝北方大泽 (zé, pond) 的水，可是还没有走到，就渴死了。夸父死以前，把手里的拐杖 (guǎizhàng, walking stick) 扔出去，拐杖一下子变成了一片桃树 (táoshù, peach tree)，树上一年四季长满了桃子。这样，后来的人们走到这里，渴了的时候就可以吃桃子了。

Kua Fu Chasing the Sun

According to legend, in ancient China, Kua Fu was a giant who lived in the northern mountains. He had two yellow snakes hanging from his ears and two more yellow snakes waving in his hands. In a year when the weather was scorching hot, Kua Fu decided to race with the sun. He followed the sun from east to west, but the sun was always faster than he was. Kua Fu ran and ran, racing until he became very thirsty. Then he would stop, and at the Yellow River and Wei River he would take a drink of water. At the instant when he was finally about to catch up with the sun, he found that he had drunk all the water in the Yellow and Wei Rivers. Not being able to find any more water to drink, Kua Fu decided to go to the Great Lake in the north. However, before he got there he died of thirst. Right before he died, Kua Fu cast his walking stick away. As the stick landed on the ground, it transformed into a lush peach grove. The peach trees in this grove bore fruit year-round. This way, when future passersby came to this spot they could simply eat a peach to quench their thirst.

YOUR TURN:

Can you think of an ancient myth that has a theme similar to Kua Fu Chasing the Sun? If so, relay the myth in Chinese to your classmates.

你知道吗？

这几年，中国最大的变化之一是路上的车子越来越多了。为了解决 (jiějué, solve)堵车问题，中国造了许多新路，一些原来只有两个车道的马路也被修成有四个或六个车道，可是堵车还是常常发生。

因此 (yīncǐ, because of this)，政府非常重视发展公共交通。比方说，在中国最大的城市上海，公交很发达 (developed)，多数的居民都坐公交。上海的公交包括公交车、地铁、轻轨和摆渡 (bǎidù, ferry) 船等等。

<u>公交车</u>：上海城里和郊区都有公交车。公交车从早上四、五点钟就开始服务，一直服务到晚上十一、二点。有些线路半夜也有服务，可是公交车比较少，需要等30到60分钟。

<u>地铁、轻轨</u>：上海的地铁和轻轨服务四通八达。在上海，这是最快最方便的交通方法。地铁和轻轨很少受到堵车的影响，可以很快地从一个地方去另外一个地方。每天的服务时间是从早上六点左右到晚上十点左右。

<u>摆渡船</u>：黄浦江上的摆渡船已经有一百多年的历史了。摆渡船虽然比较慢，可是还是有不少上海居民喜欢坐摆渡船，特别是那些骑自行车的人。摆渡船很方便，也很便宜。不少来上海旅游的游客也喜欢坐一下摆渡船，看看黄浦江和外滩的风景。摆渡船每天的服务时间是从早上五、六点钟到晚上十点左右。

黄浦江上的摆渡船

地铁站

1.4 网校 Online School

对话

玛丽娅：汤姆，你拿的是什么书？

汤姆：《数学高考题指南》和《物理高考难题分析》。

玛丽娅：你在积极准备高考吧？

汤姆：不准备也不行啊。不管是老师还是父母，见了面就对我说："高考准备得怎么样了？你一定要争取上个好大学。"听得我都烦了。但是我想了想，觉得他们说的也有道理。在中国要上大学就得参加高考。如果想进好大学，就得好好准备考试。你看中国的高中生都在积极备考，我当然也不能马马虎虎。你准备得怎么样了？

玛丽娅：除了化学课以外，别的课我都不怕。现在我每个星期六上午去参加一个化学备考班。你有没有参加备考班？

汤姆：没有。我现在常去一个网校，在那里可以得到老师的帮助。

玛丽娅：网校是网上的学校吗？

汤姆：其实，网校就是远程教育网。我现在去的那个远程教育网，不但有网上的课程，而且有许多不同的服务，帮助老师和学生教学。那儿有从小学到高中每个年级的教学辅导材料。比如说，我们在学几何。网上会有很多几何的题目。你做了题以后，马上可以知道你做得对不对。要是你做得不对，网上会告诉你哪儿做错了。

玛丽娅：那么酷啊！

汤姆：这个网校有老师负责不同的服务，比如：常见问题、备考中心、学习方法什么的。你有问题可以发电邮，老师会在24小时里给你回答。

玛丽娅：如果我希望马上得到回答呢？

汤姆：那里也有同步课堂，你需要看一下课程表。可以在上课的时候上网，这样就可以直接跟老师谈话。

玛丽娅：那个网校有许多老师吗？

汤姆：是的。他们都是从各个学校来的，而且都是很有经验的老师。对了，我在网上看到一个学生写的关于学习方法的感想，还不错。我会把那个感想发给你看看。

玛丽娅：好，谢谢。

课文

（这是汤姆发给玛丽娅的电邮。）

Send	Reply	Reply All	Forward	Print	Delete

玛丽娅，

这就是我刚才告诉你的关于学习方法的文章。我觉得这些方法我们也能用。我特别喜欢他关于数学学习方法的感想。

汤姆

网校帮我找到好的学习方法

十一中初一学生　王健如

我已经在网校学习了一个学期了。网校的老师常常回答关于学习方法的问题。现在我把我学到的好的学习方法总结一下。

一、语文

第一，要把语文课上好。上课认真地听，把老师提的问题好好想一想，认真地做作业。第二，要多看书报杂志。只有多看书，才能了解世界，学到很多课本以外的知识。这些知识也能帮助我更好地理解语文课的内容。第三，为了能在语文考试的时候得到好成绩，在看书报的时候，我应该把一些好的词句记录下来。这样以后在写作文的时候可以用。第四，要常常动动笔，可以写日记，也可以写周记，把听到的看到的有意思的事情写下来，这样可以帮助我提高语文水平。

二、数学

我觉得学数学最好的方法是举一反三。多做难题不一定有用。有用的方法是要理解基础题。这样在做难题的时候，可以根据基础题的原理，用不同的方法去做，这样就不会怕难题了。

三、英语

我觉得要学好英语，就要做到“四多”：多听、多写、多读、多说。不但上课要听，而且下课以后，可以多听英语广播，多看英语电视节目。不管一开始是不是听得懂，最后一定会越听懂得越多。多写多读是为了帮助自己记住英语。每个生词，我都应该写几遍，课文也应该读几遍，这样就比较容易记住了。多说，就是要在上课的时候积极说英语，不要怕说错。

生词

	Simplified	*Traditional*	*Pinyin*	*Part of Speech*	*English*
1.	网校	網校	wǎngxiào	*n.*	online school, school on the web
2.	难题	難題	nántí	*n.*	difficult problem, headache
3.	积极	積極	jījí	*adj.*	active, positive, vigorous
4.	不管		bùguǎn	*conj.*	regardless of, no matter (what, when, where, how…)

5.	争取	爭取	zhēngqǔ	*v.*	strive for, fight for
6.	烦	煩	fán	*adj.*	be tired of
7.	道理		dàolǐ	*n.*	reason, sense
8.	备考	備考	bèikǎo	*v.o.*	prepare for a test
9.	远程	遠程	yuǎnchéng	*adj.*	long-distance, remote
10.	几何	幾何	jǐhé	*n.*	geometry
11.	同步		tóngbù	*adj./n.*	synchronous, synchronization
12.	感想		gǎnxiǎng	*n.*	reflections, impressions
13.	总结	總結	zǒngjié	*n./v.*	summary, summarize
14.	语文	語文	yǔwén	*n.*	language
15.	动笔	動筆	dòngbǐ	*v.o.*	start writing
16.	日记	日記	rìjì	*n.*	diary
17.	周记	週記	zhōujì	*n.*	weekly journal
18.	水平		shuǐpíng	*n.*	level
19.	举一反三	舉一反三	jǔ yī fǎn sān	*s.p.*	draw inferences
20.	基础	基礎	jīchǔ	*n.*	base, foundation
21.	原理		yuánlǐ	*n.*	principle, theory
22.	广播	廣播	guǎngbō	*n./v.*	broadcast, be on the air

语言注释

1. 也 *(for emphasis)*

We know that 也 has the meaning of "also" and "moreover." Sometimes, it can be used for emphasis, with the meaning of "really," or "indeed."

汤姆也太马马虎虎了，怎么会在考试的时候少做了一页？
Tom is really too careless. How could he miss one page on the test?

你两个星期没跟父母联系了，也该给他们打打电话或者写写电邮了。
You haven't talked to your parents for two weeks, you really should call them or send them an email.

2. 不管…（都）(Regardless of, no matter (who, what, when, which, whether…))

不管 introduces a conditional clause, with the meaning of "no matter who (谁), what (什么), where (哪儿), when (什么时候)…" The main subject appears in the second clause, after the clause of 不管. 都 is usually included in the second clause.

> 不管在哪儿都应该注意安全。
> No matter where (you are, you) should pay attention to safety.

> 不管什么时候我去看他，他都在网上玩游戏。
> Regardless of when I visit him, he is always playing online games.

In the case of "no matter whether…," two or more choices need to be provided. One way is to list two or more nouns in immediate succession and the other is to put the phrase immediately after 不管 into a question format.

Using two or more nouns in immediate succession

> 不管春夏秋冬，这里的游客都很多。
> Regardless of the season, there are many tourists here.

> 不管男女老少，都喜欢这种运动。
> Everyone (regardless of sex and age) likes this sport.

In a question format

> 不管他愿意不愿意，他弟弟都要跟着他。(Predicate 不 Predicate)
> No matter whether he liked it or not, his younger brother followed him around.

> 不管是不是需要，他总是带着他的电脑。（是不是 Predicate）
> No matter whether it is needed or not, he always brings his computer.

> 不管是老师还是学生，都需要借书证才能借书。(Choice 1 还是 Choice 2)
> No matter whether you are a teacher or a student, you need a library card to check out books.

3. 都 (*For emphasis*)

We have learned that 都 has the meaning of "all," but sometimes 都 doesn't express a clear meaning, and instead is used for emphasis.

> 大家都让汤姆要好好备考，汤姆听得都烦了。
> Everyone urged Tom to prepare well for the test, but Tom is really tired of hearing this.

你看，那个小的比大的都贵。
Look, the small one is even more expensive than the big one.

4. 有道理 (Reasonable, it makes sense. . .)

有 or 没有 can take a noun to function as a predicate in a sentence, such as 有道理 (reasonable), 没有道理 (unreasonable), 有研究 (knowledgeable), 有经验 (experienced). . .

你说的有道理。
What you said makes sense.

在考试的时候学生写错一个字就不及格是没道理的。
It is unreasonable to fail a student in a test for writing one character incorrectly.

学无止境

We have learned some words about online education. Here are some additional words. Pinyin is provided for new characters only.

网络教育 *online (cyber) education*	网络教育学院 *online educational institution*	网院 *abbreviation of* 网络教育学院
网络大学 *cyber university*	远程教育 *distance learning*	在线教育 *online education*
同步教学 *synchronous education (real-time learning that takes place in an online setting such as a chat room or video conference)*	虚拟 (xūnǐ) 大学 *cyber learning community that simulates a university*	虚拟教室 *cyber learning community that simulates a classroom*
异 (yì) 步教学 *asynchronous education*	网上教学 *E-learning*	网上课程 *online course*

YOUR TURN:

After reading the online announcement, answer the comprehension questions.

> 普通高中网络课程
> 高中生上网除了聊天、游戏、查信息以外，还能做些什么？
> 为什么不在网上选修网络课程呢？
> 在线选修课程一共有九门：语文、英文、数学、
> 政治(political science)、历史、地理、物理、化学、生物。
> 教师来自重点中学。24小时网上答问。
> 欢迎学生报名、选课、上课。

1. 这个网站让高中生在网上做什么？
2. 网上课程有哪些？
3. 网上课程由谁教？
4. 上网上课和去学校上课有什么不同？

温故知新 GAIN NEW INSIGHT THROUGH REVIEW

We have learned many words about computers and the Internet. Let's review them.

1. Add five things you do online

看新闻					

2. Add five words related to computers

优盘					

3. Add five words related to E-learning

网校					

中国文化一瞥

Chinese proverbs

The following proverbs describe speed and quick actions. Pinyin is provided only for those phrases with new characters.

1. 一 日 千 里

a thousand miles a day; advance at a high speed

IN USE:

科技的进步一日千里。
Science and technology advance at a high speed.

这个新城市的建设一日千里。
Construction of the new city advances at a high speed.

YOUR TURN:

Do you feel it is appropriate to use 一日千里 to describe the progress in the following aspects? Choose an aspect and make a sentence with 一日千里.

电脑技术	教育	经济发展	城市建设	公共交通

2. 眼 明 手 快

quick of eye and deft of hand; see things clearly and act speedily

IN USE:

小王工作的时候眼明手快。大家都很喜欢跟她工作。
Xiao Wang sees things clearly and acts fast. Everyone likes to work with her.

我告诉你，玩这个电脑游戏一定要眼明手快。
Let me tell you, when you play this computer game, you must see things clearly and act quickly.

YOUR TURN:

Answer the following questions:

1. 你做什么事情眼明手快？
2. 你觉得在你的同学里，谁总是眼明手快？

3. jié zú xiān dēng
捷 足 先 登

the quick-footed arrive first; if you are quicker, you get ahead of others; the early bird catches the worm

IN USE:

每次听讲座，他总是捷足先登，坐在离讲台最近的地方。
Every time there is a lecture, he is always the first to arrive and sits closest to the podium.

我去买音乐会票子的时候，才发现别人捷足先登，好位子都卖完了。
Not until I went to buy the concert tickets did I find out that all good seats had been taken by early birds.

YOUR TURN:

Can you use 捷足先登 to describe the following situations?

同学们排队上车。大卫第一个上了车。	可以	不可以
为了上张老师的地理课，大卫很早就去排队注册课程。	可以	不可以
大卫总是很快地做好作业，交给老师。	可以	不可以
电脑房的电脑不太多，要用的学生比较多。所以，大卫常常在电脑房门口等着电脑房开门。	可以	不可以

Chinese Legends

精卫填海

传说古代的时候有一种鸟，名字叫精卫。精卫原来是炎帝 (Yándì, a legendary king of China) 最喜欢的女儿。有一天精卫去东海游泳，遇到了暴雨，结果在海里淹死 (yānsǐ, drown)。精卫死了以后，变成了一只鸟。她每天去西山用嘴搬着石子 (shízǐ, pebble) 和树枝 (twig)，飞到东海，把石子和树枝投 (tóu, throw) 到大海里，想要把东海填平。后来人们常用"精卫填海"这个成语，比喻 (bǐyù, use as a metaphor) 坚持不懈 (jiānchíbùxiè, unremitting) 的努力。

Jing Wei Trying to Fill Up the Sea

Legend has it that once upon a time there was a bird called Jing Wei. Originally Jing Wei was the favorite daughter of Emperor Yan, one of the legendary rulers of ancient China. One day, while Jing Wei was swimming in the Eastern Sea, she encountered a storm and drowned. After her death, she turned into a bird. Every day, she flew from the Western Mountain to the Eastern Sea, carrying twigs and pebbles in her mouth and dropping them into the sea, hoping to fill it up completely. This fable is often used to describe people who will not stop until they reach their goal.

YOUR TURN:

Can you think of a myth in the Western tradition that shares a similar theme with the story above? If so, relay the story in Chinese to your classmates.

你知道吗?

远程教育在中国已经有几十年的历史，可是远程教育的方法有了很大的变化。中国第一代远程教育是“函授 (hánshòu, correspondence) 教学”，老师和学生通过写信的方法来教学。第二代是电视广播教学，学生通过看电视听广播来学习。现在的网络教育是第三代远程教学。也有人把网络教育叫作“因特网在线教育”。

虽然网络走进中国普通人的生活只有十几年的时间，但是网络教育在中国发展得很快。现在中国的网络教育包括为中小学生办的网校，为大学生办的“网络教育学院”（网院），还有不少网上的职业培训课程。网上的学校越来越多，网络课程也是五花八门，科目 (kēmù, subject) 很多。中国网络教育的发展为中国人提供了更多受教育的机会。

1.5 新图书馆 A New Library

对话一

玛丽娅：凯丽，学校的新图书馆盖好了，你去过了吗？

凯丽：去过了。新图书馆的条件比旧图书馆好多了。

玛丽娅：我还没去过呢。从外边看，新馆比旧馆大得多。以前的图书馆只有三层楼，现在有六层。

凯丽：对，虽然新馆比旧馆高了三层，可是上上下下比以前快多了。新图书馆有六个电梯，这六个电梯在图书馆的不同地方，不管你在哪一层，不用走很多路，就能坐电梯上下楼。

玛丽娅：借书呢？是不是也都自动化了？

凯丽：是的，所有的目录都在电脑里。去图书馆以前，你可以先上网查一下，你要借的书在第几层，有没有被别人借走。如果被别人借走了，电脑会告诉你，借的书哪一天会到期。你可以根据还书的时间，在网上预订你想借的书。

玛丽娅：听上去非常方便。新图书馆里的书是不是比以前多了？

凯丽：其实，书报杂志没有增加很多。现在很多人都看电子书报。新图书馆的很多地方都是给学生学习用的。那里有网络学习室、阅览室、会议室什么的。我们可以去那里用电脑、学习、或者开会。你为什么不去看一看呢？

玛丽娅：今天下课以后，我就去。

上海图书馆

对话二

（在图书馆里。）

玛丽娅： 请问，参考书在几楼？

工作人员：在一楼的参考阅览室里。你往左走，右边的第一个大房间就是参考阅览室。我们图书馆一共有六个阅览室。参考阅览室除外，还有社会科学阅览室、自然科学阅览室、外文阅览室、多媒体报纸阅览室和视听阅览室。每层楼都有一个阅览室，都在电梯的左边。

玛丽娅： 谢谢。听说图书馆还有一些学习室和电脑室，也是每层都有吗？

工作人员：是的。在五楼，还有一个大教室，那儿每个星期都有讲座。你看，在一进门的地方放着一些电脑吧？那些电脑是图书馆指南。你可以去看一下。这个学期所有的讲座和活动安排都在电脑里。

玛丽娅： 我可以在那儿查图书目录吗？

工作人员：当然可以。

玛丽娅： 对了，网络学习室有没有打印机？

工作人员：有。如果你要打印，可以到服务台买电脑服务卡，然后就可以打印了。

玛丽娅： 哦，打印贵不贵？

工作人员：跟在学校的电脑房一样，打印一张纸五分钱。如果你要复印，每层楼都有一个小小的复印室。

玛丽娅： 我也需要先买电脑服务卡吗？

工作人员：是的，也是五分钱一张。

玛丽娅： 那我可以用现金打印复印吗？

工作人员：不可以。凡是要打印复印的，都得买电脑服务卡。如果你怕麻烦，可以多放一点儿钱在卡上。这个学期用不完的话，下个学期还可以用。

玛丽娅： 图书馆每天都开门吗？

工作人员：是的，你看，那个牌子上写得很清楚。

玛丽娅： 谢谢！我去看看那个牌子。

图书馆开放时间

周一到周五：	8:00 – 21:00
周六：	9:00 – 18:00
周日：	13:00 – 21:00
（国定假日除外）	

阅览室

生词

	Simplified	Traditional	Pinyin	Part of Speech	English
1.	条件	條件	tiáojiàn	*n.*	condition, qualification
2.	电梯	電梯	diàntī	*n.*	elevator
3.	自动化	自動化	zìdònghuà	*n./v.*	automation, make something automated
4.	目录	目錄	mùlù	*n.*	catalog
5.	查		chá	*v.*	check, look up, look into
6.	到期		dàoqī	*v.o.*	become due, mature, expire
7.	预订	預訂	yùdìng	*v.*	reserve, make a reservation
8.	杂志	雜誌	zázhì	*n.*	magazine
9.	增加		zēngjiā	*n./v.*	increase
10.	会议	會議	huìyì	*n.*	meeting, conference
11.	参考	參考	cānkǎo	*n./v.*	reference, consult, refer to
12.	除外		chúwài	*v.*	except, with the exception of
13.	多媒体	多媒體	duōméitǐ	*n.*	multimedia
* 14.	视听	視聽	shìtīng	*n.*	audio-video
15.	打印机	打印機	dǎyìnjī	*n.*	printer
16.	打印		dǎyìn	*v.*	print
17.	复印	復印	fùyìn	*v.*	make a photocopy, duplicate
18.	凡是		fánshì	*adj./adv.*	every, any, all
19.	国定假日	國定假日	guódìng jiàrì	*n.*	national holidays

语言注释

1. 化 (*suffix*)

When 化 is added to an adjective or a noun, it changes the word into a verb or a noun, with the meaning of "transform" or "change."

自动	automatic	自动化	make something automatic
现代	modern	现代化	modernize, modernization
西方	the West	西方化	Westernize, Westernization
商业	commerce	商业化	commercialize, commercialization

2. 除外 (Except, with the exception of)

As a verb, 除外 is used as a predicate. 除外 has the same meaning as 除了…以外. While 除了 X 以外 is often placed at the beginning of a sentence, 除外 is often at the end of a sentence. In formal writing, 除外 is often used.

除了国定假日以外，图书馆每天开放。
图书馆每天开放，国定假日除外。
The library opens every day except for national holidays.

除了背包以外，我有三件行李。
我有三件行李，背包除外。
I have three pieces of luggage, not including my backpack.

3. 凡是 (Every, any, all)

凡是 is almost always used with 都.

凡是不了解的她都想学。
She likes to learn anything that she doesn't understand.

凡是星期六星期天，这个饭店都有特价午餐。
Every Saturday and Sunday, the restaurant has a lunch special.

学无止境

We have learned the use of 化. Here are some additional words containing 化 that are often used in China today. Pinyin is provided for new characters only.

个人化 *individualize*	社会化 *socialize*	美化 *beautify*
电气化 *electrify*	数码化 *digitize*	绿化 *make an area green*
工业化 *industrialize*	大众 (zhòng) 化 *popularize (make something accessible for ordinary people)*	城市化 *urbanize*
私(sī)有化 *privatize*	个性化 *personalize*	全球化 *globalize*

YOUR TURN:

Please try to make three new words with 化. Report them to your class and your teacher will let you know if you have done them correctly.

温故知新 GAIN NEW INSIGHT THROUGH REVIEW

We have learned many words about the things we see in an office. Look at the following list of words. Some of them may be new words for you. Since there are no new characters, you should be able to guess the meaning. Group these words into three categories in any way you like. Add a heading for each of the categories.

电脑	电话	光盘	计算器	铅笔	纸
文件夹	会议桌	复印机	尺子	订书机	橡皮
练习本	书桌	信封	优盘	打印机	书架
椅子	名片	圆珠笔	铅笔盒	台灯	传真机

中国文化一瞥

Chinese proverbs

The following proverbs describe new development. Pinyin is provided only for those phrases with new characters.

1. 后 来 居 上

the latecomers surpass the old timers

IN USE:

这种通信技术后来居上，很受大家的欢迎。
This type of telecommunication technology surpasses the old types and is well received by everyone.

学校篮球队来了两个新队员。他们是后来居上，球打得比老队员还好。
The school's basketball team has two new members. The new comers surpass the old timers, and play even better than them.

YOUR TURN:

Which point of view do you support? Try to cite a few examples to support your view.

我觉得世界上什么事情都是后来居上。新的总是比旧的好。	我觉得世界上的事情不一定都是后来居上。有的是新的比旧的好，有的是新的没有旧的好。

2. hòu làng tuī qián làng
后 浪 推 前 浪
the new waves push the old waves forward; the new replaces the old

IN USE:

后浪推前浪，多数的顾客更喜欢新产品。
The new replaces the old. Most customers prefer new products.

公司里的年轻人把工作做得非常好，真是后浪推前浪啊。
Young people in the company are doing a great job. They are really pushing the older ones forward.

YOUR TURN:

Choose one of the following fields in which you believe the new has replaced the old to demonstrate 后浪推前浪.

体育	娱乐	电脑	教育	商业

3. 别 开 生 面
break a new path; start something new; break fresh ground

IN USE:

自从用了新技术以后，我们的工作别开生面。
Since we adopted the new technology, our work has broken a new path.

校长听取了师生的意见，让学校的文化活动别开生面。
The principal listened to the opinions of teachers and students and started something new in the school's cultural activities.

YOUR TURN:

Can you use 别开生面 to describe the following situations?

张老师用新的教学方法教数学。学生的数学成绩比以前好了。	可以	不可以
音乐课的林老师教我们唱了一首新歌。	可以	不可以
新图书馆把图书目录全放到电脑里去了。	可以	不可以
听了关于健康和运动的讲座以后，同学们更注意锻炼身体了。	可以	不可以

Chinese Legends

仓颉 (Cāng Jié, a proper name) 造字

传说汉字是黄帝 (Huángdì, a legendary king of China) 手下的大臣 (dàchén, minister)仓颉造出来的。黄帝统一 (tǒngyī, unify)了黄河中部以后，让仓颉造字，因为如果有了文字，管理就比较方便了。可是造字是很难的一件事，仓颉坐在河边的房子里想了好长时间也没想出来。有一天他正坐在房前想啊想啊，一只凤凰 (fènghuáng, phoenix) 叫着从天上飞过来，凤凰嘴里的一片树叶 (shùyè, tree leaf) 掉下来，树叶上有一个很清楚的动物蹄印 (tíyìn, paw print)，一位猎人 (lièrén, hunter) 告诉仓颉，这是豹子 (bàozi, leopard) 蹄印，各种动物的蹄印都不一样，他只要一看蹄印，就知道是什么动物。

猎人启发 (qǐfā, inspire)了仓颉：世界上的山河、日月，花草、鸟兽 (shòu, beasts)不都有自己的样子吗？要是把他们的样子画出来，不就是字了吗？就这样，仓颉造出了第一批 (pī, batch)文字。我们把这些字叫做"象形字" (xiàngxíngzì, pictographs)。

Cang Jie, the Inventor of Chinese Characters

Legend has it that Chinese characters were invented by Cang Jie, a minister of the Yellow Emperor, one of the legendary kings of China. After the Yellow Emperor unified the Central Plain (the middle range of the Yellow River), he asked Cang Jie to create a writing system so that bookkeeping for the royal palace would become easier. However, creating a writing system was no easy task. Cang Jie would sit in his home by the river devoting much time and effort to this question, but was still unable to think of anything. One day, while thinking in front of his house, Cang Jie saw a phoenix flying in the sky. The leaf the bird was carrying in its mouth fell to the earth, and a paw print could be clearly seen upon it. A hunter told Cang Jie that the paw print belonged to a leopard, and that every species of animal had a distinctive paw print. All the hunter had to do was look at the paw print, and he would know what animal had made it.

The hunter inspired Cang Jie: Didn't the mountains and streams, sun and moon, flowers and plants, birds and beasts all have their own unique shapes? If these shapes could be drawn, would that not count as writing? In this way, Cang Jie created the first batch of characters. We call these characters "pictographs."

YOUR TURN:

Do you still remember the six categories of Chinese characters? To refresh your memory, please refer to the "Do You Know?" section in *Huanying*, Volume 1 textbook, Lesson 1.3. After reviewing the section, prepare an oral presentation on the formation of Chinese characters. Make sure to include some concrete examples in your presentation.

你知道吗？

世界各国的人最喜欢上网做什么？有人调查了一下，发现中国的网民 (Internet user) 最喜欢做的是上网聊天；美国网民最常做的事情是去社交网站，比如“脸书” (Facebook)、“微博” (Twitter)、“我的空间” (Myspace)等等；法国网民中有许多人喜欢上网写博客，十个法国网民里就有一个人写博客。所以我们可以说，各国网民的上网习惯有一点儿不同。

因为因特网发展得很快，所以我们生活中的许多方面已经离不开网络了。尽管各国网民最喜欢做的事有点儿不一样，可是多数人都上网做各种各样的事，比如上网购物、理财、查看地图、跟朋友和家人联系、查天气、看新闻、订票买票、查地址或电话号码、查体育比赛的结果、玩游戏等等。还有不少人上网找工作、找住房、申请学校。

以前，上网的多数是年轻人，可是现在男女老少都上网。当然，每个国家上网的人数有多有少。如果网络在一个国家比较普及 (pǔjí, widespread)，那个国家的网民就会比较多。

1.6 第一单元复习
Unit 1 Review

对话

凯丽： 昨天我经过学校旁边的建设工地，发现工人已经盖好很多楼了。

大卫： 是吗？我怎么没看到呢。

凯丽： 不是前边的大楼，是后边三层楼的别墅楼。

大卫： 那也够快的。上海什么都快，几个月就能盖好一个大楼，几个星期就能修好一条马路。你们看，学校门口的马路也快修好了，好像下个月就可以通车了。

汤姆： 如果要我用一个字来总结现代生活，那就是"快"。现在交通很方便，去哪儿都很快。因为有了网络，跟别人联系也很快。技术发达了，盖房子修马路也变得很快。你们说呢？

玛丽娅： 我觉得还可以用一个字："小"。

汤姆： 小？

玛丽娅： 是啊，你不觉得世界变得越来越小了吗？因为可以很快地从一个地方去另外一个地方，地方的远近变得不重要了。在网上，这个国家发生的事，别的国家马上就知道了。如果你想买点东西，不管是中国的还是美国的，都可以在网上买到。我们虽然生活在地球不同的地方，但是就象在一个地方一样。

大卫： 我会用一个字"冷"来总结。

凯丽： 冷？天气没有越变越冷啊。

大卫： 我的意思是，现在大家把多数的时间都花在网络和电视上，不像以前每天会花很多时间跟家人朋友邻居谈话，所以人跟人的关系比以前冷了，也远了。

玛丽娅：大卫说的也有道理。凯丽，你会用哪个字？

凯丽：好的字都被你们用过了。要是非要我说，我就用“多”。现在什么都比以前多了，人、车、房子、东西、信息、新闻、技术什么的。

汤姆：我们的总结都挺有意思的。我看，我们可以让班上的每个同学都来参加这个“一字游戏”，听听大家对现代生活的看法。

玛丽娅：好主意。

上海的大楼

课文

在美国中部的一个高中里，有一个“中国：网络电话俱乐部”。这个俱乐部是四五年以前成立的。那时候，这个高中的校长访问了北京附近的一个高中。这两个校长在谈话的时候，觉得现在网络技术发展了，网上交流很方便。他们就想，能不能用网络技术让两个学校的学生互相学习，互相帮助呢。

在一些电脑工程师的帮助下，这个美国高中成立了“中国：网络电话俱乐部。”俱乐部里有十几个学生。每星期有两个晚上，他们通过网络电话跟中国高中的学生联系，帮助中国学生学英文。

有些中国学生会把他们做好的英语作业给美国学生看。有时候，他们也会让美国学生帮助回答英语课本里的一些问题。但是最常见的是，中美学生会在一起讨论大家都有兴趣的话题，比如高中生最喜欢的课程、运动、课外活动等等。一个中国学生告诉他的美国朋友："在你的帮助下，我的英文考试成绩越来越好了。对中国学生来说，考试是非常重要的。但是你们除了帮助我们学习英文以外，还让我们有机会了解美国。谢谢！"

这个俱乐部成立以后，有些俱乐部的学生已经去中国访问过了。在中国，他们受到中国高中生的欢迎。这些美国学生说："虽然我们在电视上看到过中国，也在历史课里学习过中国历史，但是'百闻不如一见'，我们到了中国，看到了许多在电视上和书上看不到的东西，让我们更了解中国了。"现在，一些中国学生正在打算访问美国。他们也希望能更好地了解美国。

中国的小镇

中国式花园

生词

	Simplified	*Traditional*	*Pinyin*	*Part of Speech*	*English*
1.	通车	通車	tōngchē	*v.o.*	be open to traffic
2.	地球		dìqiú	*n.*	the earth, the globe
3.	网络	網絡	wǎngluò	*n.*	net, network (in mainland China)
	网路	網路	wǎnglù	*n.*	net, network (in Taiwan)
4.	百闻不如一见	百聞不如一見	bǎi wén bù rú yī jiàn	*s.p.*	seeing is believing

生词扩充

Many Chinese words are formed by combining two or more characters. If you know the characters in a word, you can often guess the meaning of that word. See if you understand the meaning of the following words.

网店		天然		牛车	
村民		建造		古文化	
查找		网友		查看	
自动电梯		视觉		听觉	
海景		铁轨		月球	

SELF-ASSESSMENT

In Unit 1, you have learned to describe travel, everyday objects, buildings, and phenomena in some detail. You have also expanded your ability to narrate and summarize past and present events in a logical, detailed sequence. Have you achieved the learning goals of Unit 1? After completing the exercises for Unit 1 in your Workbook, fill out the following self-assessment sheet.

Yes/No	*Can you say and write these things in Chinese?*
	Give detailed descriptions of travel
	Give detailed descriptions of everyday objects
	Give detailed descriptions of various places
	Give detailed descriptions of facilities
	Give detailed descriptions of common practices
	Talk about computer technology in some detail
	Narrate a present event in a logical, detailed sequence
	Narrate a past event in a logical, detailed sequence
	Summarize the major characteristics of a phenomenon

8–9	yes	excellent
5–7	yes	good
1–4	yes	need some work

第二单元：民以食为天

UNIT 2 Bread Is the Staff of Life

LEARNING GOALS OF UNIT 2

By the end of this unit, you will learn how to:

- Talk briefly about China's agriculture
- Describe the relation between agriculture and diet
- Talk about the major cuisines in China
- Talk briefly about Muslims in China
- Talk about food that is popular around the world
- Discuss the advantages and disadvantages of food globalization
- Describe, in some detail, a specialty dish
- Describe the differences between food labels
- Describe briefly the general process of growing and manufacturing food
- Describe Chinese cultural customs related to eating
- Describe, in some detail, how Chinese view food

2.1 农业和饮食 Agriculture and Food

对话一

凯丽：这个学期你在上经济课吧？那门课怎么样？

汤姆：我原来以为经济课会比较枯燥，可实际上不是这样。我们正在学习中国的农业。为了让我们了解农业的情况，老师带我们去参观了农业展览馆，下个星期五，我们还要去一个村子做校外考察。

凯丽：历史书上常常说，中国是一个农业大国。可是我们现在住在上海，看到的都是现代化的大楼、商场、公司等等。我很难想象中国是个农业大国。

汤姆：是啊。其实，中国的现代化和工业化是最近一两百年的事。如果我们看一下中国五千多年的历史，就会发现五千多年来，中国的经济主要都是农业经济。再说，中国非常大，我们在上海，看到的只是一个城市的情况。实际上，中国的大多数地区今天还是农业区。

农业区

凯丽： 上中国地理课的时候，我们学到过，中国山地多，平原少。这样的地理情况是不是会影响到农业发展呢？

汤姆： 当然会。总的来说，中国是人口多，耕地少。中国的人口占世界的百分之二十，可是中国的耕地只占世界的百分之七。要在很少的耕地上养活这么多人非常不容易。过去的五千年来，中国一直努力发展农业，解决人民的吃饭问题。

凯丽： 我常常听人说，中国的南方人吃米饭，北方人吃面食，这也跟中国粮食生产有关系吧？

汤姆： 是的，粮食作物在南方主要是大米，在北方主要是小麦。

凯丽： 听上去，中国的农业非常值得我们了解。等你考察回来，应该把结果给我们班的同学介绍一下。

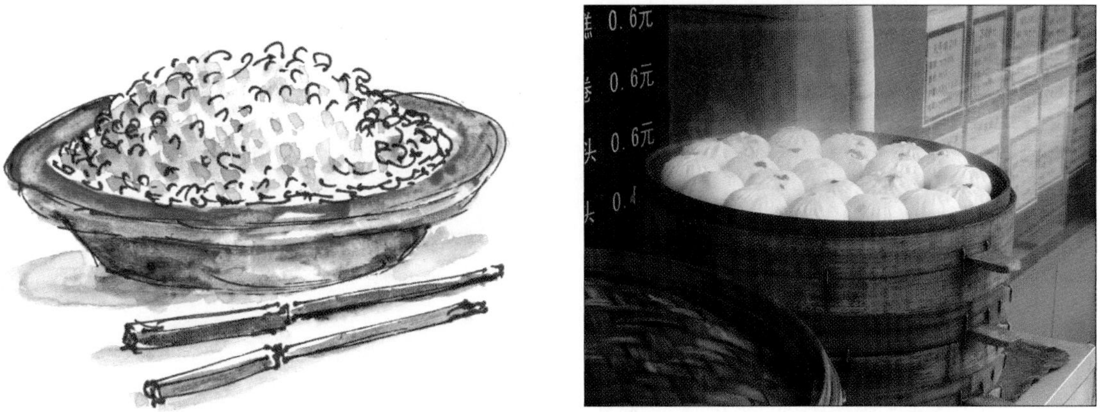

米饭和包子

对话二

汤姆： 昨天我们去做校外考察了。

凯丽： 哦，就是你说的经济课的校外考察吧？你们去参观了一个村子，是吗？

汤姆： 是的。这个村子离我们学校不远，就在浦东。

凯丽： 浦东有村子吗？我看到的都是高楼、商店和一些居民小区。

汤姆： 这个村子看上去跟一般的居民小区差不多，有一些六层楼的公寓楼，这些公寓楼都是九十年代以后盖的。二十多年以前，这个村子的附近都是菜地，村里的农民主要种蔬菜。九十年代的时候，浦东开始发展了，不少工厂和公司搬到浦东来，菜地被用来盖房子、造马路了，不少农民去做别的工作了。有的去工厂工作，有的当建筑工人，有的做绿化工作，现在只有很少的农民还在种地。

凯丽： 他们还种蔬菜吗？

浦东的绿化

汤姆： 对。你知道浦东有不少菜场，在那里，大家可以买到各种各样新鲜的蔬菜。这个村子的农民常常一大早骑着自行车去菜场卖菜。还有一些浦东的超市、饭店也跟农民定了合同。他们种的菜可以直接送到超市和饭店去。那儿的农民告诉我们，他们不但种一些上海居民喜爱吃的菜，而且还种了一些新的蔬菜品种。这些新品种的蔬菜特别受到饭店的欢迎，因为如果饭店的菜单上有一些不同一般的菜，常常可以吸引更多的顾客。

凯丽：　万一他们生产的蔬菜太多，怎么办呢？
汤姆：　在这种情况下，村民就把一部分蔬菜加工以后再卖给超市。
凯丽：　你怎么可以买到这个村子加工的食品呢？
汤姆：　他们加工的食品是"新浦东"牌的。下次我去超市，一定去找一下。如果有，我就买一些。
凯丽：　好，万一你吃了觉得很好，别忘了告诉我。
汤姆：　行。

生词

	Simplified	*Traditional*	*Pinyin*	*Part of Speech*	*English*
1.	民以食为天	民以食為天	mín yǐ shí wéi tiān	*s.p.*	bread is the staff of life, food is the most important part of life
2.	枯燥		kūzào	*adj.*	dry, boring, uninteresting
3.	实际上	實際上	shíjìshàng	*conj.*	actually, as a matter of fact, in fact

4.	想象		xiǎngxiàng	*v.*	imagine
5.	工业化	工業化	gōngyèhuà	*n./v.*	industrialization, industrialize
6.	山地		shāndì	*n.*	hilly area
7.	平原		píngyuán	*n.*	plain
8.	总的来说	總的來說	zǒngdeláishuō	*s.p.*	in summary, in the final analysis
9.	耕地		gēngdì	*n.*	arable land, farm land
10.	占	佔	zhàn	*v.*	take up, occupy
11.	百分之		bǎifēnzhī	*n.*	percent, percentage
12.	养活	養活	yǎnghuó	*v.c.*	support, feed
13.	解决		jiějué	*v.*	solve
14.	面食	麵食	miànshí	*n.*	food made of wheat
15.	粮食		liángshí	*n.*	grain
16.	作物		zuòwù	*n.*	crop
17.	小麦	小麥	xiǎomài	*n.*	wheat
18.	值得	値得	zhídé	*adj.*	worthwhile
19.	合同		hétóng	*n.*	contract
20.	不同一般		bùtóngyībān	*s.p.*	extraordinary, special
21.	吸引		xīyǐn	*v.*	attract
22.	顾客	顧客	gùkè	*n.*	customer
23.	加工		jiāgōng	*v.*	process

语言注释

1. 实际上 (Actually, as a matter of fact, in fact)

父母希望我当电脑工程师，实际上，我对电脑没有兴趣。

My parents want me to become a computer engineer. As a matter of fact, I am not interested in computers.

这些数学题看上去很难，实际上不太难。

These math problems look difficult, but in fact, they are not that hard.

2. Time word/phrase + 来 (Ever since...)

五千年来，中国人一直住在黄河边。
For five thousand years, the Chinese have lived along the Yellow River.

许多年来，他希望有机会去一次北京。
For many years, he hoped to have an opportunity to go to Beijing.

3. 总的来说 (In summary, in sum)

下星期有数学、语文、英文、物理和化学的考试。总的来说，大家都会很忙。
Next week there are tests on math, Chinese, English, physics, and chemistry. In sum, everyone will be very busy.

总的来说，人们的生活比三十年前好多了。
In summary, people's lives are much better than they were 30 years ago.

4. 占 (Constitute, occupy)

占 is a verb, with similar meaning to 是. It is used when we talk about ranking and percentage.

中国人口差不多占世界人口的百分之二十。
China's population constitutes approximately 20% of the world's population.

在我们学校，外国学生占一半。
In our school, 50% of the students are foreigners.

高三的同学在跳高比赛中占了前两名。
Members of the senior class held the top two places in the high jump competition.

在世界的经济大国中，美国、中国和日本占了前三名。
Among the world's largest economies, the United States, China, and Japan comprise the top three.

5. 百分之 (Percent)

Unlike the English way of saying 30% (number + percent), the Chinese way is 百分之三十 (百分之 + number). Here are some more examples:

5%	百分之五	25%	百分之二十五
46.1%	百分之四十六点一	50.88%	百分之五十点八八
100%	百分之（一）百		

6. 怎么办 (What should be done? What shall we do?)

怎么办 is a set phrase commonly used in spoken Chinese, with the meaning of "what to do," "what should be done," or "what shall we do?"

A: 我今天明天都没空，你说怎么办?
B: 那我们下个星期再去吧。
A: I don't have time either today or tomorrow. What shall we do?
B: In that case, we can go next week.

A: 我的手机没电了，怎么办?
B: 我们去找个公用电话吧。
A: My cell phone is out of power. What should we do?
B: Let's look for a payphone.

学无止境

We have learned some words about agriculture. Here are some additional words related to the topic. Pinyin is provided for new characters only.

农田(tián) *farmland*	农地 *farmland*	土(tǔ)地 *land*
农作物 *agricultural crops*	农产品 *agricultural produce*	农业生产 *agricultural production*
耕种 *plough and sow, cultivate*	收成 *crop harvest*	产量 *yield, output*
农场 *farm*	农业科学 *agricultural science*	农业技术 *farming techniques*

YOUR TURN:

Answer the following questions based on your country's situation:

1. 在你们国家，耕地多吗？
2. 你们国家的农民多吗？
3. 农业区在哪儿？
4. 有哪些主要的农作物？
5. 你们国家的人民主要吃什么粮食？

温故知新 GAIN NEW INSIGHT THROUGH REVIEW

- In *Huanying*, Volume 2 Lesson 2.2, we learned 种瓜得瓜，种豆得豆. Do you remember the meaning of this Chinese saying?
- Season, weather, and climate are extremely important for agriculture. See how many words you can come up with that describe the four seasons. After you have finished, share the results in class.

春天					
夏天					
秋天					
冬天					

中国文化一瞥

Chinese proverbs

For many years, Chinese people have hoped for a better life. Here are some proverbs relating to basic needs and common desires.

1. fēng yī zú shí
丰 衣 足 食
have enough food and clothing; be well-fed and well-clothed

IN USE:

那个地区农业非常发达，农民丰衣足食。
That area's agriculture is well developed and the farmers there are well-fed and well-clothed.

我希望世界上的人都可以丰衣足食。
I wish everyone in the world could have enough food and clothing.

YOUR TURN:

Write two ideas about how to make everyone in the world have enough food and clothing. Share your ideas with your class.

我们可以用这两个方法让世界上的人都丰衣足食：

2. guó fù mín qiáng
国 富 民 强
The nation is prosperous and the people are strong

IN USE:

最近几十年来，科学和经济发展让许多国家变得国富民强。
In the last few decades, scientific and economic development has made many countries become prosperous and helped their people become powerful.

YOUR TURN:

Name one country that you believe exemplifies 国富民强. You should cite a couple of reasons to explain your choice.

3. rén jǐ jiā zú
人 给 家 足
everyone is well-provided for and every family has enough;
people and families are well provided for

IN USE:

不管在什么国家，一般人的理想生活是人给家足。
No matter in which country, the ideal life for ordinary people is to have everyone and every family well provided for.

我觉得人给家足还不够，还应该让每个人都生活得很快乐。
I feel having everyone and every family well provided for is not enough. Everyone should live happily.

YOUR TURN:

Work with a peer and find two challenges for reaching the goal of 人给家足. Write the challenges in Chinese and share them in class.

Symbolism in Chinese Food

Introduction:

In Unit 2 you will be exploring the role food plays in Chinese culture. You will learn that food—its cultivation, supply and production—not only is the central concern of people's daily lives, but also informs government policy. In fact, food is so important to the Chinese that food metaphors are among the most commonly used metaphors in the Chinese language. Moreover, symbolism of food is displayed in daily meals, especially during festivals and celebrations. In this section, you will be introduced to some traditional festival foods and their symbolic meaning.

Since the content is quite different from the texts you have learned so far, a loose translation in English is provided to facilitate your understanding.

月饼的传说

中秋节的时候，中国人大多全家聚 (jù, get together) 在一起，一边赏月 (shǎngyuè, appreciate the Moon) 一边吃月饼。月饼常常是圆的，象征 (xiàngzhēng, symbolize) 着团圆。月饼里的馅儿 (xiànr, stuffing)，常常是莲蓉 (liánróng, lotus seed paste) 做的，里面还包着一个鸭蛋黄。当你把月饼切开 (qiēkāi, cut open) 时，这个大大的鸭蛋黄就象又大又圆的月亮一样，祝福你全家中秋快乐。

关于月饼，还有这样一个传说。在中国元朝 (Yuán Cháo, the Yuan Dynasty, AD 1271–1368) 的时候，汉人在蒙古人 (Měnggǔrén, Mongolian) 的统治 (tǒngzhì, rule) 下，生活很不自由。元朝末年，很多汉人为了推翻(tuīfān, overthrow) 蒙古人的统治，决定组织起义 (qǐyì, uprising)。可是由于元朝的统治者禁止 (jìnzhǐ, forbid) 汉人聚会，起义的信息很难传播 (chuánbō, to spread)。于是，汉人就利用 (lìyòng, use) 中秋节的机会，互相送月饼。在这些月饼里面都夹着一个小纸条，上面写着起义的时间。就这样，汉人把起义的信息传给亲戚朋友。起义者 (qiyìzhě, the rebels) 经过多年的努力，终于 (zhōngyú, finally) 推翻了元朝，建立 (jiànlì, establish) 了明朝 (Míngcháo, the Ming Dynasty, AD 1368–1644)。

The Moon Cake

During the Moon Festival, Chinese people generally reunite with their families, and gaze at the moon while eating moon cakes. A typical moon cake is round. The word for "round" in Chinese is "yuan," which is a homophone of "yuan" in "tuanyuan"—reunion. The round moon cakes, therefore, symbolize reunion and togetherness. The filling of the moon cakes is usually made of sweet lotus seed paste wrapping a large salted duck egg yolk. When you cut open the moon cake, the large duck egg yolk resembles the large and round moon, sending the holiday blessings to families and friends.

There is a legend about moon cakes as well. During the Yuan Dynasty (AD 1271–1368), when China was ruled by the Mongols, life was very restricted. In the last years of the Yuan Dynasty, a group of Chinese decided to wage an uprising against Mongol rule. However, the rebels needed to find a way to distribute the message of rebellion, as the Yuan rulers forbade the Chinese from gathering in public. Knowing that the Moon Festival was drawing near, the leaders of the rebellion ordered special moon cakes be made. Stuffed into each moon cake was a message about the time of the uprising. On the night of the Moon Festival, the rebels successfully attacked the government army. One victory led to another. The Yuan Dynasty was overthrown and the Ming Dynasty (AD 1368–1644) was established.

YOUR TURN:

Choose one holiday food from your own culture. What is the history of this holiday food? Is there a legend about it? Prepare an oral presentation in Chinese on this holiday food, describe what it is and explain its cultural significance.

你知道吗?

中国是一个山地很多的国家，差不多有百分之六七十都是山地。世界上有十二座8,000米 (meter) 以上的高山，其中七座在中国。比如，世界上最高的珠穆拉马峰 (Zhūmùlāmǎfēng, Mount Everest, 8,848m) 也在中国的西藏。

除了中国中部的山地以外，中国有四大高原 (plateau)。最大的高原是青藏 (Qīngzàng, Qinghai-Tibet) 高原，在中国西部的西藏和青海 (Qinghai province)。青藏高原是世界上最高最大的高原，所以有人把它叫作"世界的屋脊 (wūjí, roof)"。中国的北部有内蒙古高原。内蒙古高原是中亚高原的一部分 (bùfèn, part)。这个高原差不多有900米到1200米那么高。还有两个高原，一个叫云贵高原，在中国西南部的云南和贵州。另一个叫黄土高原，在中国的西北部。

2.2 中国的地方菜系
Regional Cuisines in China

对话

玛丽娅：周末过得好吗？

汤姆：不错。星期六我爸爸的一位老同学钱叔叔请我们去吃饭。我爸爸说，钱叔叔在上大学的时候，就是一位美食家，他对吃什么、怎么吃特别有研究。

玛丽娅：他在家请你们吃饭吗？

汤姆：不，我们去了一个回族饭店。

玛丽娅：回族是少数民族吧？

汤姆：对，回族是中国主要的少数民族之一，大概有一亿人口，住在中国各地。历史书上说，在唐朝的时候，一些中亚国家和波斯的商人就开始到中国来做生意，有些人后来就留在中国了。

中国西部的少数民族

玛丽娅：这么说，这些人是回族的祖先。

汤姆：是的。他们把中亚和波斯的文化带到了中国。因为回族人信伊斯兰教，所以都不吃猪肉。我们去的那个回族饭店只有牛肉、羊肉和鸡肉。钱叔叔说，那家饭店最好吃的菜是涮羊肉。涮羊肉就是把一片一片的生羊肉先放在热汤里涮一下，然后拿出来吃。涮羊肉特别嫩，也特别鲜美。

清真（回族）饭店

玛丽娅：“涮羊肉”是回族的特色菜吗？好像现在不少饭店都有这道菜。

汤姆：涮羊肉本来是蒙古族的菜。那是元朝的时候，蒙古军队杀好了羊，正准备做饭，突然听到军队马上要出发。为了能马上吃到饭，他们就把羊肉切成一片一片的放在水里涮一下。结果大家都觉得这样做的羊肉非常好吃，后来就有了“涮羊肉”这道菜。中国各族人民在一起生活了几百年，饮食习惯互相影响，所以现在许多民族的人都吃涮羊肉。对了，我在回族饭店喝了一种特别的茶，是一般的饭店没有的，叫“十二味香茶”。

玛丽娅：你是说，那种茶有十二种味道吗？

汤姆：从名字上看，应该有十二种味道，可是我没喝出那么多味道来。钱叔叔说，这种茶里不但有茶叶，而且有果干和糖，所以喝起来又香又甜，非常可口。

玛丽娅：除了回族的食品，钱叔叔还给你介绍了别的地方菜吗？

汤姆：介绍了。哟，三点二十五了，我得马上去参加数学小组的活动。活动完了以后，我给你发电邮吧。

玛丽娅：好，谢谢。

果干

课文

Send	Reply	Reply All	Forward	Print	Delete

玛丽娅：

对不起，刚才我急急忙忙的，话没说完就走了，现在我再给你介绍别的地方菜。

钱叔叔说，中国各地的饮食很不一样，这是因为中国很大，各地的气候、地理都会影响到农业生产，也决定了各地的饮食。

中国各地做的菜各有特点。一般来说，中国菜被分为八大菜系。总的来说，中国菜可以说是南甜、北咸、东辣、西酸。南方的主食是米饭，北方的是面食。

江南人，就是住在长江南边的人喜欢吃得比较清淡，还喜欢菜里带一点儿甜味。他们喜欢吃得好一些少一些。如果你去上海人家吃饭，他们常常用小盘子放一点儿菜，但是菜的品种会比较多。

住在中国北部和东北的人，喜欢菜的味道浓一些，所以做得菜比较油，也比较咸。而且他们认为让大家吃饱是非常重要的。要是我们去东北饭店吃饭，就会看到都是用大盘子放菜，数量特别多。所以到了东北饭店，我们应该少点几个菜，要不然一定会吃不完。

中国西部的菜，特别是山西菜，带一点酸味，因为做菜的时候，山西人喜欢放一点儿醋。

湖南、四川等地的菜都比较辣。如果你喜欢吃辣的，可以选湖南饭店或者四川饭店。

广东菜非常有特色。广东在中国的南部，那里气候好，一年四季都有新鲜的蔬菜，广东又在海边，所以广东菜用许多新鲜的蔬菜和海鲜。钱叔叔还说，广东人是中国最敢吃的人，他们什么都愿意尝一尝。有一句笑话说，“除了飞机以外，天上飞的东西广东人都敢吃；除了桌子以外，有四条腿的东西广东人都敢吃。”

钱叔叔的介绍非常有意思。我们应该向钱叔叔学习，去吃一下中国各地不同的菜，这样我们就知道哪些是我们最爱吃的了。怎么样，明天下课以后，我们是不是一起去小吃街逛一逛？

汤姆

生词

	Simplified	Traditional	Pinyin	Part of Speech	English
1.	美食家		měishíjiā	*n.*	food connoisseur
2.	对…有研究	對…有研究	duì… yǒu yánjiū	*v.p.*	knowledgeable, well learned
3.	亿	億	yì	*n.*	a hundred million
4.	商人		shāngrén	*n.*	businessman
5.	生意		shēngyì	*n.*	business, business transaction

6. 祖先		zǔxiān	*n.*	ancestor
7. 羊肉		yángròu	*n.*	lamb
8. 涮		shuàn	*v.*	dip in boiling water, rinse
9. 生		shēng	*adj.*	raw, uncooked
10. 嫩		nèn	*adj.*	tender, delicate
11. 鲜美	鮮美	xiānměi	*adj.*	delicious, fresh and tasty
12. 特色		tèsè	*n.*	special characteristics/ features
13. 军队	軍隊	jūnduì	*n.*	army, troops
14. 杀	殺	shā	*v.*	kill
15. 果干	菓乾	guǒgān	*n.*	dried fruit
16. 菜系		càixì	*n.*	cuisine
17. 清淡		qīngdàn	*adj.*	light (of food)
18. 浓	濃	nóng	*adj.*	strong, dense, thick
19. 数量	數量	shùliàng	*n.*	quantity
20. 敢		gǎn	*v.*	dare, venture
21. 尝	嘗	cháng	*v.*	taste

专名

22. 回族		Huí zú	Hui (Muslim) ethnic group
23. 唐朝		Tángcháo	the Tang Dynasty (618-907)
24. 中亚	中亞	Zhōng Yà	Central Asia
25. 波斯		Bōsī	Persia
26. 伊斯兰教	伊斯蘭教	Yīsīlánjiào	Islam
27. 蒙古族		Ménggǔ zú	Mongolian, the Mongolian ethnic group
28. 元朝		Yuáncháo	the Yuan Dynasty (1271–1368)
29. 十二味香茶		shíèrwèi xiāngchá	tea with 12 flavors

语言注释

1. 对···有研究 (Knowledgeable in..., well learned in...)

You can add an adverb, such as 很、非常、没···, before 有研究.

王老师对中国少数民族的历史很有研究。
Teacher Wang is very knowledgeable in the history of Chinese minorities.

我对中国菜系没有研究。
I have no knowledge of Chinese cuisines.

2. 从···看 (From the perspective of..., through)

This is a prepositional phrase, and it is usually placed before a verb phrase.

我们可以从教育看一个国家的将来。
We can see a nation's future through its education.

从外面看，这座大楼很一般。可是大楼里面漂亮极了。
From the outside, the building looks ordinary. But it is extremely beautiful inside.

3. 一般来说 (Generally speaking, in general)

一般来说，中国网民喜欢上网聊天。
Generally speaking, Chinese Internet users like to chat online.

一般来说，这儿的秋天不常下雨。
In general, it doesn't rain very often in the autumn here.

学无止境

We have learned some words about doing business. Here are some additional words. Pinyin is provided for new characters only.

做买卖 *do business (informal)*	经商 *do business (formal)*	市场 *market*
商机 *business opportunity*	商品 *commodity*	商务 *business*
客户 (hù) *client*	业务 *business, professional work*	业务员 *sales person*
销售 (xiāoshòu) *sales*	营销 *sales*	货运 *shipping*
广告 *advertisement*	创 (chuàng) 业 *start a business*	商法 *business law*

温故知新 GAIN NEW INSIGHT THROUGH REVIEW

We have learned many words about food. Now let's review some words. Place the following words into three categories. Compare your list with a peer after you have finished it.

酸	炸	鸡肉	蔬菜	海鲜
牛肉	辣	饮料	涮	甜
米饭	面条	汤	醋	春卷
鱼	盐	糖	蛋糕	素菜
点心	羊肉	水果	茶	饺子

食品	食品的味道	做食品的方法

中国文化一瞥

Chinese proverbs

The following proverbs describe food. Pinyin is provided only for those phrases with new characters.

1. 家 常 便 饭

home-cooked food; a common meal (*this proverb also means "common occurrence"*)

IN USE:

(To show modesty, a Chinese host often uses the phrase 家常便饭 *when inviting guests over for meals.)*

请你和我们一起吃点儿家常便饭吧。

Please have some simple food with us.

对他来说，周末工作是家常便饭。

For him, it is common to work on the weekends.

YOUR TURN:

Answer the following questions based on your own situations:

1. 做作业是家常便饭吗？
2. 锻炼身体是家常便饭吗？
3. 打工是家常便饭吗？
4. 对你来说，什么事是家常便饭？

2. cū chá dàn fàn

粗 茶 淡 饭

simple food; bread and water; humble fare (this proverb also means "live a simple life")

IN USE:

虽然他很有钱，可是每天粗茶淡饭。他觉得简单的生活比较好。

Although he is wealthy, he lives a simple life. He feels a simple life is better.

我们家总是粗茶淡饭。就是客人来了也一样。

Our family always has simple food. It is the same even when guests come.

YOUR TURN:

Can you use 粗茶淡饭 to describe the following situations?

王老师每天中午只吃一碗素菜面条。	可以	不可以
丁老师每天早上去一个法国点心店吃早饭。每次，她都要吃三种不同的点心、一个鸡蛋、一些肉、还要喝一杯牛奶和一杯咖啡。	可以	不可以
张老师吃饭很随便。如果菜多就多吃，菜少就少吃。有肉就吃肉，没肉就不吃。	可以	不可以
钱老师每次做饭，最多只做一个菜。他说吃饱就行了。	可以	不可以

3. shān zhēn hǎi wèi
山 珍 海 味

Exotic food from the mountains and seas; nice dishes of every kind; all kinds of costly food

IN USE:

每天山珍海味对你的健康不一定好。

It is not necessarily good for your health if you have all kinds of nice dishes every day.

酒席上山珍海味，有许多我从来没吃过的东西。

The banquet is full of exotic food from mountains and seas, many of which I have never had before.

YOUR TURN:

Circle around the classroom and ask three students the following question.

你觉得什么食品是山珍海味？

Record their answers in the space below. Later share your findings in class and compile a list of exotic foods.

山珍海味：

1.	2.	3.

Symbolism in Chinese Food

腊八粥 (là bā zhōu, La Ba porridge)

北京人很讲究过年。在北京，过年的活动其实从腊月 (làyuè, the twelfth month on the Lunar calendar) 八日，也就是第十二个月的第八天就开始了。有一个北京的民谣 (mínyáo, folk rhyme) 说："小孩儿小孩儿你别馋 (chán, gluttonous)，过了腊八就是年；腊八粥 (zhōu, porridge)，过几天，漓漓拉拉 (līlilāla, the pattering sound) 二十三；…" 这民谣里说的腊八粥，是什么呢？

传说农历的十二月八日是佛祖 (fózǔ, the Buddha) 得道 (become enlightened)的日子。当年佛祖释迦牟尼 (Shìjiāmóní, Sakyamuni Buddha) 出去化缘 (huàyuán, receive alms)，化到的是五谷杂粮 (wǔgǔ záliáng, grains and cereals)。后来的人们为了纪念他，在每年腊月初八也用各种各样的米和豆子熬 (áo, boil) 粥供佛 (gòngfó, to give offerings to the Buddha)。清代北京的雍和宫 (Yōnghégōng, the Yonghe Buddhist Temple) 里专门有一个为皇室 (huángshì, the Royal family)、大臣和喇嘛 (lǎma, Lama) 熬腊八粥用的大铜 (tóng, copper) 锅。在民间，人们常常把熬好的腊八粥放到盒子里，送给亲友。

La Ba Porridge

Beijingers care a lot about the New Year. In Beijing, the Spring Festival celebrations actually start as early as *la ba*, the eighth day of the twelfth month on the lunar calendar. There is a folk rhyme in Beijing that goes like this:

Little children, don't be greedy for food.
The New Year is not long after *la ba*.
(But for now) you will be having the *la ba* porridge
Until the twenty-third day of the month.
…

According to legend, the eighth day of the twelfth lunar month is the day that the Buddha became enlightened. At that time, Sakyamuni Buddha went out to beg for alms and received a variety of grains and cereals. Later, to remember the Buddha's life and teaching, the Chinese started the tradition of boiling rice and beans to make porridge on the anniversary of the Buddha's enlightenment. During the Qing Dynasty, the lamas at the Yonghe Buddhist Temple in Beijing used to make *la ba* porridge for the royal family and government ministers in a giant copper pot. Ordinary people often made *la ba* porridge at home and then gave it to friends and family.

YOUR TURN:

Choose one food that has special religious or spiritual significance from your own culture. Prepare an oral presentation in Chinese on this food, describing what it is and explaining its religious or spiritual significance.

你知道吗？

在中国，很容易就能找到一个饭店。不管是大城市还是小镇，总是有一些大大小小的饭店。如果你打算去一个比较高级(upscale)的饭店，那里的服务跟美国一般饭店的服务差不多。进了饭店，有人领座(seat you)。在你看菜单的时候，服务员会为你送来一些茶水。然后，服务员会过来问你要点什么菜，还会把饭店特别的菜介绍给你。跟美国不同的是，中国饭店的服务员比较多。所以在你吃饭的时候，常常会有一些服务员来为你上茶水、换盘子。等你吃完饭以后，服务员会为你送来账单(zhàngdān, bill)。虽然在中国不一定要付小费(tip)，但是许多高级饭店都会在账单上加上10%–15%的“服务费”。

如果你去一个小饭店吃饭，情况就会不太一样。有些小饭店请顾客先付钱再吃饭。你点完菜以后，马上就得付钱。有些饭店不印(print)菜单，他们把菜单写在一个牌子上，挂在门口或者付钱的地方。一些农村和小镇的小饭店是家庭开的。有的没有菜单，每天做的菜都不一样。春天做春天有的菜，夏天做夏天有的菜。你去吃饭的时候，需要先问一下，那天有什么菜。你也可以把想吃的菜告诉饭店的主人，他们会马上去食品店把这些菜买回来为你做。在小饭店吃饭，不需要付小费。

小饭店

2.3 饮食全球化 The Globalization of Food

对话一

汤姆：我妈妈说，现在中国各地的饮食差别越来越小了。以前，中国南方人吃米饭，北方人吃面食。可是现在呢？南方北方都差不多。不少南方人为了方便，常常吃面食。北方人为了品尝各种各样的菜，在酒席上一定吃米饭。所以，虽然说各地都有一些特色食品，但是我们吃的多数食品已经没有地方特色了。

凯丽：其实，现在无论在哪个国家，吃的东西都越来越相似了。比方说，意大利面，不但意大利人在吃，世界各地的人都在吃。

大卫：拿中国饭来说，无论你去哪个国家，都找得到中国饭店。

玛丽娅：在许多国家都有汉堡、可乐、比萨这样的快餐食品，它们已经变成世界食品了。

凯丽：这么说，饮食也全球化了。

大卫：我觉得饮食全球化会带来一些别的问题。因为每个国家的饮食是由那儿的农业决定的。如果一个地方一年四季都生产新鲜的水果蔬菜，住在那儿的人就会多吃一点儿水果蔬菜。如果一个地方养的牛比较多，那儿的人就会多吃一点儿牛肉。现在虽然交通发达了，可以把食品很快地从一个国家运到别的国家去，可是运食品需要用能源，还要用冰箱冷冻食品。我认为，最简单的方法还是吃在当地生产的食品。这样不但方便，吃的东西新鲜，而且对环境有好处，不会浪费能源。

凯丽：哦，我在超市里看到过一个牌子，上面写着“种在当地，吃在当地”。我觉得这种方法有好处，也有坏处。好处是可以帮助当地的农业生产，不浪费能源，也不需要改变传统的饮食习惯。坏处是，当地人没有机会品尝外国食品，这不是很可惜吗？

汤姆：不一定吧？如果当地的食品很好吃，吃不到外国食品也没有关系。

玛丽娅：可是那些能够全球化的食品一定是比较容易得到、比较容易准备、也比较好吃的食品。要是不好吃，谁要吃啊？

对话二

大卫：星期五下午我们有汉语考试，考完了试，我们是不是应该出去轻松一下？

玛丽娅：好啊，我们可以一起去吃晚饭。

凯丽：吃中餐还是西餐？

汤姆：在学生餐厅每天吃中餐。我们去吃西餐，换换口味吧。

凯丽：离学校不远有几家西餐店，那儿有汉堡、三明治、比萨、意大利面什么的，你们要去哪一家？

大卫：你说的是那几家快餐店吧？快餐店里的西餐不地道。我们要吃就要吃地地道道的西餐。怎么样，你们想吃烤肉吗？

汤姆：新疆烤肉吗？哦，不对，新疆烤肉是中餐，不是西餐。我们去吃韩国烧烤吗？

大卫：不，听说世纪公园附近新开了一家巴西烤肉店。我们可以去那儿尝尝巴西烤肉。

玛丽娅：我吃过巴西烤肉。巴西的烤肉实在是太鲜美了!有牛肉、猪肉、羊肉和鸡肉，随便你选用。服务员把不同的肉串在一起，拿着肉串在饭店里走来走去。谁要吃肉，只要告诉服务员，他就根据你的选择，把肉切下来，放到你的盘子里，你要多少，他就切多少。

汤姆：　你是说，随便你要吃多少肉都可以吗？

玛丽娅：是的，只要你吃得下，三盘、五盘、十盘都没有关系。

凯丽：　可是，吃得太多会让人不舒服吧？

汤姆：　别担心，虽然我很喜欢吃肉，但是为了健康，我不会暴吃的。

玛丽娅：我觉得生活在上海挺好的。无论要吃哪国的饭，都能吃到。

汤姆：　其实，现在住在哪儿都没有关系。世界各国的食品差别越来越小了，尤其是那些好吃的东西，很快就会全球化。

大卫：　对，巴西烤肉也一样。巴西是南美洲最先养牛的国家。从十六世纪开始，就开始养牛，烤肉是巴西的传统食品，后来才慢慢地传到了别的国家，各国的人都觉得好吃，所以今天在每个大城市，差不多都能吃到巴西烤肉。

凯丽：　那么有名的食品，我还没吃过！真对不起我自己。星期五，我们一定去品尝一下。

生词

	Simplified	*Traditional*	*Pinyin*	*Part of Speech*	*English*
1.	全球化		quánqiúhuà	*n./v.*	globalization, globalize
2.	品尝	品嘗	pǐncháng	*v.*	taste
3.	无论	無論	wúlùn	*conj.*	regardless of, no matter (what, whether…)
4.	相似		xiāngsì	*adj.*	similar

5. 运	運	yùn	*v.*	ship, transport
6. 能源		néngyuán	*n.*	energy
7. 冷冻	冷凍	lěngdòng	*adj.*	frozen
8. 简单	簡單	jiǎndān	*adj.*	simple
9. 好处	好處	hǎochù	*n.*	advantage, benefit
10. 种	種	zhòng	*v.*	plant, grow
11. 当地	當地	dāngdì	*adj.*	local
12. 坏处	壞處	huàichù	*n.*	disadvantage, harm
13. 地道		dìdào	*adj.*	authentic, real
14. 烧烤	燒烤	shāokǎo	*n.*	barbecue, roast
15. 串		chuàn	*n./v.*	string, string together
16. 选择	選擇	xuǎnzé	*n./v.*	choice, choose, select
17. 暴		bào	*adv.*	excessively
18. 差别		chàbié	*n.*	difference, discrepancy
19. 尤其		yóuqí	*adv.*	particularly, especially

专名

20. 南美洲	Nán Měizhōu	South America

语言注释

1. 无论 [Regardless of; no matter (what, when, whether…)]

We have learned 不管 in Lesson 1.4. 无论 has the same basic meaning as 不管; the only difference is 无论 is used more in written Chinese.

无论在什么地方，都有很多车。
No matter where it is, there are many cars.

无论在哪个国家，都有一些风景点。
No matter which country it is, there are some scenic spots.

无论你是初中生还是高中生，都要参加毕业考试。
Whether you are a middle school student or a high school student, you have to take the graduation exam.

2. 对···有好处 (Be beneficial to...)

“种在当地，吃在当地”对当地的经济有好处。
“Growing locally and eating locally” is beneficial to the local economy.

多吃蔬菜水果对身体有好处。
Eating more vegetables and fruits is good for your health.

If something is harmful, we can use 对···有坏处:

暴吃暴喝对健康有坏处。
Eating and drinking excessively is harmful to health.

3. 尤其 (Particularly, especially)

那家饭店的菜做得很好，尤其是牛肉。
That restaurant’s dishes are very well prepared, particularly their beef dishes.

这张光盘上的歌非常好听，尤其是那首名字叫“春天”的歌。
The songs on this CD are great, particularly the one called “Spring.”

4. 对不起（人）(Let someone down)

我爸爸为了帮助我上大学，每天下班以后还去打工。如果我不好好学习，就太对不起他了。
In order to help me go to college, my father has taken a part-time job after work. If I don’t study well, I would let him down.

让我们好好生活。这样才对得起我们自己。
Let’s lead great lives. This way we won’t let ourselves down.

学无止境

We have learned the names of some popular food around the world. Here are some additional ones. Pinyin is provided for new characters only.

肉串 *kabobs*	泡(pào)菜 *pickled vegetables*	玉米饼 *taco, corn tortilla*
炸鸡 *fried chicken*	甜甜圈(quān) *donut*	布(bù)丁蛋糕 *muffin*
馅(xiàn)饼 *pie (sweet or salty)*	咖喱(gāli)鸡 *curry chicken*	寿(shòu)司 *sushi*
炸鱼 *fried fish*	炸薯(shǔ)条 *French fries*	中东口袋(dài)面包 *pita bread*

YOUR TURN:

Write down what you ate yesterday for breakfast, lunch, and dinner. See if your meals contained any food that is popular around the world. Share your findings with your peers.

早餐	午餐	晚餐

温故知新 GAIN NEW INSIGHT THROUGH REVIEW

We have learned some proverbs that have something to do with "transportation" and "travel." Do you know the meaning of the following proverbs?

车水马龙	读万卷书，行万里路	老马识途
轻车熟路	一路平安	走马观花

中国文化一瞥

Chinese sayings

The following sayings give advice on taking actions. Pinyin is provided only for those phrases with new characters.

1. shào zhuàng bù nǔ lì, lǎo dà tú shāng bēi
少 壮 不 努 力，老 大 徒 伤 悲

if one does not exert oneself in youth, one will regret it in old age

IN USE:

老师和家长常常说，年轻的时候应该好好学习，要不然就会“少壮不努力，老大徒伤悲。”

Teachers and parents often say that (we) should study hard when we are young. Otherwise, we will be in the situation of “not working hard in our youth and regretting it in an old age.”

YOUR TURN:

Answer the following two questions and share your answers in class.

1. 你觉得“少壮不努力，老大徒伤悲”有道理吗？
2. 年轻的时候应该在哪些方面努力？

2. 言 必 行，行 必 果

what is said must be put into action, what is put into action must succeed; promises must be kept and actions must show results

IN USE:

不管是谁，都应该言必行，行必果。

No matter who you are, you should keep your promises and work until you reach your goals.

要做好生意，公司就应该言必行，行必果。

To do business well, the company should keep its promises and make sure its actions lead to results.

YOUR TURN:

Decide which of the following correctly explains the meaning of 言必行，行必果.

A. 说过的话和做过的事都会有结果。

B. 说过的话就应该去做，做一件事一定要有结果。

C. 说过的话会带来很好的结果。

D. 先说话再做事，最后就会有好结果。

3. 有 志 者，事 竟 成

where there is a will, there is a way; those with a will are sure to be successful

IN USE:

如果你想当班长，就应该参加竞选。“有志者，事竟成”嘛。

If you would like to be class president, you should run for it. Where there's a will, there's a way.

“有志者，事竟成”。经过一年的努力，他终于会说中文了。

"Where there's a will, there's a way." After a year's hard work, he can speak Chinese at last.

YOUR TURN:

Did you do something that was difficult but you succeeded in the end? This is an example of 有志者，事竟成. Share your experience with a peer.

Symbolism in Chinese Food

春卷和“咬(yǎo, bite)春”

春卷算是在美国的中餐馆里最常见的食品了。可是你知道吗？传统上中国人只有在立春 (lì chūn, Beginning of Spring) 那一天才吃春卷，叫做“咬春”。吃春卷的习俗是在唐朝的时候开始的。古书上说，唐人在立春那一天做春饼，里面包上春蒿 (chūnhāo, spring wormwood)、黄韭 (huángjiǔ, spring chives) 等等在立春的时候最先发芽 (fāyá, sprout) 的青菜。用这些菜做春卷里的馅儿，一口咬下去不但味道鲜美，而且有「咬春」的涵义 (hányì, implication)。有一部明朝的历史书上说，立春那天，北京城里的男女老少，无论贫富贵贱 (pín fù guì jiàn, rich or poor, noble or ordinary)，都互相送春卷，祝亲友们春天快乐。

Spring Rolls and "Biting Into the Spring"

Spring rolls may be one of the most popular appetizers in the Chinese restaurants in the U.S. But did you know that traditionally the Chinese only had spring rolls on the day of *li chun*, or the Beginning of Spring according to the lunar calendar. The custom of eating spring rolls known as *yao chun* (biting into the spring), first became popular during the Tang Dynasty. Ancient texts recorded that on *li chun* people in the Tang Dynasty ate a kind of flat bread made of wheat flour which they wrapped around a selection of the first vegetables that sprout in the spring, such as wormwood leaves and chives. As these vegetables were used to fill up the roll, a bite would not only have a very fresh taste, but also would imply that you were "biting into spring." A Ming Dynasty text recorded that, on the day of *li chun*, people in Beijing—regardless of their age and social status—would give each other spring rolls as gifts, wishing each other a happy New Year.

YOUR TURN:

Choose one food that must be eaten during a particular season according to your own cultural tradition. Prepare an oral presentation in Chinese on this food, describe what it is and explain its cultural significance.

你知道吗？

回族是中国人口最多的少数民族之一。回族住在中国的各地，差不多每个城市都有回族。回族的祖先是从许多不同国家来的。公元7世纪，许多波斯和阿拉伯商人来中国做生意，一些人后来就留在中国。他们主要住在中国南部靠海的地区，或者中国北部。后来到了公元13世纪，蒙古军队西征 (zhēng, Western expedition)。那时候，不少中亚的居民搬到中国来住。可以说，中国的回族主要来自中亚、波斯和阿拉伯国家。这些移民都信伊斯兰教，慢慢地变成了一个民族：回族。

回族的饮食有三个特点。一是回族人不吃猪肉，在他们的饮食中，牛羊肉比较多。二是回族主要吃面食，面食的品种很多。三是回族受到阿拉伯饮食的影响，有不少美味的甜食。

2.4 “绿色食品”和“健康食品” “Green Food” and “Health Food”

对话一

玛丽娅：周末我去超市买东西，发现很多食品上都有“绿色食品”或者“健康食品”的标志。绿色食品和健康食品的意思是一样的吧？为什么要有两个不同的名字呢？

凯丽：这个问题很有意思。在超市我还看到过“有机食品”和“天然食品”。这些是不是也是健康食品呢？

玛丽娅：不知道别人怎么看，反正我一看到这些标志，就会觉得这样的食品对我们的健康有好处。

大卫：不见得吧？有些食品，像炸薯片、饼干，也被说成是“绿色食品”。多吃这些食品对我们的健康是没有好处的。

汤姆：食品标志太多，容易让人糊里糊涂。不管怎么说，“健康食品”的意思应该很清楚：吃这些食品对健康有好处，让人不容易生病。

大卫：“天然食品”也不难理解，里边都是天然产品，没有其他的东西。

玛丽娅：可是“有机食品”跟“天然食品”有什么不一样呢？

汤姆：食品生长的时候不用化学品，就是“有机食品”。

凯丽：听你们这么一说，我认为“天然食品”是废话。食品不都是天然生长的吗？

汤姆：那不一定。有些食品，比如香精、糖精、味精就不是天然的，是用化学品制造的。

玛丽娅：我们越说越糊涂了。还是上网去找找信息吧。

超市里的不同食品

对话二

玛丽娅：哎，你们看，我在绿色生活网站找到关于食品标志的回答了。

大卫：真的？网上说，“绿色食品”是什么？

凯丽：“有机食品”呢？

玛丽娅：别急，我们一个一个地看。“绿色食品”就是没有受到污染的食品。在生产这些食品的时候，没用过或者只用过很少的化学品，这些食品没有被化学品污染。

大卫：所以我们可以说，吃绿色食品比较安全。

凯丽：我们再来看一下“天然食品”。天然食品常常是生的蔬菜水果，鱼肉鸡鸭等等。这些食品没有被加过工或者只经过很少的加工。这是什么意思？

汤姆：加过工的食品就是买回来就能吃的东西，还有那些只要简单做一下就能吃的东西，像点心啊、饮料啊、熟肉啊、还有那些冷冻食品。

加工过的肉食

玛丽娅：这么说，天然食品就是买回来以后，要我们自己洗洗、切切、烧烧以后才能吃的食品。

汤姆：哦，就是那些我爷爷奶奶，姥爷姥姥在菜场买的食品。他们为了做饭，每天要花很多时间。

凯丽：也就是说，天然食品和"有机食品"还不一样。天然食品虽然是自然生长的，可是也可能用过化学品。"有机食品"在生长的时候，一定没有用过化学品。

大卫：我看，所有这些食品跟"健康食品"可能有关系，也可能没有关系。"健康食品"应该是不会影响我们身体健康的。绿色食品、天然食品、有机食品只是告诉我们，在种食品和加工食品的时候，发生了什么情况。

玛丽娅：大卫，你真会总结。我们现在知道这些食品标志有哪些不同了。

生词

	Simplified	*Traditional*	*Pinyin*	*Part of Speech*	*English*
1.	标志	標誌	biāozhì	*n.*	label
2.	有机	有機	yǒujī	*adj.*	organic
3.	天然		tiānrán	*adj.*	natural
4.	不见得	不見得	bùjiàndé	*s.p.*	not necessarily
5.	炸薯片		zháshǔpiàn	*n.*	fried potato chips
6.	饼干	餅乾	bǐnggān	*n.*	cookies, crackers
7.	糊里糊涂	糊裡糊塗	húlihútu	*s.p.*	muddle-headed, puzzled, mixed up
8.	化学品	化學品	huàxuépǐn	*n.*	chemical product
9.	废话	廢話	fèihuà	*n.*	nonsense, rubbish
10.	香精		xiāngjīng	*n.*	artificial flavor
11.	糖精		tángjīng	*n.*	artificial sugar
12.	味精		wèijīng	*n.*	monosodium glutamate (MSG)
13.	制造	製造	zhìzào	*v.*	make, manufacture
14.	糊涂	糊塗	hútu	*n.*	muddle-headed, puzzled, mixed up
15.	信息		xìnxī	*n.*	information
16.	污染		wūrǎn	*n./v.*	pollution, pollute
17.	熟		shú	*adj.*	cooked
18.	烧	燒	shāo	*v.*	cook, burn

语言注释

1. 不见得 (Not necessarily)

The meaning of 不见得 is similar to 不一定. 不见得 is often used in spoken Chinese.

贵的东西不见得好。

Expensive things are not necessarily good.

天然食品不见得都对健康有好处。
Not all natural food is necessarily beneficial to your health.

2. 像 (Such as)

When citing an example, we can use 像 to list things.

中国的少数民族，像回族、蒙古族、白族等，都有自己的节日。
China's minorities, such as Hui, Mongolian, Bai and other ethnic groups, all have their own festivals.

有些事，像打扫房间、洗衣服、买东西什么的，可以让孩子学着做。
(You) can let your child learn to do a few chores, such as cleaning up the room, doing laundry, shopping, and so on.

学无止境

We have learned some food labels. Here are some words that usually appear on food packaging. Pinyin is provided for new characters only.

生产日期 *manufacturing date*	到期 *expiration date*	保质期 *good until*
配料 (pèiliào) *ingredients*	营养成分表 *nutrition facts*	热量 *calories*
蛋白质 *protein*	脂肪 (zhīfáng) *fat*	保存方法 *storage (method)*
制造商 *manufacturer*	生产厂家 *manufacturer*	净含 (hán) 量 *net weight*

YOUR TURN:

Look at a food package and use the above words to describe the product inside.

温故知新 GAIN NEW INSIGHT THROUGH REVIEW

We have learned some proverbs and sayings about learning and studying. See if any of the following doesn't belong to this category.

学而不厌	三人行，必有我师	书不释手
只要功夫深， 铁棒磨成针	严师出高徒	三天打渔， 两天晒网
青出于蓝， 而胜于蓝	不知肉味	好好先生

中国文化一瞥

Chinese proverbs and sayings

Here are some proverbs and sayings about nature. Pinyin is only provided for those phrases with new characters.

1. 青 山 绿 水

green hills and blue waters; beautiful scenery; green mountains and rivers

IN USE:

他的老家青山绿水，风景非常美丽。

His hometown has green hills and blue waters. The scenery there is beautiful.

我们应该保护这儿的青山绿水，不让它们受到污染。

We should protect the mountains and rivers here, and not let them be polluted.

YOUR TURN:

Answer the following question:

你去过一个有青山绿水的地方吗？请给我们介绍一下那个地方。

2. 海　无　边，江　无　底

The ocean is boundless, the river is bottomless; something profound; something without boundary

IN USE:

他的知识非常丰富，就像海无边，江无底。

His knowledge is very rich, like boundless oceans and bottomless rivers.

YOUR TURN:

Use 海无边，江无底 to talk about one of the following.

Model: 父母对我的感情是海无边，江无底。

爱情	友情	新技术	亲情	自然资源

3. 人　不　知　春　草　知　春

spring is sooner recognized by plants than people

IN USE:

我们到了山上，看到草已经绿了，才感觉到春天已经来了。真是“人不知春草知春”啊。

Only after we climbed up the hill and saw the grass had turned green did we realize that spring had come. Plants really recognize spring faster than people do.

YOUR TURN:

你同意"人不知春草知春"的说法吗？说一下，你是怎么知道春天到了。

4. bǎi chuān guī hǎi
百 川 归 海
all rivers flow into the sea; all things go in one direction

IN USE:

全世界的人民都希望世界和平，就像百川归海。
People all over the world hope for world peace. This is just like all rivers flowing in a single direction.

YOUR TURN:

Work with a peer. After you have found something that everyone wishes for, use 百川归海 to describe it.

除了和平以外，还有哪些事情也是大家都希望的？

Symbolism in Chinese Food

"好吃不过年饺子"

在中国的北方有一句俗语 (súyǔ, common saying)，叫做"好吃不过年饺子"。饺子是每个家庭春节的年夜饭上都必须有的美餐，这是因为饺子的样子很像元宝 (yuánbǎo, ingots made of silver or gold)，吃饺子象征着把财宝招 (zhāo, hail)进家门。除夕吃饺子的习俗在明清 (the Ming and Qing Dynasties) 的时候已经很盛行 (shèngxíng, popular) 了。过年的饺子一般要在年三十的晚上先包好，等到半夜子时 (midnight) 才可以煮 (zhǔ, boil)了吃。子时是"更岁交子" (the new year replaces the old at midnight on New Year's Eve) 的时刻 (shíkè, moment)，也就是新年到来的时候。在这个时候吃饺子，是因为"饺子"和"交子"听上去一样，有"更岁交子"的意思。年夜饭吃了饺子，一年都会象饺子一样圆圆满满 (yuányuán mǎnmǎn, fulfilling) 了。

Dumplings: The Best Food

There is a saying in Northern China: No food can be better than the dumplings made for the New Year. Indeed, a New Year's Eve meal is not complete without dumplings. One reason why the Chinese must have dumplings during the New Year is that the shape of dumplings resembles *yuanbao*, or gold and silver ingots that were used as currency in ancient China. Eating dumplings takes on the symbolic meaning of bringing prosperity into one's house. The custom of having dumplings on New Year's Eve was already quite popular during the Ming and Qing Dynasties. New Year's dumplings should be wrapped ahead of time and cooked at midnight on New Year's Eve. Midnight in Chinese is *zi shi*, or the *zi* hour, which is the hour when the old year ends and the new year begins. The transition from the old year to the new year is called "*gengsui jiaozi*" (the new year replaces the old at midnight on New Year's Eve) in Chinese. At this time you eat dumplings, as *jiaozi* (dumplings) has the same pronunciation as *jiaozi* (the passing of the *zi* hour), so that "dumplings" comes to have the meaning of "the changing of the years." By eating dumplings at midnight on New Year's Eve, the next year is then hoped to be as fulfilling as the dumplings.

YOUR TURN:

Choose a food item that is indispensible on the New Year's Eve dinner menu in your own country. Prepare an oral presentation in Chinese on this food, describe what it is and explain its significance.

你知道吗？

在中国人的饮食中，粮食（米饭和面食）和蔬菜占大多数。他们也吃一点儿肉或者鱼，可是数量不太多。在中国，吃甜食的人不多。传统的点心和小吃一般都是咸的，像包子、炸豆腐、豆腐干(dòufŭgān, dried bean curd)、花生(peanut)、春卷、饺子什么的。

以前，一般的中国人吃水果吃得不太多。那是因为虽然中国地方很大，可是不是每个地方都生产水果。水果需要从一个地方运到另外一个地方。这样，水果不但比较贵，而且也不是很新鲜。现在不一样了，因为有了冷冻技术，交通也越来越方便，可以很快地把水果运到各个地方。这样，无论在哪儿都可以买到新鲜的水果。在中国人的饮食中，水果也比以前增加了。

中国最常见的饮料是茶。茶有红茶、绿茶、花茶。喝绿茶的人比较多。中国人喝茶不放糖，也不放牛奶。

各种各样的茶

2.5 中国的饮食文化 China's Food Culture

对话一

大卫：昨天教育频道有一个关于中国食文化的电视节目，介绍了文化传统对饮食的影响。这个节目说，有时候，一个国家的饮食习惯是由文化传统决定的。

凯丽：文化传统有那么大的作用吗？饮食应该是由一个国家的农业决定的吧？

大卫：虽然吃什么可能主要是由农业决定的，但是文化传统对怎么吃一定是有影响的。那个电视节目举了一个例子说，从古代开始，中国人就喜欢在一起吃饭，常常是一个家庭、或者亲戚朋友聚在一起吃饭。这种传统影响到中国人对吃饭的看法。他们觉得，吃饭不但是为了吃饱，也是为了培养人跟人的感情。

汤姆：这种说法很有道理。自从搬家来中国以后，我父母差不多每个星期不是请人吃饭就是被人请去吃饭。不像我们住在美国的时候，没有那么多请客吃饭的情况。

大卫：这个电视节目还介绍说，中国的文化传统之一是好客，如果有朋友从很远的地方来看你，这是非常让人愉快的。所以客人来了，中国人总是要做很多菜给客人吃。在吃饭的时候，会一再让客人多吃一点儿，并且把菜夹到客人的碗里。

玛丽娅：中国人的确很喜欢请朋友吃饭，一有机会大家就在一起吃饭。为了庆祝结婚、毕业、找到工作、过生日、生孩子什么的，一般的中国人常常在饭店办酒席。要是你去朋友家玩儿，他们也常常留你吃饭。

汤姆： 我有点儿怕跟中国人去吃饭，他们总是让你多吃一点儿。哪怕客人说已经吃饱了，他们还是会把许多吃的东西夹到你的碗里。

凯丽： 我刚到中国的时候，也觉得这样做有点儿奇怪，别人吃不下了，为什么还非要别人吃呢？后来才知道，这是中国人的传统习惯，这样做会让主人和客人都很愉快。

大卫： 凯丽，现在你同意了吧？文化传统会影响一个国家的饮食方式。

对话二

玛丽娅： 我常常听人说，中国有一句名言“民以食为天”，这是什么意思？

大卫： 人们觉得吃饭是生活中最重要的事。

汤姆： 怪不得我姥姥常常说，“开门七件事，柴米油盐酱醋茶。”这七样东西都跟做饭吃饭有关。

大卫： 的确是这样。我看的那个电视节目还说，文化也影响到人们怎么吃。比方说，从古代开始，中国人就喜欢吃热的和熟的食品，不喜欢吃冷的和生的。几千年来，中国人用不同的方法烹调食品，一种菜可以作出几十种不同的味道来，所以中国人的烹调技术非常高。

凯丽： 而且中国人做菜的时候，很注意菜的颜色、香味和味道。一个好的菜应该有各种颜色，红、绿、黄、白、黑等等。这样就需要用不同的蔬菜、鱼、肉，才能让一个菜有许多不同的颜色。

玛丽娅：要让一个菜有香味，就需要加一些不同的香料吧？

汤姆：对，实际上，许多国家的菜都讲究香味，做菜的时候加香料是很平常的事。

大卫：要让一个菜味道好，就需要放不同的调料。中国主要的调料是油、盐、酱、醋、糖。

玛丽娅：现在网上电视上常常介绍"营养学"，说是通过吃，可以让大家少生病，更健康。你们相信吗？

大卫：当然相信。那个电视节目说，两千多年以前，中国人就发现不同的食品里有不同的营养，人们应该吃不同的东西。可是有些东西没有味道不好吃，所以可以用甜、酸、苦、辣、咸这五种味道来烹调食品，让它们变得好吃一些。同时，中国人觉得不同的季节应该吃不同的食品。他们把食品分成"热性"、"中性"、"凉性"等等。比方说，热性的食品，夏天天气太热，就应该少吃一些，冬天可以多吃一些。

凯丽：哪些食品是热性的？

大卫：一般来说是辣的东西。中国人觉得热性食品吃得太多了对身体不好，容易发烧，长痘子。

汤姆：啊呀，我的脸上长了两个痘子，是不是因为上个星期吃了两次四川菜？

玛丽娅：不会吧？能那么"立竿见影"吗？

各种各样的食品

生词

	Simplified	Traditional	Pinyin	Part of Speech	English
1.	举例子	舉例子	jǔlìzi	*v.o.*	give an example, cite an example
2.	古代		gǔdài	*n.*	ancient times
3.	聚		jù	*v.*	gather
4.	好客		hàokè	*adj.*	hospitable
5.	愉快		yúkuài	*adj.*	pleasant, happy
6.	并且	並且	bìngqiě	*conj.*	moreover, furthermore
7.	夹		jiā	*v.*	press from both sides (pick up food with chopsticks)
8.	留		liú	*v.*	ask someone to stay
9.	哪怕		nǎpà	*conj.*	even, even if, even though
10.	名言		míngyán	*n.*	well-known saying
11.	柴		chái	*n.*	firewood
12.	米		mǐ	*n.*	rice (uncooked)
13.	酱		jiàng	*n.*	sauce
14.	香料		xiāngliào	*n.*	spices
15.	调料	調料	tiáoliào	*n.*	seasoning
16.	营养学	營養學	yíngyǎngxué	*n.*	nutritional science, nutrition
17.	热性	熱性	rèxìng	*n.*	hot type (of food or medicine)
18.	中性		zhōngxìng	*n.*	neutral type (of food or medicine)
19.	凉性		liángxìng	*n.*	cool type (of food or medicine)
20.	痘子		dòuzi	*n.*	pimple
21.	立竿见影	立竿見影	lì gān jiàn yǐng	*s.p.*	set up a pole and see its shadow—get instant results

语言注释

1. 举例子 (Give an example, cite an example)

王老师上课的时候常常举例子。听他的课比较容易懂。
Teacher Wang often cites examples when giving a class. It is easier to understand his lessons.

在谈到饮食全球化的时候，你能举两个例子吗？
When talking about food globalization, can you give a couple of examples?

2. 像 (Similar to, resemble)

In Lesson 2.4 we learned 像 has the meaning of "such as." It has another meaning of "look like, or "resemble."

他很像他爸爸。
He resembles his father.

这儿的天气很像我老家。冬天老下雨。
The weather here is similar to my hometown. It always rains in winter.

我像你一样，很注意食品标志。
Like you, I also pay a lot of attention to food labels.

3. 并且 (Moreover, furthermore)

他们去校外考察的时候，参观了历史博物馆，并且看了一个历史电影。
When they took a field trip they visited the history museum, moreover, they also saw a history movie.

购物中心里有一个健身中心，并且有一个溜冰场。
Inside the shopping mall, there is a gym. Moreover, there is also a skating rink.

4. 哪怕 (Even if, even though)

哪怕 is a conjunction, and it is often used with 也.

哪怕刮风下雨，他也去跑步。
Even if it is windy and rainy, he still jogs.

哪怕电脑坏了，你不是还有笔吗？为什么不做作业呢？
Even if the computer was down, didn't you still have a pen? Why didn't you do your homework?

学无止境

To demonstrate that the Chinese make one type of food into many different flavors, the following is a list of chicken dishes that are commonly served in restaurants. Pinyin is provided for new characters only.

炸鸡	fried crispy chicken
盐水鸡	boiled salted chicken
葱 (cōng, onion or scallion) 油鸡	steamed chicken with scallions
香叶鸡	basil chicken
川酱鸡	chicken in Sichuan spicy sauce
甜酸鸡	sweet and sour chicken
辣子鸡	spicy chicken
咖喱鸡	curry chicken
柠檬 (níngméng, lemon) 鸡	lemon chicken
陈皮鸡	Mandarin chicken
宫 (gōng) 保鸡	Kung Pao chicken
铁板 (tiěbǎn, sizzling plate) 鸡	sizzling chicken
豉汁 (chǐzhī, black bean sauce) 鸡	chicken in black bean sauce

YOUR TURN:

Next time you eat at a Chinese restaurant, see if you can recognize any chicken dishes on the menu.

温故知新 GAIN NEW INSIGHT THROUGH REVIEW

We have learned many words and phrases that contain the characters 天 and 地. See if you remember the meaning of the following words and phrases.

谢天谢地	地区	地铁	冬天	地理
夏天	天下一家	星期天	桃李满天下	地图
天气	地方	改天换地	天下为公	阴天
天翻地覆	聊天	地道	晴天	天气预报

中国文化一瞥

Chinese proverbs

Here are some proverbs and sayings about different flavors. The Chinese often use flavors as an analogy for experiences in life. Pinyin is only provided for those phrases with new characters.

1. kǔ jìn gān lái
苦 尽 甘 来
after the bitterness comes the sweetness; the bitterness is gone and the sweetness is here; a good life comes after hardship

2. 先 苦 后 甜
sweetness follows bitterness; after some hardship, life has become sweet

IN USE:

中国父母常常对孩子说，先苦后甜/苦尽甘来。年轻的时候要努力学习，将来才可能生活得好。

Chinese parents often tell their children that a good life comes after some hardship. Study hard when you are young, and you will have a good life in the future.

老王努力工作了很多年，终于苦尽甘来，建立了自己的公司。

Old Wang worked hard for many years. Finally, a good life came after hardship and he established his own company.

YOUR TURN:

Can you use 先甜后苦 or 苦尽甘来 to describe the following situations?

1. 他年轻的时候有非常理想的工作，可是后来生病了，不能工作，所以现在他的生活不太好。	可以	不可以
2. 她离婚了，一个人养两个孩子，生活很难。可是她的两个孩子都上了大学，现在都生活得很好。她非常高兴。	可以	不可以
3. 小时候，她家很有钱，所以她每天吃喝玩乐。现在她把家里的钱都用完了，她又找不到工作，只好住在马路上。	可以	不可以
4. 他小时候努力学习，成年以后努力工作，他的生活一直很好。	可以	不可以

3. wǔ wèi jù quán
五 味 俱 全

with five flavors (sweet, sour, bitter, spicy, and salty); all flavors; all kinds of life experiences

IN USE:

健康饮食应该五味俱全。这样可以吃各种各样的食品。

A healthy diet should include all flavors. This way, one can eat all kinds of food.

这个饭店的菜是五味俱全。谁都能找到自己喜欢吃的菜。

The restaurant's dishes have all five flavors. Everyone can find his favorite dish.

YOUR TURN:

Discuss the following questions with your peers.

1. 你觉得生活里也可能五味俱全吗？
2. 生活中哪些经历给人带来苦味或者甜味？

A Chinese joke

古时候，有一个人去朋友家做客。他在朋友家住了很久了，还不打算离开。主人想，这个客人在我家住了那么长时间了，什么时候才打算走呢？一天，主人看到外边在下雨，就想，今天下雨，客人又走不了了。他写了两句诗，“下雨天留客，天留我不留”，可是他没有写标点符号 (biāodiǎn fúhào, punctuation)，所以他的诗看上去是这样的：“下雨天留客天留我不留。”

那个客人看到了以后，就把标点符号加在这两句诗里：“下雨天，留客天，留我不？留。”

YOUR TURN:

Translate the two versions of the poem into English.

Symbolism in Chinese Food

枣 (zǎo, dates) 栗子 (lìzi, chestnuts) 和早立子

中国人在举办婚礼的时候，常常用枣和栗子做成果盘，向新婚夫妇 (fūfù, a married couple) 表示祝福 (zhùfú, blessing)，祝福他们“早立子” (zǎo lìzǐ, being blessed with a son soon)，或者“早生贵子”。这是因为“枣”和“早日”的“早”谐音，“栗子”和“立子”谐音。把枣和栗子放在一起，是希望新婚夫妇早一天生儿子。

“早立子”（枣栗子）这个习俗后面还有这样一个故事。古时候有一对姓陡 (dǒu, a surname) 的夫妻 (fūqī, husband and wife)。他们结婚多年，感情很好，可是没有孩子。他们的生活很简单：丈夫 (zhàngfū, husband) 每天到海里打渔 (dǎyú, go fishing)，妻子(qīzǐ, wife)在山上种枣树。每次丈夫出门打渔，妻子总是让丈夫带着一袋干枣 (dried dates)，饿的时候可以吃。有一天，丈夫出去打渔的时候遇到暴风雨 (bàofēngyǔ, severe thunderstorm)，一夜没有回家。妻子看到丈夫没有回来，就请村里人划着船去找丈夫。大家找了三天三夜，终于在一个小岛上找到了她丈夫。丈夫回家以后告诉妻子，他是靠着 (kàozhe, rely on) 妻子给他的干枣活下来的。这件事发生后的第二年，这对夫妻终于生下了一个可爱的小男孩。慢慢儿地，后人就把陡氏夫妇 (dǒushì fūfù, the Dous) 吃枣生子的故事，和“早立子”的祝愿 (zhùyuàn, wish) 联系了起来。

Dates, Chestnuts, and Being Blessed with a Son

When Chinese people have weddings, they often will put together a plate of dates and chestnuts for the newlyweds as a blessing, wishing that they will soon give birth to a son. The pronunciation of dates and chestnuts in Chinese is exactly like "to be soon blessed with a son." In Chinese, "dates" and "early" have the same pronunciation, as do "chestnuts" and "raise a son."

Behind the custom of giving dates and chestnuts to newlyweds is an old story. In ancient times there was a couple by the name of Dou. They were happily married for many years, but were childless. Their lives were very simple: every day the husband went to the sea to fish while the wife went up the mountain to tend to her date trees. Every time the husband went out to fish, the wife would give him a bag of dried dates to carry with him, so that he could eat them whenever he was hungry. One day, the husband ran into a thunderstorm while fishing in the ocean and did not come home at night. When the wife saw that he did not come home, she asked the villagers to take their boats and go look for him. Everyone searched for three days and nights, when finally they found the husband on a remote island. After the husband returned home, he told his wife that he had survived on nothing but the dried dates that she gave him. The second year after this incident, the couple gave birth to a lovely boy. Over time, many came to conflate the story of the Dous with the wish "to be soon blessed with sons."

YOUR TURN:

Choose a food item that is commonly seen at a wedding. Prepare an oral presentation in Chinese on this food, describe what it is and explain its significance.

你知道吗？

有客人来家里访问的时候，中国人习惯用茶水招待客人。只要来了客人，主人 (host) 都会为客人送来一杯茶。客人为了表示 (biǎoshì, express) 对主人的尊敬 (zūnjìng, respect)，无论是不是想喝茶，都应该喝一两口。但是要注意，客人喝茶不能喝得太快，也不能把杯子里的茶水都喝完。

到了吃饭的时候，主人会留客人一起吃饭。主人会说："跟我们一起吃一点家常便饭吧。"不留客人吃饭是不客气的。客人这时候应该谢谢主人的好意，并且表示要离开主人家。客人可以说，"谢谢，可是我还有事，我该走了。"为了表示客气，主人和客人一个非要留客，一个非要离开，这样常常会花去一些时间。最后，客人会接受主人的邀请，跟主人一起吃饭。当然，如果客人不打算在主人家吃饭，就应该在午饭前一个小时左右就离开主人家。

吃饭的时候，大家又要为谁先坐下，坐在哪儿花去一些时间。客人应该坐在上座（面对门口的座位），主人坐在下座（靠近门口的座位）。在吃饭的时候，客人不能吃得太快，也不能吃得太多或者太少。主人总是让客人多吃一点儿，并且把菜夹给客人。主人夹菜的时候，客人常常会说自己已经吃饱了，吃不下了。可是不管客人说什么，主人都觉得为了表示客气，应该把更多的菜夹到客人的碗里，因为让客人吃饱是非常重要的。吃完饭以后，客人会说："谢谢，饭好吃极了。"主人回答："哪里哪里。一点家常便饭，真是不好意思。"

2.6 第二单元复习 Unit 2 Review

对话

凯丽：大卫，你是从香港来的。有人说，“吃在香港”。这是为什么呢？

大卫：我在香港的时候，也常常听人说，香港是“美食天堂”。他们说，香港的食文化结合了东方文化和西方文化。除了各地的中国菜以外，在香港我们还能吃到世界各国的菜，欧洲、亚洲、美洲、非洲的菜都能吃到。

凯丽：可是只要是大城市，不是都能吃到各国的菜吗？为什么说香港是美食天堂，别的城市就不是呢？

大卫：可能每个城市都认为自己是“美食天堂”吧。不过，香港人的确是非常重视吃，香港的食品种类特别多。香港的居民来自世界各国和中国各地，而且这些居民也很不同，有的非常有钱，有的没有钱，所以他们的饮食很不一样。在香港，你可以花很多钱，去非常高级的饭店吃饭，也可以花很少钱，去买传统的“街头食品”。那些街头食品简单、好吃、便宜，非常有特色。

香港的一条街

凯丽：街头食品品种多吗？

大卫：非常多，冷的、热的、干的、湿的都有，各地各国的都有。

凯丽：香港离广东很近。香港人和广东人的饮食是不是很相似？

大卫：香港的广东餐馆的确很多，因为广东人比较多。可是香港还有许多从中国各地来的移民，他们也带来了各地的特色菜。一般来说，广东来的移民在家做广东菜，上海来的在家做上海菜，山东来的在家做山东菜。

凯丽：广东人爱饮茶，香港也有许多可以饮茶的餐厅吧？

大卫：对，这样的餐厅在香港叫“茶楼”，一般的中国餐厅叫“酒楼”。为了让食品比较卫生，现在街头食品都放在小饭店里卖，这样的小饭店叫“茶餐厅”。这是因为茶餐厅不但供应点心和小吃，而且还供应咖啡、奶茶、冷饮等等。

凯丽：奶茶？香港人喝茶放牛奶吗？一般的中国人喝茶不放奶，也不放糖。

大卫：香港人学习了英国的饮食文化，许多人习惯喝英国的“下午茶”，也习惯象英国人一样，在茶里加牛奶和糖。

凯丽：香港的饮食文化听上去太有意思了。希望我有机会去香港，尝尝各种食品。

课文

Send	Reply	Reply All	Forward	Print	Delete

凯丽：你好！

我这几天正在准备大考，你呢？寒假你有什么计划吗？如果有兴趣，欢迎你来大理做客。

我在大理生活差不多半年了，非常喜欢这个城市。大理的气候好，四季如春，风景也很美丽。一年四季都有许多游客来大理。游客们到了大理，除了参观这儿的风景以外，都想品尝一下云南菜。我的同学告诉我，大理菜可以说代表了云南菜。

中国人常说，“靠山吃山，靠水吃水。”意思是，住在山附近的人常常吃山里生长的东西，住在江河和大海旁边的人常常吃水里生长的东西。拿大理来说，这儿有高山也有大湖，所以天然的绿色食品很多。选用绿色食品是大理菜的一个特点。同时，大理菜的味道一般都比较浓，辣的很辣，酸的很酸。

到了大理，游客们也都希望参加一些少数民族的文化活动。不少人喜欢去尝一下白族的“三道茶”。白族人家无论是过节、庆祝生日、还是结婚，都要请客人喝“一苦二甜三回味”的三道茶。三道茶就是让客人喝三种不同的茶。第一杯是苦的，第二杯是甜的，第三杯有不同的味道，需要客人回味。这代表了人的生活，先苦后甜，给人很多可以回味的经历。如果你来大理，我一定带你去喝三道茶。

请问玛丽娅、汤姆、大卫好！

明英

大理街头的白族

生词

	Simplified	*Traditional*	*Pinyin*	*Part of Speech*	*English*
1.	美食		měishí	*n.*	delicious food
2.	天堂		tiāntáng	*n.*	paradise, heaven
3.	结合	結合	jiéhé	*n./v.*	combination, combine
4.	高级	高級	gāojí	*adj.*	high-class, high-ranking
5.	街头食品	街頭食品	jiētóu shípǐn	*n.*	street food, food sold on street
6.	湿		shī	*adj.*	wet
7.	生长	生長	shēngzhǎng	*v.*	grow
8.	回味		huíwèi	*n./v.*	aftertaste, retrospect

专名

9.	白族	Bái zú	Bai ethnic group

生词扩充

Many Chinese words are formed by combining two or more characters. If you know the characters in a word, you can often guess the meaning of that word. See if you understand the meaning of the following words.

餐饮业		美食街	
聚会		浓汤	
湿热		亿万	
菜干		品茶	
污水		农作物	
合同工		海运	
简化		果酱	

营养师		废气	
工业品		暴雨	
怪味		欢天喜地	

SELF-ASSESSMENT

In Unit 2, you have learned about various aspects of agriculture, food, and diet. Specifically, you can talk about major cuisines in China, some specialty dishes, the foods eaten by Chinese Muslims, popular foods around the world, the advantages and disadvantages of food globalization, good labels, and Chinese customs related to food. Have you reached the learning goals of Unit 2? After completing the exercises for Unit 2 in your Workbook, fill out the following self-assessment sheet.

Yes/No	*Can you do these things in Chinese?*
	Talk briefly about China's agriculture
	Describe the relation between agriculture and diet
	Talk about the major cuisines in China
	Talk briefly about Muslims in China
	Talk about food that is popular around the world
	Discuss the advantages and disadvantages of food globalization
	Describe, in some detail, a specialty dish
	Describe the differences of food labels
	Describe briefly the general process of growing and manufacturing food
	Describe Chinese cultural customs related to eating
	Describe, in some detail, how Chinese view food

9–11	yes	excellent
6–8	yes	good
1–5	yes	need some work

第三单元：发展和环境

UNIT 3 Development and the Environment

LEARNING GOALS OF UNIT 3

By the end of this unit, you will learn how to:

- Describe, in some detail, a greener way to celebrate holidays
- Describe different types of pollution
- Describe general economic development
- Describe various ways to protect the environment
- Describe, with some examples, a green life
- Compare globalization and localization
- Discuss the impact of commercialization, particularly commercial advertisements
- Describe, in some detail, an online business transaction
- Describe China's geographic environment
- Discuss the relationship between geography and economic development

3.1 绿色的春节
A Green Spring Festival

对话一

汤姆：　春节过得怎么样？

玛丽娅：很不错，我姥爷姥姥也来上海过年。大年夜，跟一般的中国家庭一样，我们全家在一起吃了年夜饭，看了"春节晚会"的节目。过春节的时候，不是我们去访问朋友，就是朋友来我们家，非常热闹。

汤姆：　大年夜，你们放鞭炮了吗？

玛丽娅：没有。因为放鞭炮不但声音很大，带来噪音污染，而且烟尘很大，容易带来空气污染。为了过一个绿色的春节，今年我们小区的居民建议，谁都不放鞭炮。

汤姆：　这样不影响你们睡觉了吧？以前到了半夜十二点，大家都出来放鞭炮。放几个还没什么，可是这几年越放越多，有人一次就放几千个，乒乒乓乓，让人睡不了觉。过年的时候出门去，地上到处都是纸屑，看上去很脏。不放鞭炮就没有这些问题了。可是我也担心过年放鞭炮是中国的传统，代表送旧迎新，要是不放鞭炮，会不会影响大家愉快地过年？

玛丽娅：我们小区的居民讨论了这个问题，大家觉得，可以用其他的方法来送旧迎新，比如，写春联，挂气球，在小区各个地方放一些花，这样庆祝春节也很好。今年过完春节以后，大家都说，不放鞭炮是个好主意。新年的时候，小区不但很安静，也很干净，一点也没有影响大家高高兴兴过春节。你的春节过得怎么样？

庆祝春节

汤姆：　春节的时候，我们一家去海南岛旅游了。
玛丽娅：海南岛天气暖和，风景又好，春节的时候，去那里旅游的人一定很多吧？
汤姆：　是的。因为游客比较多，所以不少旅游景点都请大家要注意保护环境，不要乱丢垃圾，要保护景点的一草一木。有个牌子上写着，“美丽的海南岛，我只留下了我的脚印，带走了你的照片。”
玛丽娅：哦，你的意思是说，我们都要做绿色的旅游者，要保护旅游景点的环境。
汤姆：　对。要是海南岛上都是垃圾，谁还想去呢？
玛丽娅：所以每个人都应该从小事做起，从自己做起，来保护环境。

对话二

凯丽：　过年以前我去超市买年货，看到墙上写着：让野生动物平平安安地过年。这是不是有点儿奇怪？野生动物跟过年有什么关系？
汤姆：　这有什么奇怪的！乱放鞭炮，不就把野生动物都吓跑了？
凯丽：　可是城市里本来就没有什么野生动物。除了动物园里住着一些野生动物的后代以外，城市里哪有野生动物？
汤姆：　对，真是莫名其妙。
大卫：　谁说的？我们先想想，超市和野生动物有什么关系？
汤姆：　哦，我知道了，你是说不应该吃野生动物，是不是？
大卫：　是的。因为有些人喜欢吃野味，所以超市要他们注意最好不吃野味。
凯丽：　听说有的人，除了桌子以外，四条腿的东西都吃。怪不得超市要让大家保护野生动物。
汤姆：　野生动物已经越来越少了，需要大家保护它们，所以最好不要吃野味。

凯丽：除了不吃野味以外，过年的时候最好也别大吃大喝。大吃大喝不但对身体不好，而且对环境也不好。生产食品需要用资源，大吃大喝会浪费资源。今年过春节，我们家就跟平时一样，吃得很简单。而且今年去看朋友的时候，大家都不送礼物。

大卫：不送礼物是不是不客气呢？

凯丽：我家的亲戚朋友都说，过春节本来就是为了要跟家人和朋友在一起，不是为了送礼物。

汤姆：对，我最不喜欢去买礼物了，要浪费很多时间。有时候出去逛了半天，也不知道买什么礼物好。

大卫：这是因为多数的人都不需要什么东西。结果又浪费时间又浪费钱，而且还浪费资源。不送礼物，就可以节约钱和时间，并且还可以让春节不受商业化的影响。

凯丽：我觉得这样过春节非常好。可以说，大家都过了一个绿色的春节。

生词

	Simplified	Traditional	Pinyin	Part of Speech	English
1.	放鞭炮		fàng biānpào	*v.o.*	light firecracker
2.	噪音		zàoyīn	*n.*	noise
3.	烟尘	煙塵	yānchén	*n.*	smoke dust
4.	乒乒 乓乓		pīngpīng pāngpāng	*ono.*	bang, ping
5.	纸屑	紙屑	zhǐxiè	*n.*	shredded paper
6.	送旧 迎新	送舊 迎新	sòng jiù yíng xīn	*s.p.*	greet the new year
7.	春联	春聯	chūnlián	*n.*	Spring Festival couplets
8.	气球	氣球	qìqiú	*n.*	balloon
9.	景点	景點	jǐngdiǎn	*n.*	scenic point, scenic spot
10.	垃圾		lājī	*n.*	trash, rubbish
11.	一草一木		yī cǎo yī mù	*s.p.*	all plants, every plant
12.	脚印		jiǎoyìn	*n.*	footprint
13.	野生		yěshēng	*adj.*	wild
14.	动物	動物	dòngwù	*n.*	animal
15.	平平安安		píngpíng'ān'ān	*adv.*	safely, quietly
16.	后代	後代	hòudài	*n.*	descendant
17.	莫名 其妙		mò míng qí miào	*s.p.*	baffling, absurd, be baffled
18.	野味		yěwèi	*n.*	game (as food)
19.	生产	生產	shēngchǎn	*n./v.*	production, produce
20.	资源	資源	zīyuán	*n.*	resource
21.	浪费	浪費	làngfèi	*n./v.*	waste
22.	礼物	禮物	lǐwù	*n.*	gift, present
23.	节约	節約	jiéyuē	*v.*	save, practice thrift
24.	商业化	商業化	shāngyèhuà	*n./v.*	commercialization, commercialize

语言注释

1. 没什么 (It's nothing; It's not a big deal)

没什么 is usually used in spoken Chinese.

做作业的时候做错了题没什么，可是到了高考的时候做错题就是大问题了。

It's not a big deal to make a few mistakes when doing homework, but it will be a big problem to make a few mistakes in the college entrance exam.

A: 谢谢你，为了开晚会，你买这买那，忙了好几天。

B: 没什么。我喜欢逛商店、买东西。

A: Thank you. You were busy for several days buying different things for the party.

B: It's nothing. I enjoyed going to the stores and shopping.

2. 受···影响 (Influenced by…; affected by…)

传统节日不应该受商业化的影响。

Traditional holidays should not be influenced by commercialization.

受了他父母的影响，张京生决定要上北京大学。

Influenced by his parents, Zhang Jingsheng has decided to attend Beijing University.

有些青少年在网上交了一些坏朋友，安全受到很大的影响。

Some teenagers made friends with some bad people online and their safety was greatly affected.

受西方快餐的影响，不少中国的青少年现在喜欢吃汉堡和比萨。

Influenced by Western fast food, these days many Chinese teenagers like to eat hamburgers and pizzas.

学无止境

We have learned several ways of celebrating Chinese festivals. Here are some additional activities that people like to do during festivals. Pinyin is provided for new characters only.

走亲访友 *visit relatives and friends*	家庭聚会 *family gathering*	老同学聚会 *reunion with former classmates*
开联欢会 *have a get-together*	游行 *parade*	游山玩水 *go to scenic spots*
购物 *shopping*	看文娱表演 *watch entertainment shows*	看体育比赛 *watch sports competitions*
看灯 *look at lights and lanterns*	看焰 (yàn) 火 *watch fireworks*	休闲 (xián) *rest and relax*

节日的晚上

恭喜发财

温故知新 GAIN NEW INSIGHT THROUGH REVIEW

In Lesson 2.1 of *Huanying,* Volume 2, we learned some Chinese festivals. Throughout the book, we also learned about some festivals celebrated in the United States. Now it is time for a review. Do you remember what and when these festivals are? Work with a peer to fill out the missing information in the following table.

中国和美国的节日

元旦	公历一月一日	New Year's Day
	农历一月一日	
元宵节	农历一月十五日	
总统节	公历二月的第三个星期一	
国际妇女节	公历三月八日	
国际劳动节		International Labor Day
端午节	农历五月五日	
国际儿童节		International Children's Day
	公历七月四日	
	公历九月的第一个星期一	Labor Day
	农历八月十五日	
中国国庆节		
		Thanksgiving Day
	公历十二月二十五日	

中国文化一瞥

Chinese proverbs

The following proverbs use animals to make analogies. These animals illustrate the proverbs' meanings vividly. Pinyin is provided only for those phrases with new characters.

1. huà hǔ lèi gǒu
画 虎 类 狗

to try to draw a tiger but end up with a dog; to make a poor imitation; to lack the skills necessary to draw a tiger, but then insist on drawing one only to instead end up with the likeliness of a dog (describes those who are overly ambitious but without the ability to succeed)

IN USE:

小高做的事常常是画虎类狗。他应该根据自己的能力来做事。
What Xiao Gao does is usually overly ambitious and doesn't lead to any good results. He should do things according to his ability.

YOUR TURN:

Can you use 画虎类狗 to describe the following situations?

小弟很喜欢大哥的滑板。他买了一个同样的滑板。	可以	不可以
小弟觉得自己玩滑板玩得跟大哥一样好。可是在玩滑板的时候，他摔倒了，腿受了伤。	可以	不可以
小弟天天练习玩滑板，现在他跟大哥玩得差不多一样好了。	可以	不可以
小弟想因为他玩滑板玩得很好，应该不用练习就可以像运动员一样玩滑雪板了。	可以	不可以

2. wō xíng niú bù
蜗 行 牛 步

at a snail's pace; as a snail moves and a cow walks; at a very slow pace

IN USE:

你们这样蜗行牛步，什么时候才能把这件事做完？

You are working at a snail's pace. When will you get the job done?

YOUR TURN:

Answer the following questions based on your own situation:

1. 你做什么事情都很快吗？有没有蜗行牛步的时候？说一下为什么那件事情你做得很慢？
2. 在你认识的人中，有没有人常常蜗行牛步？举一个例子。

3. hú qún gǒu dǎng
狐 群 狗 党

a pack of foxes and a bunch of dogs; an evil lot; a bad bunch; a gang of crooks

IN USE:

来找他的都是狐群狗党。他们总是在一起做坏事。

Those who come to see him are a bunch of crooks. They always do bad things together.

YOUR TURN:

狐朋狗友 and 狐朋狗党 have the same meanings as 狐群狗党. You can use any one of them to answer the following questions.

1. 如果一个人总是跟狐群狗党在一起，她可能受到哪些坏影响？
2. 如果你朋友跟狐朋狗党在一起，你会给朋友哪些建议？
3. 在你们学校，有没有狐朋狗友的问题？如果有，学校怎么解决这个问题？

The Chinese View of Nature

Introduction:

In this unit you will be discussing the complex relationship between economic growth and environmental protection in contemporary China. You might be wondering how a country that was known for its belief in living in harmony with nature transformed itself into a country that seeks the domination of nature. To help you formulate your own analysis on how the Chinese might be able to create a sustainable development, we have included in this section some traditional Chinese stories or views about the relationship between people and nature.

Since the content is quite different from the texts you have learned so far, a loose English translation is provided to facilitate your understanding.

中国的五岳 (yuè, mountain)

中国有五座最有名的高山，人们把它们叫做五岳。这五岳都和“盘古开天地”(see Lesson 1.1) 的故事有关系。传说盘古是创造 (chuàngzào, create) 天地的人。他死了以后，他的呼吸 (hūxī, breath) 变成了风和云，他的眼睛变成太阳和月亮，他的血 (xuè, blood) 变成江河，他的头、胳膊、和腿变成了五座山。这五座山是：东岳泰山 (Tàishān)，在今天的山东省；西岳华山，在今天的陕西省；南岳衡山 (Héngshān)，在今天的湖南省；北岳恒山(Héngshān)，在今天的山西省；中岳嵩山 (Sōngshān)，在今天的河南省。这五座山后来成了道教 (Dàojiào, Daoism) 的圣地 (shèngdì, sacred place)。按照道教的说法，东岳主 (be in charge of) 生，代表春天；南岳主长，代表夏天；西岳主收，代表秋天；北岳主藏 (cáng, preserve)，代表冬天；中岳主化养 (nurture)，代表长夏，也就是从夏到秋的转折 (zhuǎnzhé, turning point)。有了五岳，天地就有了定位 (rightful place)，四季就可以分明 (fēnmíng, have a clear division)，人们在四季中的活动就有了方向。

The Five Great Mountains of China

There are five famous mountains in China, known as the *wuyue*. The formation of these five mountains is part of the Chinese creation myth, "Pan Gu Creates the World" (see Lesson 1.1). According to the myth, Pan Gu created the world. After he died, his breath became the wind and the clouds; his eyes became the sun and the moon; his blood formed rivers; and his head, arms and legs turned into five mountains: Mt. Tai in the east, Mt. Hua in the west, Mt. Heng (balance) in the south, Mt. Heng (permanence) in the north, and Mt. Song in the center. These five mountains later became known as the holy mountains of Daoism. According to Daoist thought, the eastern mountain is responsible for birth, and so it represents the spring; the southern mountain is responsible for growth, and thus it represents the summer; Mt. Hua guards the harvest, making it represent the autumn; Mt. Heng in the north watches over preservation, and represents the winter; and Mt. Song in the center is in control over nurturing, representing the late summer and the transition from summer to fall, and therefore from growth to harvest. The five mountains together provide orientation to all things in the world, form distinct seasons, and give direction to human activities throughout the year.

YOUR TURN:

Choose one of the mountains of your own country. Prepare an oral presentation in Chinese about this mountain, including its location and significance.

你知道吗？

春节（中国新年）是中国最重要的传统节日。春节从农历一月一日开始，一直过到农历一月十五日的元宵(xiāo)节 (Lantern Festival)。

春节前的一两个星期，中国人把家里打扫得干干净净 (gāngānjìngjìng, clean)，因为这样可以把一年的坏运 (bad luck) 扫地出门。新年来的时候，就可以把好运带到家里来。

春节的前一天晚上，全家要在一起吃年夜饭 (New Year's Eve dinner)。如果家里的人住在四面八方，这一天都要回家来。中国人非常注意年夜饭应该吃什么，因为那是一年中最重要的晚饭。年夜饭一定要有鱼，这是因为“鱼”和“余”(yú, abundance)同音，鱼代表了“年年有余”。在中国的北方，一般的家庭都要吃饺子，因为饺子代表金钱。在南方，许多家庭会吃年糕，“糕”和“高”同音，代表了一年比一年“高”，也就是说，一年比一年好。吃完年夜饭以后，全家人在一起看中央电视台的“春节联欢晚会”。等到半夜12点，大家就到外边去放鞭炮，送旧迎新。这几年，有些城市建议大家不要放鞭炮，因为放鞭炮不但会污染空气，也可能带来火灾 (zāi, disaster)。

过年的时候，小孩和年轻人要给家里年纪大的人“拜年”(wish someone a Happy New Year)。拜年的时候，爷爷、奶奶、姥爷、姥姥、爸爸、妈妈、叔叔、阿姨、舅舅等会给孩子和没有结婚的年轻人一个“红包”。红包是一个红颜色的信封 (envelope)，里边放着一些钱。中国人在过年的时候也喜欢走亲访友。去亲戚和朋友家的时候，不少人都带一点儿礼物。礼物常常是一些吃的东西，比如水果、甜点心、年糕、蛋糕等等。

春联

3.2 全球化和本土化 Globalization and Localization

对话一

（在一个美国连锁快餐店里。）

玛丽娅：你想吃什么？

汤姆：到了美国快餐店，当然就是吃汉堡，喝可乐了。我就要一个特价套餐吧，这样吃的喝的都有了。

玛丽娅：等一等，这儿有好几个特价套餐，你要哪个？第一个是：牛肉汉堡、玉米色拉、红茶。第二个是：猪肉汉堡、黄瓜色拉、绿茶...

汤姆：我要第六个。那是地道的美国快餐：牛肉汉堡、炸薯条、可乐。

玛丽娅：这家快餐店的不少食品都中国化了，又有中国色拉，又有红茶绿茶。

汤姆：这家快餐店你没来过吧？我挺喜欢这家的，中西餐都有。要是你来吃早饭，这里早上还卖豆浆、油条、饭团。

玛丽娅：这些不都是传统的中国早餐吗？

汤姆：是啊，这家美国快餐店已经入乡随俗了。

玛丽娅：哦，到什么山上唱什么歌嘛。

汤姆：这句话是什么意思？

玛丽娅：意思是，我们说话做事都应该根据一个地方的情况做出改变。这家快餐厅已经根据中国人的饮食习惯改变了菜单。

汤姆：我们来看看甜品菜单，上面有绿茶冰激凌、炸苹果，的确很有中国特色。正因为是这样，所以来这家快餐店吃饭的人特别多。

玛丽娅：对啊，别的美国快餐店常常是年轻人多，老年人少。这家真不一样，你看，男女老少都有。这大概就是经济课老师说的，一个跨国公司要想在国外发展，就需要“本土化”。比如，我去兼职的那个小公司，为了让国外的顾客了解他们的产品，就让我把公司的网页翻译成英文。这就是“本土化”，是吧？

汤姆：哎，我们是不是应该先吃饭再研究“全球化”和“本土化”啊？我快饿死了。

玛丽娅：好吧，好吧，我们快点菜吧。

对话二

玛丽娅：你已经吃完了？怎么吃得那么快？

汤姆：因为我快饿死了，所以一下子就吃完了。你慢慢吃吧。

玛丽娅：行，我吃，你跟我说说话。上个周末你做什么了？

汤姆：我正要告诉你呢。上个周末，两个旧金山的老邻居到上海来旅游，顺便来看看我们。

玛丽娅：他们是跟旅行团来的吗？

汤姆：不是。他们觉得，跟旅行团旅游是“走马观花”，看不到真正中国人的生活，所以不愿意参加旅行团。到了中国，他们也不是坐着旅游车到处走，而是跟一般的中国人一样，坐公共交通去各地旅游。因为我在上海，当然就由我当他们的导游了。

玛丽娅：你们去哪儿了？

汤姆：上海的历史古迹本来就不多，再说，这两位邻居也不怎么喜欢去博物馆，因为他们要看“活的文化”。我只能带他们在街上走走，去市中心、外滩、和浦东看了看，还去黄浦江坐了游船。

黄浦江上的游船

玛丽娅：他们玩得高兴吗?

汤姆：玩得非常高兴，看到了现代的上海，也看到了中国人现在是怎么生活的。可是，他们也有点儿失望。

玛丽娅：失望？为什么呢?

汤姆：他们喜欢了解外国文化，一来就说，到了中国一定要“入乡随俗”。也就是说，吃饭要吃中国饭，穿衣要穿有中国特色的，买东西要买中国造的。反正一句话，在中国说话做事都要中国化。

玛丽娅：在中国要达到中国化应该不难。

汤姆：听上去容易，做起来难。在上海，吃中国饭不是个问题，哪儿都有中国饭店。穿有中国特色的衣服可能就有问题了。你去大街上看看，有几个人穿传统的中国衣服?

玛丽娅：对啊，现在世界各国的人穿得都差不多一样。

汤姆：　我带他们逛了市中心和购物中心。在那里，他们看到许多外国的连锁店。还有不少商店，不管是外国的还是中国的，都用英文名字。商店里卖的也不都是中国商品，外国商品非常多。一句话，在美国能买到的东西在中国都买得到。我的老邻居看了有点儿失望，觉得中国和许多别的国家一样，都西方化了。

玛丽娅：这有什么奇怪的！我们时代的特点就是全球化。各个国家的文化都在互相影响。各国的差别越来越小，吃的东西、穿的衣服、用的东西、做的活动，都越来越相似了。

汤姆：　对啊，我的老邻居也是这么说的。他们觉得，如果到处都差不多，不就没有必要去国外旅行了吗？

生词

	Simplified	*Traditional*	*Pinyin*	*Part of Speech*	*English*
1.	本土化		běntǔhuà	*n./v.*	localization, localize
2.	连锁(店)	連鎖(店)	liánsuǒ (diàn)	*n.*	chain (store)
3.	套餐		tàocān	*n.*	set meal, set menu
4.	玉米		yùmǐ	*n.*	corn
5.	猪肉	豬肉	zhūròu	*n.*	pork
6.	黄瓜		huángguā	*n.*	cucumber
7.	中国化	中國化	Zhōngguóhuà	*v.*	make something Chinese
8.	豆浆	豆漿	dòujiāng	*n.*	soy milk
9.	油条	油條	yóutiáo	*n.*	fried bread stick
10.	饭团	飯糰	fàntuán	*n.*	rice ball (usu. w/stuffing)
11.	入乡随俗	入鄉隨俗	rù xiāng suí sú	*s.p.*	when in Rome, do as the Romans do
12.	改变	改變	gǎibiàn	*n./v.*	change
13.	死		sǐ	*v.*	die

14. 顺便	順便	shùnbiàn	*adv.*	in passing, conveniently
15. 走马观花	走馬觀花	zǒu mǎ guān huā	*s.p.*	glance over things in a hurry
16. 古迹	古跡	gǔjī	*n.*	ancient site
17. 失望		shīwàng	*n./v.o.*	disappointment, lose hope
18. 达到	達到	dádào	*v.*	reach
19. 西方化		Xīfānghuà	*n./v.*	Westernization, Westernize

语言注释

1. 正 (Exactly, precisely)

正 is used in front of a verb, an adjective, or a phrase for emphasis.

这件大衣不大不小，你穿了正合适。
The overcoat is not too large or too small. It fits you very well.

这正是我要告诉你的。
This is exactly what I am about to tell you.

正为了保护环境，他们才决定春节不放鞭炮。
It was precisely for the purpose of protecting the environment that they decided not to light firecrackers during the Spring Festival.

2. Adjective + 死了 (Extremely)

Adjective + 死了 expresses the meaning of "extremely." It is similar to "Adjective + 极了," which we learned in *Huanying*, Volume 2, Lesson 6.2. "Adjective + 死了" is used in informal speech.

工作了六个小时以后，我累死了。
After working for six hours, I was extremely tired.

听说学校要组织大家去加拿大旅行，他高兴死了。
When he heard the school would organize a tour to Canada, he was extremely happy.

3. 顺便 (In passing, conveniently)

顺便 is usually used in front of a verbal phrase to indicate that the action was taken without making any special effort. When other people thank you for doing something for them, you can also use this expression to show politeness and modesty.

在去学校的路上，我顺便买了一张电话卡。
While on my way to school, I bought a prepaid phone card.

A: 我要去图书馆，可以顺便帮你还书。
B: 太谢谢你了。
A: 别客气，我是顺便。
A: I am going to the library, while I'm there I can return the books for you.
B: Thank you very much.
A: You are welcome. It will be convenient for me.

4. 正要···(呢) (About to...)

正要 is placed before a verbal phrase to indicate that one is about to do something. 呢 is optional. It is placed at the end of a sentence.

他正要出去打网球，外边开始下雨了。
He was about to go out and play tennis when it started to rain.

我正要给他写电邮呢，他给我来电话了。
I was about to send him an email when he called me.

5. 一句话 (To sum up, in sum, in summary)

一句话 is usually used in informal speech.

这个学期，他修了六门课，参加了学校的篮球队，周末还要去博物馆做义工。一句话，他比上学期忙多了。
This semester, he has taken six courses, joined the school's basketball team, and volunteered in the museum on the weekends. In sum, he is much busier than last semester.

她一会儿说有事不能来，一会儿说车坏了，一会儿又说生病了。一句话，我看她不愿意见你。
At one time she said she was busy and couldn't come, then said her car was broken, and later said she was sick. In a word, I don't think she wants to see you.

学无止境

We have learned more words about diet in this lesson. The following are some popular sayings about eating and health. Try to figure out the meanings by yourself. Pinyin is provided for new characters only.

早饭吃得饱，午饭吃得好，晚饭吃得少。

饭吃七分饱。

人是铁，饭是钢 (gāng, steel)。

饭前喝汤，胜过药方 (shèng guò yào fāng, better than any medicine)。

吃不言，睡不语。

病从口入。

饭后百步走，活到九十九。

温故知新 GAIN NEW INSIGHT THROUGH REVIEW

We have learned a few Chinese proverbs with the word 马 in them. Take a look at the following list and see if you have remembered these proverbs.

马到成功	马马虎虎	车水马龙	老马识途	马不停蹄

中国文化一瞥

Chinese proverbs

The following proverbs are about variety. Pinyin is provided only for those phrases with new characters.

1. 万 紫 千 红

innumerable flowers of purple and red; a vast display of diverse colors; a variety of colors

IN USE:

春天的时候，花园里万紫千红，美丽极了。
During the spring, the garden has a vast array of colors. It is extremely beautiful.

YOUR TURN:

Answer the following question:

在什么地方，你可以看到万紫千红的景色？

2. 气 象 万 千

a majestic scene in all its variety; a great variety of scenes; things change in countless ways

IN USE:

长江的自然景色气象万千。我们应该坐游船去看一下。
The Yangtse River has a great variety of scenes. We should take a cruise ship to see it.

最近十年来，这个城市的变化可以说是气象万千。
In the last decade, a great variety of changes have taken place in the city.

YOUR TURN:

Use 气象万千 to describe one of the following:

天气	高科技	城市	大海	自然景色

3. 五 花 八 门

a wide variety; many different kinds (an ancient Chinese military strategy adjusted the troop formation into five rows and eight exits in order to provide a flexible attack or defense)

IN USE:

这个网站的网上游戏五花八门。

The website has a wide variety of online games.

同学们对将来生活的计划五花八门。

Students have a great variety of plans for their future lives.

YOUR TURN:

Answer the following questions based on your situation:

1. 你的同学打工吗？他们的工作是不是五花八门？
2. 同学们喜欢的音乐是不是五花八门？
3. 在你的城市，可以去哪儿买到五花八门的食品？
4. 电视上有哪些五花八门的节目？

The Chinese View of Nature

风水

随着中国传统文化在西方国家的流传 (liúchuán, spread)，越来越多的人开始对风水感兴趣。很多人都知道，风水跟中国古人的天人合一，与 (yǔ, and, with) 自然和谐 (héxié, harmony)的思想有关。

风水指的是气和水的流动。古人认为，气是一种自然的精华 (jīnghuá, essence)。气遇到风就会疏散 (shūsàn, evaporate)，遇到水就会聚集 (jùjí, gather)。气分成阴阳两种，阴和阳本身是中性(neutral) 的。气对人的影响根据自然中的季节、时间、饮食、身体情况而变化。考虑风水，目的是要把对人有好处的气聚集起来，把对人有害的气疏散出去。在日常生活中，风水的好坏主要表现在居住环境中的空间 (space)、山、水，树木等等自然环境，如果这些自然环境帮助增进 (zēngjìn, increase) 人和自然的沟通 (gōutōng, communication)，那风水就比较好。不然，就需要通过重新(chóngxīn, again, anew) 安排空间、颜色、家具等等的方法改进(gǎijìn, improve) 风水。

Feng Shui

Following the introduction of Chinese culture into Western countries, more and more people have become interested in *feng shui*. Many people now know that *feng shui* relates to the creation of a harmonious environment.

Feng shui refers to the movement of *qi* and water. The ancient Chinese believed that nature has its own essence called *qi*. *Qi* evaporates in the wind and gathers in the water. *Qi* presents itself in two forms: the *yin* (the female principle) and the *yang* (the male principle); they are by themselves neither good nor bad. The impact of *qi* on human beings changes depending on the seasons, hours, food eaten and the state of a person's health. The main purpose of *feng shui* is to gather the *qi* that is beneficial and disperse the *qi* that is harmful. In daily life, one can recognize if the *feng shui* is good or bad by observing the living space and its relation to the natural environment such as mountains, rivers and forests. If the location has a fluid space and its natural surroundings enhance the communication between people and nature, then the *feng shui* of this place is good. If not, then one would need to rearrange the space, colors, furniture or other characteristics of the room in order to improve the *feng shui*.

YOUR TURN:

Do you think that *feng shui* speaks of truth about the relationship between human beings and nature or it is only a superstition? Present your argument in Chinese in the form of an oral presentation.

你知道吗？

中国的商店可以说是五花八门。在许多城市，商业区和居住区分得不太清楚，所以在居民小区里，有很多个人或者家庭开的小商店。中国政府鼓励 (gǔlì, encourage) 大家自己找工作，一些住在底楼 (ground floor) 的居民会去申请一个商业执照，然后在家里开一个小店，卖一些日常用品。这些小店除了卖东西以外，也是邻居们聚会聊天的地方。对一些中国人来说，去商店不仅是为了买东西，也是为了社交(socialize)。这些小店常常是一大早就开门，一直营业到晚上十点。

除了这些在居民小区的小店以外，不少街道上有许多小商店和小饭店，卖各种各样的东西，比如书店、食品店、衣服店、鞋子店、厨房用品店、音乐光盘店、行李店、礼品店什么的。在城市的中心，常常有许多大商店和百货公司。最近，不少城市还建起了很大的购物中心。市中心和购物中心的商店卖的东西质量(zhìliàng, quality)比较好，所以比小店的东西要贵一些。这些大商店的营业时间一般是上午十点到晚上十点。受了全球化的影响，现在不少中国商店卖各国商品。还有不少外国公司也来中国开了专卖店 (retail store that sells only one brand of products)。

同时，城市里还有不少西式的大超市和便利(biànlì, convenient)店。不少超市早上七八点开门，晚上十点关门。便利店是每天开门，二十四小时为顾客服务。

各种不同的商店

3.3 到处都是广告 Commercials Everywhere

对话一

凯丽：电视上的广告那么多，看一个电影，中间要放几十个广告，真讨厌！

玛丽娅：我也最讨厌广告了。广告上要卖的那些东西，多数都是我不需要的。对我来说，看广告是浪费时间。

大卫：你不需要，不等于别人不需要。

凯丽：大卫说得也有道理。可是如果一个人真的需要一样东西，不看广告也会去买的。

大卫：要是只有在需要的时候才去买东西，那百分之五十的商店都会没有顾客了。一个人去买东西，不一定是因为他真的需要东西，而是因为他想要最新最时髦的东西。这跟需要不需要没有关系。

玛丽娅：你说得对。我看，现代人的东西都太多了。拿我来说，我有十几双鞋子。其实，只要有三四双就够穿了。

大卫：那你为什么要买这么多呢?

玛丽娅：我也说不清楚，有时候是因为看到广告说那种牌子的鞋子很好，也有时候是因为觉得鞋子很时髦，这样不知不觉就买了十几双鞋子。

大卫：所以你买那么多的鞋子是受了广告的影响。

玛丽娅：可以这么说吧。虽然我知道不应该听广告的，但是也免不了受广告的影响。

大卫：这不能怪你。我们都会受影响。广告上说这个牌子的东西好，又有一些名人用这些东西，我们去买东西的时候，就会不知不觉去找那个牌子。

凯丽：广告常常让人觉得，现代生活就应该买、买、买。结果，大家的东西都越来越多。旧的东西还没有用坏，新的已经来了。

买，买，买

大卫： 就是。不少人家东西放不下了，就搬到大房子里去住。到了大房子以后，又有空的地方了，又可以买很多东西，最后又放不下了，再搬更大的房子……

玛丽娅：我看要保护环境，节约资源，广告公司就应该少做一些广告。

大卫： 你们也别太理想主义了，广告公司不做广告，那还要广告公司做什么？

对话二

玛丽娅：昨天发生了一件特别奇怪的事，让我们都大吃一惊。

凯丽：怎么了？

玛丽娅：我们正在吃晚饭，一个人来敲门，说要找妮娜。那个人推着一辆自行车，车上放着一个很大的纸盒子。我们问他为什么要找妮娜。他说是为妮娜送货上门。

凯丽：你是说，妮娜在商店买了东西，让人送回来吗？

玛丽娅：问题就在这里啊，妮娜怎么会有钱买东西呢？我们想那个人一定是送错地方了。可是他说，他是替一家网上公司来送货的。妮娜在那儿买了一辆自行车，现在应该一手交钱，一手交货。

凯丽：妮娜才七八岁，怎么可以去网上买东西呢？

玛丽娅：我们开始也不相信，可是送货的人把打印出来的订单给我们看，上面的确写着妮娜的名字。于是，我们就问妮娜，“这是你买的吗？”她说，“我没有买这个大盒子，我买的是红色的自行车，车上画着一只白猫。”那个送货的人听了就说，“你们听到了吧？是这个小朋友买的东西。一手交钱一手交货吧。”我妈妈向他解释了半天，虽然家长也有责任，不应该让孩子上网买东西，可是这件事主要应该由公司负责，他们的网页有问题，那么小的孩子怎么可以随便上网订货呢？

凯丽：一般公司的网页上不是都写着吗？如果你不到十八岁，不能订货。这家公司怎么没写？

玛丽娅：那个送货的人告诉我妈妈，他不太清楚公司网页的情况，他只管送货。既然我们不要，他就把货拿回去。

玛丽娅：他走了以后，我妈妈一再对妮娜说，没有经过爸爸妈妈的同意，她不可以上网去买东西。再说，她已经有自行车了，为什么还要再买一辆？

凯丽：妮娜一定是看到了广告，觉得自行车很好看吧？

玛丽娅：是的，她说她的自行车上没画着可爱的白猫，所以要买新的。我对她说，如果她要白猫，我可以帮她画。可是不能因为她要白猫就要买新的自行车，要是她喜欢黑猫了，看到有黑猫的自行车，难道也要买一辆吗？一个人要那么多自行车做什么？不需要的东西，就不应该买，这样对环保有好处，不浪费资源，也不会增加垃圾。

凯丽：你说得对。那你帮她画猫了吗？

玛丽娅：画了，可是画得不太像。我把猫的耳朵画得太长了，看上去像一只兔子。妮娜说没关系，兔子也挺可爱的。

生词

	Simplified	Traditional	Pinyin	Part of Speech	English
1.	到处	到處	dàochù	*adv.*	everywhere, in all places
2.	广告	廣告	guǎnggào	*n.*	advertisement
3.	讨厌	討厭	tǎoyàn	*adj./v.*	disgusting, dislike, be disgusted with
4.	等于	等於	děngyú	*v.*	equal to, be equivalent to
5.	时髦	時髦	shímáo	*adj.*	fashionable
6.	不知不觉	不知不覺	bù zhī bù jué	*s.p.*	unconsciously, unknowingly
7.	免不了		miǎnbùliǎo	*s.p.*	can't avoid, be unavoidable
8.	理想主义	理想主義	lǐxiǎngzhǔyì	*n.*	idealism
9.	发生	發生	fāshēng	*n./v.*	occurrence, occur, happen
10.	敲门	敲門	qiāomén	*v.o.*	knock on the door
11.	推	推	tuī	*v.*	push
12.	相信		xiāngxìn	*v.*	believe
13.	订单	訂單	dìngdān	*n.*	order (form)
14.	于是	於是	yúshì	*conj.*	hence, consequently, as a result

15. 订货	訂貨	dìnghuò	*v.o.*	order goods
16. 既然		jìrán	*conj.*	now that, since, as
17. 兔子		tùzi	*n.*	rabbit

语言注释

1. 对我来说 (As far as I am concerned)

The personal pronoun in this prepositional phrase can be changed. For example, 对你们来说，对他来说，对王老师来说…

对中国人来说，春节是很重要的传统节日。
As far as the Chinese are concerned, the Spring Festival is an important traditional festival.

对一些外国公司来说，中国有十三亿人口，是一个非常大的市场。
As far as some foreign companies are concerned, China has 1.3 billion people and is a huge market.

2. 不是…而是… (Not...but...)

我不是不想跟你一起去旅游，而是没有时间。
It is not that I don't want to travel with you, but that I don't have time.

环保不是一天两天要做的事，而是每天都要做的事。
Environmental protection is not something that we do for one or two days, but every day.

3. 于是 (Consequently, as a result)

于是 is a conjunction. It introduces a sentence to indicate a result or a consequence.

现在大家都知道环保很重要，于是大家都注意不浪费资源。
Now everyone knows it is important to protect the environment. Consequently everyone pays attention not to waste resources.

他很喜欢新式的电脑，于是就买了一台。
He likes the new style computer, so he bought one.

4. 既然 (Now that, since, as)

既然 introduces a conditional clause. It is usually placed at the beginning of a sentence.

既然你想考上一个好大学，为什么现在还不准备高考呢?
Since you want to get into a good university, why aren't you preparing for the college exam now?

既然你不需要那些东西，你就别买了。
Since you don't need these things, don't buy them.

学无止境

We have learned some words about doing business. Here are some additional ones. Pinyin is provided for new characters only.

邮购 *mail order*	电子商业 *e-commerce*	运费 *shipping cost*
发票 *sales receipt*	促 (cù) 销 *(promote) sales*	货到付款 *cash on delivery*
免费运货 *free shipping*	供应商 *supplier*	商家 *business (company, store)*
退货 *return (goods)*	换货 *exchange (goods)*	网店 *online store*
直销店 *outlet store*	消(xiāo)费者 *consumer*	商城 *shopping center, big store*

YOUR TURN:

Read the following website, and answer the comprehension questions.

万紫千红网

您好，欢迎来我们网站！

我要买	购物 车	搜 索	联系我们

女装	男装	泳装	童装	内衣
女鞋	男鞋	童鞋	运动鞋	牛仔

网上交易

免费注册
购物流程
信用卡支付
网上银行支付
货到付款
安全可靠

客户服务

提供发票
闪电发货
7天退换
100%正品
假一赔三客
户服务电话

1. What products does this website sell?
2. How many ways are there for making a payment?
3. Is there a time limit to return or exchange goods?

温故知新 GAIN NEW INSIGHT THROUGH REVIEW

The following are some animals. See how many you know. Some are new words, but you may be able to guess them.

猫	老虎	狗	兔子	野猪
乌龟	熊猫	牛	羊	马
猪	河马	大象	熊	海龟

中国文化一瞥

Chinese proverbs

The following proverbs all have something to do with looking at things. Pinyin is provided only for those phrases with new characters.

1. yī mù liǎo rán
一 目 了 然
clear at a glance; perfectly obvious; easy to see

IN USE:

你可以上电话公司的网站看一下，电话费用一目了然。
You can take a look at the phone company's website. Phone charges are clear at a glance.

YOUR TURN:

Can you use 一目了然 to describe the following situations?

1. 这本书只要一看书名就知道书的内容了。	可以	不可以
2. 这本书我看了半天，还不清楚在讲什么。	可以	不可以
3. 电影里有一个很难看的人，我想他是个坏人，可是他是个好人。	可以	不可以
4. 机场的出口非常清楚，一下飞机就能看见。	可以	不可以

2. yī lǎn wú yú
一 览 无 余

see everything at one glance; a glance catches the whole picture

IN USE:

站在山上往下看，山下的景色一览无余。

Looking down from the hill, one can see the whole scene clearly.

YOUR TURN:

Answer the following questions based on your own situation:

1. 你有没有看过一览无余的电影？
2. 为什么你觉得那个电影是一览无余？
3. 你喜欢看一览无余的电影吗？为什么？

3. 东 张 西 望

look to the east and west; look around

IN USE:

进了博物馆，大卫东张西望，不知道从哪儿开始看。

After getting into the museum, David looked around and didn't know where to begin.

小明上课的时候东张西望，老师说的都没听进去。

During class, Xiao Ming looked east and west. He didn't hear what the teacher said.

YOUR TURN:

Answer the following questions based on your own situation.

1. 去了一个新的地方，你喜欢东张西望吗？
2. 在什么时候，一个人不应该东张西望？为什么？

4. mù bù zhuǎn jīng
目 不 转 睛

look at something without turning one's eyeballs; look at something intensely; look with fixed eyes

IN USE:

我的狗看到了别的狗，就目不转睛。
When my dog sees other dogs, its eyes are fixed on them.

他父母很担心，因为他每天都目不转睛地看着电脑。
His parents are worried because every day he stares at the computer.

YOUR TURN:

Answer the following question based on your own situation.

你看到什么东西的时候，会目不转睛？

The Chinese View of Nature

茶马古道

在云南的丽江地区有一个很有名的旅游点，叫做“茶马古道”。这条道路是古代中国、西藏、和其他南亚国家交流的一条重要通道 (tōngdào, passage)。

茶马古道的建立和唐宋时期的茶马互市 (hùshì, exchange with each other) 有关。唐朝和宋朝 (Sòng Chaó, Song Dynasty, AD 960-1279) 时期，因为西藏和南亚国家希望买到中国的茶，中国希望买到西藏和中亚的马，所以在离西藏和南亚最近的云南开辟 (kāipì, open up) 了一条贸易 (màoyì, trade) 道路。这条古道穿过云南和青藏高原，在中国和西藏商业的历史上一直很活跃 (huóyuè, active)，只有到了清朝中期才慢慢衰落 (shuāiluò, decline) 了。茶马古道不但是中国西南对外贸易的通道，也是中国古代利用自然为人服务的一个例子。

The Ancient Tea-Horse Trading Road

There is a famous tourist attraction on the bank of the Li River in Yunnan Province: the ancient Tea-Horse Trading Road. This road was an important commercial passage mainly for trading tea and horses between China, Tibet, and other South Asian countries.

The opening of the Tea-Horse Trading Road was related to the trade of horses and tea during the Tang and Song Dynasties. During that time, Tibetans and South Asians sought to buy Chinese tea, while the Chinese wanted to purchase horses from Tibet and Central Asia. As Yunnan was closest to both Tibet and South Asia, a trade route was opened there. The route passes through Yunnan and the Qinghai-Tibet plateau, and was very active in China and Tibet until the mid-Qing Dynasty, when the route fell into decline. The Tea-Horse Trading Road was not simply a route for passing goods between the various regions of Asia; it also serves as an example of how the ancient Chinese used nature in the service of human needs.

YOUR TURN:

Prepare an oral presentation on the Silk Road. In your presentation, first describe the trade route and traded goods, and then discuss the significance of this trading path to various ancient civilizations.

你知道吗？

受到商业化和全球化的影响，中国的商业广告也越来越多。现在哪儿都有广告：电视上、网页上、报纸上、杂志上、马路上、建筑上、公交车上都有广告。要想不看广告是不可能的。

广告也影响到中国的高中生。因为不少广告是关于名牌产品的，让有些高中生认为买东西就应该买名牌的。还有些学生觉得穿了名牌衣服，用名牌产品不但代表他们有比较高的社会地位 (social status)，而且容易得到别人的认可 (acceptance)。于是同学穿了名牌的运动鞋，我也要穿；同学用最新的手机，我也要用；同学有最时髦的手表，我也要买。为了解决这个问题，中国多数的学校都让学生穿校服去上学。这样可以减少学生之间的时髦竞争，也可以减少广告对学生的影响。

公共汽车上的广告

3.4 环境保护，从我做起
Environmental Protection Starts with Me

对话一

汤姆：昨天我去天天超市买完了东西，营业员问我要不要塑料袋。如果要的话，我得付六毛钱。以前天天超市的塑料袋都是免费的，怎么现在要顾客付钱了呢？

凯丽：你大概很久没去超市了吧？为了保护环境，超市让顾客自己带袋子，不用或少用一次性的塑料袋。

汤姆：哦，是这样。

凯丽：昨天你买塑料袋了吗？

汤姆：没有，我把东西放在书包里。有一包饼干放不下，我就拿在手里。

凯丽：我们可以在书包里放一个购物袋，买了东西以后可以拿出来用。要不然，手里拿着一大堆东西，走路坐车都不方便。

汤姆：你说得也是。还好我昨天买的是饼干，如果是牛奶、蔬菜什么的，抱着一瓶牛奶或者一大堆蔬菜坐地铁，看上去一定很可笑。

凯丽：对啊，这太影响你的形象了。抱着蔬菜坐车一点儿都不酷。

汤姆：别开我的玩笑了。不过，说到一次性的塑料袋，这的确对环境不好。用过一次就扔，一定会增加垃圾。再说，生产塑料袋需要用各种资源，这样也会浪费资源，所以一次性的产品都应该少用。

凯丽：在我们学校的餐厅，有不少一次性的餐巾、筷子、盘子、杯子什么的。这些一次性产品不是都在增加垃圾、浪费资源吗？

汤姆： 你说得对。我们应该建议少用一次性产品，大家可以自己带筷子和碗，吃过饭以后洗一洗，不就可以再用了吗？我们可以写一个标语，“再见了！一次性产品。”对了，还可以写一个“减少，重复，回收”的标语。

凯丽： 这是什么意思啊？

汤姆： 不就是三个R吗？Reduce, Reuse 和 Recycle。

凯丽： 你这么翻译，意思不太清楚。我看应该翻译成：“减少污染，重复使用，回收再生。”

汤姆： 行啊，你的翻译可真是画龙点睛。

凯丽： 哪里哪里。

对话二

玛丽娅：环保日马上要来了。学校要组织一些活动，我们班负责宣传节约能源。

大卫：这不难做，我们可以提一些节约能源的建议，并且把这些建议做成幻灯片，在环保日放给大家看。

玛丽娅：行啊。我们先计划一下，节能大概有哪些方面，这样我们可以去找些图片照片，把幻灯片做得比较吸引人。

凯丽：我看，交通是一个方面。应该请大家少开车，多用公共交通，或者走路骑自行车，这样不但可以节约能源，而且可以减少空气污染。

汤姆：对。如果大家都不开车，就不会有堵车的问题了，这样可以少造一些公路，不会影响农业发展。

玛丽娅：让大家都不开车是不可能的，我们应该建议大家最好少开车。如果一定要开，最好拼车。

大卫：我们也应该说一下不开车对健康的好处。现在不少人一天到晚都坐在电脑前，如果骑自行车或走路上班，不是对环保和大家的健康都有好处吗？

公共汽车站

玛丽娅：除了交通以外，我们可以让大家注意节约用电。冬天的时候，暖气不要开得太高，夏天的时候，空调不要开得太低。

大卫：还有，能不坐电梯，就不坐或少坐电梯。

汤姆：我们还可以建议大家用节能灯泡。在买冰箱、电脑、洗衣机的时候，最好都买节能产品。

玛丽娅：别忘了，我们还应该节约用水。

大卫：行，我们要请大家注意，在生活中有许多地方可以节约能源。

凯丽：另外，我们要建议大家最好别买太多的东西，因为造东西都要用能源。

玛丽娅：如果可能，就去二手店买东西。让每一样东西都物尽其用。

凯丽：可是，有些人不喜欢二手店的东西。

大卫：那我们可以建议，如果一个东西坏了，修一下再用。

汤姆：最后我看还应该加一条建议，不用或者少用一次性产品。去超市买东西，别用一次性塑料袋。

凯丽：对了，我们可以在幻灯片里，放一张汤姆的照片，他从超市出来，手里抱着牛奶和一大堆蔬菜，旁边写着：“环保第一，形象第二。”

大卫：或者我们可以写：“谁说他不酷？环保才最酷。”

汤姆：行啊，随便你们写什么，只要保护环境就行。

回收利用

生词

	Simplified	Traditional	Pinyin	Part of Speech	English
1.	塑料		sùliào	*n.*	plastic
2.	袋（子）		dài (zi)	*n.*	bag, pocket
3.	抱		bào	*v.*	embrace, hold with arms
4.	可笑		kěxiào	*adj.*	laughable, ridiculous, funny
5.	形象		xíngxiàng	*n.*	image
6.	扔		rēng	*v.*	throw, toss, cast
7.	标语	標語	biāoyǔ	*n.*	poster, slogan
8.	重复		chóngfù	*v.*	repeat
9.	回收		huíshōu	*v.*	recycle, recover
10.	使用		shǐyòng	*v.*	use
11.	再生		zàishēng	*v.*	regenerate, revive
12.	画龙点睛	畫龍點睛	huà lóng diǎn jīng	*s.p.*	add the final touch
13.	宣传	宣傳	xuānchuán	*v.*	give publicity to
14.	幻灯片	幻燈片	huàndēngpiàn	*n.*	slide
15.	节能	節能	jiénéng	*v.o.*	save energy
16.	拼车	拼車	pīnchē	*v.o.*	share a ride
17.	暖气	暖氣	nuǎnqì	*n.*	heater, warm air
18.	灯泡	燈泡	dēngpào	*n.*	light bulb
19.	二手店		èrshǒudiàn	*n.*	second-hand store
20.	物尽其用	物盡其用	wù jìn qí yòng	*s.p.*	make the best use of everything

专名

21.	环保日	環保日	huánbǎorì	*n.*	Earth Day

语言注释

1. 你说的也是 (You are right)

This is an idiomatic expression, with the meaning of 你说得对. It is usually used in spoken Chinese to express agreement.

A: 有时候坐公交车挺挤的，特别是上下班的时候。
B: 你说的也是。所以我常常早一点儿出门。
A: Sometimes the buses are crowed, particularly during rush hour.
B: You are right. That's why I often leave home a little earlier.

A: 张老师的课挺难的，而且作业也比较多。
B: 你说的也是。正因为他是个好老师，所以对学生很严格。
A: Teacher Zhang's class is quite difficult. Moreover, there is rather a lot of homework.
B: You are right. Precisely because he is a good teacher, he is very strict with students.

2. 还好 (Fortunately, luckily)

In Lesson 5.3 of *Huanying*, Volume 2, we learned the expression of 好在. 还好has the same meaning and usage as 好在, and it is usually placed at the beginning of a sentence.

还好我们来得早，要不然就来不及了。
Luckily we came early. Otherwise, we wouldn't have enough time.

还好你准备了幻灯片。这样我们关于环保的讲演就有意思多了。
Fortunately you had prepared slides. This made our presentation on environmental protection much more interesting.

学无止境

We have learned some words about environmental protection. Here are some additional words and phrases related to the topic. Pinyin is provided for new characters only.

电子垃圾 *electronic waste (e-waste)*	垃圾分类 (lèi) *sort waste (trash)*	污水 *wastewater*
绿色消费 *green consumption*	水源 *water resources*	废气 *exhaust gas, tail gas*
酸雨 *acid rain*	大气层 *atmosphere*	绿色生产 *green production*
地下水 *underground water*	再生能源 *regenerated energy resources*	生态 (tài) 环境 *ecological environment*

温故知新 GAIN NEW INSIGHT THROUGH REVIEW

We have learned many words with the character 电. Do you remember the following words?

电灯	电话	电脑	电子产品	电灯泡
电脑房	电视	电视机	电梯	电影
电影院	电视台	电视剧	电子邮件	电冰箱

中国文化一瞥

Chinese proverbs

The following proverbs are related to saving or using resources carefully. Pinyin is provided only for those phrases with new characters.

1. xì shuǐ cháng liú
细 水 长 流

water flowing out in a trickle takes a long time to exhaust; a small but steady stream; plan on a long-term basis

IN USE:

父母总是让他要细水长流，不要大手大脚地花钱。

His parents always tell him to plan on a long-term basis and not to spend money recklessly.

YOUR TURN:

Answer the following questions based on your own situation:

1. 你能做到在花钱的时候，细水长流吗？细水长流有哪些长处和短处？
2. 有人说，在谈恋爱的时候，爱情也应该细水长流，这样两个人的爱情会比较长久。你同意这种看法吗？为什么？

2. jié yī suō shí
节 衣 缩 食
economize on food and clothing; live frugally

IN USE:

他们全家节衣缩食了两三年，才买了一辆车。
The whole family cut back on food and clothing for two or three years before they bought a car.

为了让他上大学，他父母节衣缩食帮助他交学费。
To enable him to go to college, his parents live frugally and help him with tuition.

YOUR TURN:

Choose one goal from the following list that you believe is worth living frugally for and give a reason.

我可以为了______________节衣缩食，因为______________。

上大学	结婚	谈恋爱	买车	旅游
听音乐会	父母	买新电脑	帮助别人	跟朋友出去玩

3. jīng dǎ xì suàn
精 打 细 算
careful calculation and strict budgeting; be very careful with the budget; count every cent and make every cent count

IN USE:

虽然他每个月的零花钱不多，但是因为他很会精打细算，所以钱还花不完。
Although his monthly allowance is small, because he is good at budgeting, he doesn't spend all of the money.

如果你精打细算，这些钱应该够你去北京旅行了。
If you budget carefully, this amount of money should be enough for you to travel to Beijing.

YOUR TURN:

Answer the following questions based on your own situation:

1. 在你的家人和朋友中，谁花钱的时候精打细算？
2. 精打细算，这对他/她的生活有没有帮助？
3. 要做到精打细算容易吗？可以用哪些方法帮助一个人精打细算？

The Chinese View of Nature

Zhú Lǐ Guǎn
竹 里 馆

[Táng] Wáng Wéi
[唐] 王 维

Dú zuò yōu huáng lǐ,
独 坐 幽 篁 里，

tán qín fù cháng xiào.
弹 琴 复 长 啸。

Shēn lín rén bù zhī,
深 林 人 不 知，

míng yuè lái xiāng zhào.
明 月 来 相 照。

In a Retreat Among the Bamboo
Wang Wei (Tang Dynasty)

Sitting alone in the quiet of the bamboo grove,
I am playing my lute and humming a song.
In the deep forest no one is aware—
The bright moon comes to shine on me.

YOUR TURN:

1. Read and recite the poem. Pay special attention to the imagery it creates. Then create a picture presentation based on the poem.
2. Make a new translation of the poem. Your translation should reflect the understanding of the relationship between nature and man that forms the underlining theme of the poem.

你知道吗?

在中国，“绿色生活”变得越来越重要。对许多中国人来说，绿色生活的一个方面是节约能源。媒体 (méitǐ, media) 常常给大家一些节约能源的建议。比如：

- 使用节能电器，这样可以节约百分之五十到九十的电能。
- 使用节能灯泡，可以节约百分之七十五的电能。
- 在家随手关灯 (turn off the lights when you leave a room)。
- 使用节能洗衣机，这样可以节约百分之五十的电能和百分之六十的水。
- 别把空调的温度开得太低。
- 如果你住得不太高，可以多走楼梯，少坐或者不坐电梯。
- 节约使用电脑和打印机。不用的时候，可以把电脑和打印机关上。
- 节约使用电视机。不看的时候就关上。或者可以多运动，少看电视。
- 买绿色的电子产品，这样比较环保。
- 回收旧电器。
- 多用电邮、电子书报，这样可以节约纸，保护森林。
- 双面打印、复印，可以节约纸。
- 用节水的水龙头 (faucet)。
- 洗澡 (xǐzǎo, bath, shower)的时间不要太长。
- 洗澡的水不要太热。
- 洗东西的时候用水盆。不要开着水龙头洗。
- 如果有可能，多用太阳能和风能。

3.5 地理环境和发展
Geographic Environment and Development

对话一

凯丽：　大卫，你在忙什么呢？

大卫：　我在准备报告呢。这个星期五，我要去红红的幼儿园参加“大哥哥大姐姐”活动。每个大哥哥大姐姐都要教小朋友做一件事。我觉得学会看地图非常有用，所以我要给他们介绍一下怎么看地图。

凯丽：　那你带几张地图不就行了吗？为什么还要做幻灯片呢？

大卫：　我打算一边教他们用地图，一边介绍中国地理。你看，这是我要用的地图。幼儿园的孩子认识的字不多，所以我还做了一些幻灯片，把各地的风景照片放在上边。这样，他们在听我介绍的时候，还能看到那个地方的风景。

凯丽：　这张是什么地图？跟我们平时看到的地图不太一样。

大卫：　这是中国的地形图。棕色代表高原，浅绿色代表山地，深绿色代表平原。

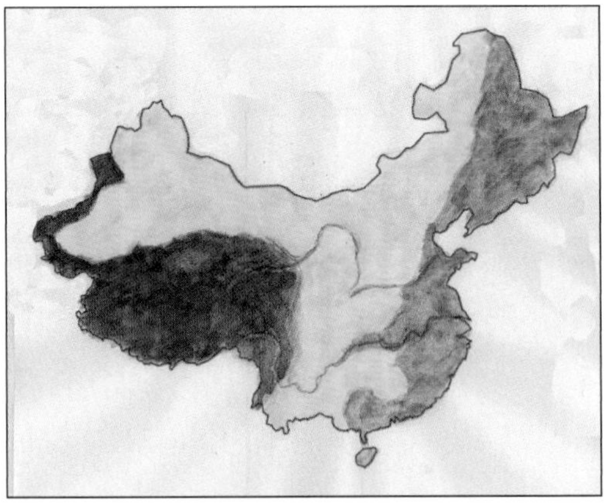

凯丽：　中国的地形图很有意思。中西部都是棕色的。难道说那儿有很多高原和山地吗？

大卫：　是的。你看，中国虽然很大，可是多半都是高原和山地。你看，我这样写可以吗？“中国地形的第一个特点是：山地多，平原少。”

凯丽：　当然可以。这些蓝色的线代表江河吧？

大卫：　对，你看，中国有两条主要的大河，一条是长江，另一条是黄河，都从西往东流。

凯丽：　为什么中国的大河都从西往东流呢？

大卫：　这个问题问得好。我可以写第二个特点了，“西部高，东部低”。你看，中国的高原和山地都在中部和西部，平原在东部。黄河和长江都是从西部的高山往东流。

凯丽：　那你还可以写第三个特点，就是“越往西，山越高。”

大卫：　对，对。还有别的特点吗？

凯丽：　你是不是应该告诉大家，中国只有一面靠海，其他的三面都是陆地？

大卫：　不错，我把这个特点也写上去。谢谢你帮我做幻灯片。

凯丽：　谢什么呀，你太客气了。

对话二

玛丽娅：凯丽，在经济课讨论的时候，你说了地理环境和经济发展的关系。我觉得你说得很有道理。

凯丽：　是吗？其实，我是受到了大卫的启发。前几天他给我看了中国的地形图，我突然发现中国的地形非常有特点，这对中国各地的经济发展一定有影响。后来我上网做了一些研究，今天就把我了解到的情况告诉了大家。

玛丽娅：原来我不太清楚为什么中国东西部的发展会有那么大的差别，现在知道因为地形的关系，西部有些地区发展经济非常困难。

凯丽：　是的。比方说，西部有些高原平均海拔在4000米以上，有些地区一年四季都有雪，这样的地区很难发展农业。

玛丽娅：不光是农业，发展工业也有困难。山那么高，要造一条公路或者铁路都很不容易。这样，交通一定不方便。

凯丽：交通不方便，经济不发达，地理条件又不好，那些地区的人口就比较少。相比之下，中国东部的地形就比较适合人口居住和经济发展。

玛丽娅：怪不得中国多数的人都住在东部和中部。

凯丽：再说，东部有平原，可以种粮食。东部的交通也比西部发达，而且又靠海，跟国外交流方便。这些都对经济发展有好处。

云南的一个村子

玛丽娅：所以中国的大城市都在东部吧？

凯丽：对，主要的大城市都在东部，比方说，北京、上海、天津、广州。但是中部也有一些大城市，比如重庆。

玛丽娅：那是因为中国的中部有一些盆地吗？

凯丽：是的。中部有四川盆地，四川盆地的面积很大，四面都是高山，那里的气候很好，不常下雪，非常适合农业生产。四川盆地的人口也很多。重庆就在四川盆地，是中国中部的一个经济中心。

四川的风景区

玛丽娅：我觉得你还提到一个很重要的方面。那就是，因为地形的不同，各地可以发展各种经济。

凯丽：对，在高原和山地，因为风景美丽，可以建设旅游区。

玛丽娅：希望我在中国的时候，有机会去看看高原的美丽风景。

凯丽：我也是。这样吧，可能的话，我们俩一起去旅游。

玛丽娅：太好了。

生词

	Simplified	*Traditional*	*Pinyin*	*Part of Speech*	*English*
1.	报告	報告	bàogào	*n./v.*	report
2.	地形		dìxíng	*n.*	topography, landform
3.	棕色		zōngsè	*n.*	brown
4.	代表		dàibiǎo	*v.*	represent
5.	高原		gāoyuán	*n.*	plateau
6.	浅	淺	qiǎn	*adj.*	light (color), shallow
7.	深		shēn	*adj.*	deep (color), deep
8.	陆地	陸地	lùdì	*n.*	land
9.	启发	啓發	qǐfā	*n./v.*	enlightenment, enlighten, illuminate
10.	发现	發現	fāxiàn	*n./v.*	discovery, discover
11.	平均		píngjūn	*n.*	mean, average
12.	海拔		hǎibá	*n.*	height above sea level
13.	不光		bùguāng	*conj.*	not only
14.	相比之下		xiāng bǐ zhī xià	*s.p.*	in comparison
15.	适合	適合	shìhé	*v.*	suit, fit, be appropriate for
16.	交流		jiāoliú	*n./v.*	exchange, interchange
17.	盆地		péndì	*n.*	basin
18.	提到		tídào	*v.*	mention

语言注释

1. 不光 (Not only, not merely)

不光 has the same meaning as 不只. It can be used before a noun or a verbal phrase.

不光居民参加了社区环保日的活动，我们学校的师生也参加了。
Not only residents attended the community's Earth Day activities, teachers and students from our school also attended.

四川不光有高山，而且有盆地。
Sichuan not only has high mountains, but also has basins.

2. 相比之下 (In comparison)

To make a comparison between A and B, we can make a statement about A, and then use 相比之下 to introduce B.

中国的西部是高原。相比之下，中国的东部山地不多。
In western China there are plateaus. In comparison, there are not too many mountainous areas in the eastern part of China.

坐机场专线车很方便，一个小时可以到机场。相比之下，坐地铁更快一点儿，大概四十五分钟就可以到了。
It is convenient to take the airport shuttle. It arrives at the airport in an hour. In comparison, it is a little faster by the subway. It arrives in about 45 minutes.

机场专线车

学无止境

We have learned about China's topography and geography. The following are some geographic areas in China. Pinyin is provided for new characters only.

青藏高原 *Qinghai-Tibet Plateau*	黄土高原 *The Loess Plateau*	云贵高原 *Yunnan-Guizhou Plateau*
内蒙古高原 *Inner Mongolia Plateau*	华北平原 *North China Plain*	长江中下游 *Middle and Lower Reaches of the Yangtze River*
东北平原 *Northeast China Plains*	戈壁沙漠 (Gēbì shāmò) *The Gobi Desert*	台湾海峡 (xiá) *The Taiwan Straits*

戈壁沙漠

YOUR TURN:

Find these areas on a map of China.

温故知新 GAIN NEW INSIGHT THROUGH REVIEW

We have learned some words about geography and landforms. Categorize the following words into two groups. After you have finished, compare notes with your peers.

农村	江河	南部	山区	平地
草原	平原	城市	盆地	北部
村子	城市	高原	西部	高山
地区	东部	湖	小镇	山地

地理	地形

中国文化一瞥

Chinese proverbs

The following proverbs describe gigantic forces. Pinyin is provided only for those phrases with new characters.

1. dì dòng shān yáo
地 动 山 摇
the earth trembles and mountains sway

IN USE:

在这个电影里，外星人到地球的时候，地球上地动山摇。
In this movie, when the aliens arrived on Earth, the ground trembled and mountains shook.

YOUR TURN:

Choose one of the situations and make a sentence with 地动山摇.

台风	地震 (zhèn) earthquake	爆炸 (bàozhà) explosion	龙卷 (juǎn)风 tornado	房子倒了

2. pái shān dǎo hǎi
排 山 倒 海
move the mountains and overturn the seas; remove mountains and upset seas; gigantic power

IN USE:

我们的球队赢了，欢呼声排山倒海。
Our team won and the cheers were so loud that they could move mountains and overturn seas.

YOUR TURN:

Match the parts in Columns A and B to make sentences.

A	B
歌星到了音乐广场，	每个公司都开始用新技术。
新技术来得排山倒海，	很多房子都倒了。
发大水的时候，大水排山倒海，	歌迷 (fans) 们发出排山倒海的欢呼。

3. dǎo hǎi fān jiāng
倒 海 翻 江

Turn over the sea and rivers; world-shaking; a gigantic force

IN USE:

最近一百年的变化可以说是倒海翻江。

The changes over the last hundred years can be described as world-shaking.

YOUR TURN:

Answer the following question based on your own situation:

什么事会让你的感情倒海翻江？

The Chinese View of Nature

桃花源

中国人常常把风景很美丽，生活很安宁 (ānníng, leisurely) 的地方叫做“世外桃源”(shìwài táoyuán, the Paradise of the Peach Blossom Spring)。我们在《欢迎2》第3.3课里给大家提到过这个故事。这跟晋朝(Jìncháo, the Jin Dynasty) 的诗人陶渊明 (Táo Yuānmíng)的散文(sǎnwén, prose)《桃花源记》(Táohuāyuán jì, Record of the Peach Blossom Spring) 有关。陶渊明在这篇散文里写道，在晋朝太元年 (376年–396年) 的时候，有一个渔夫 (yúfū, fisherman) 打渔的时候迷路了。他的船在河上漂 (piāo, float) 啊漂啊，穿过 (pass through)

了一片桃花林，他突然看到了一个非常美丽的村子。这里土地肥沃(féiwò, rich)，房屋整齐，村子里种着很多桑树(sāngshù, mulberry trees)和竹子(zhúzǐ, bamboo)。这里的人们看起来都很快乐，过着很朴素(pǔsù, simple)的自然生活。他们从来不出门旅行，也不知道世界上有战乱(zhànluàn, wars)和灾害(zāihài, disasters)。渔夫在这个小村子里住了好几天，过得非常快乐。他离开这个村子的时候，一路上作了很多标记(biāojì, marks)，打算以后再回来访问的时候，可以找到路。可是，过了一段时候，当他再要访问桃花源的时候，发现自己的标记都不见了。桃花源永远找不到了。

很多学者认为，《桃花源记》是受了老子的顺应 (shùnyìng, be one with) 自然，小国寡民 (xiǎoguó guǎmín, a small state with a small population) 的思想的影响写成的。桃花源其实就是中国人想象的乌托邦 (Wūtuōbāng, Utopia)。

The Peach Blossom Spring

The Chinese like to compare a place of beautiful scenery where people live peaceful lives with the Peach Blossom Spring. We mentioned this story in Lesson 3.3 of *Huanying,* Volume 2. This paradise comes from the Jin Dynasty poet Tao Yuanming, who wrote the essay "Record of the Peach Blossom Spring." In this story, Tao Yuanming wrote that in the Jin Dynasty, between 376 and 396 A.D., a fisherman went out fishing and lost his way. His boat floated on the river aimlessly. As he passed through a forest of peach blossoms, he suddenly spotted a beautiful little village hidden deep within the valley. The village had beautiful houses, and its streets were lined with mulberry trees and bamboo. The villagers all seemed to be quite content. They lived a simple life and were in harmony with nature. They had never gone out traveling, and did not know about the wars and disasters in the rest of the world. The fisherman enjoyed a happy few days in the village before heading back home. On his way home, he made some marks on the road for himself in case he wanted to come back. However, when he did try to go back to the Peach Blossom Spring, all the marks that he had made disappeared. The Peach Blossom Spring was forever lost.

Many scholars believe that the "Record of the Peach Blossom Spring" was written under the influence of the Chinese philosopher Lao Zi. The village described in the prose reminds people of Lao Zi's ideal world, one that consists of a small state with a small population. Indeed, the Peach Blossom Spring is the Chinese version of Utopia.

YOUR TURN:

Choose one imaginary place from a children's story that you are familiar with. Prepare a presentation in Chinese about this place and explain why you have chosen this place for the presentation.

你知道吗?

虽然中国的水资源占全球的百分之六，在世界各国中占第四位，但是因为中国的人口非常多，所以每个人的平均水资源只有世界人均 (per capita) 水资源的1/4。也就是说，中国是世界上最缺 (quē, lack) 水的国家之一。

中国各地都有缺水的情况，特别是在北方。那是因为中国的水资源百分之八十在南方，只有百分之二十左右在北方。可是，中国有百分之四十六的人住在北方。

还有一个原因是，中国北方的许多地区只有夏天和秋天下雨，到了冬天和春天，北方的一些河就干了。这时候，北方缺水的问题变得更严重。

为了解决水的问题，中国政府建造了一些水库 (shuǐkù, reservoir)。同时也让大家节约用水，保护水资源。

黄浦江

3.6 第三单元复习
Unit 3 Review

对话一

（在汤姆家。）

妈妈：爸爸回来了吗？

汤姆：还没有。平时他六点就到家了，现在快六点半了，他怎么还没回来？也许因为路上堵车吧。

妈妈：哦，我想起来了，今天是"环保日"，鼓励大家都不开车，只用公共交通，走路，或者骑自行车上班。

汤姆：原来是这样。我们家除了爸爸以外，大家都挺注意环保的。我和杰米每天都坐地铁去学校。您每天都骑自行车去上班。

妈妈：你爸爸因为上班的地方比较远，公司附近没有公交车，所以他只好开车。要是公共交通比较方便，他一定也会坐公交车的。

汤姆：不是说离他们公司不远，正在盖地铁站吗？地铁要什么时候才能通车？

妈妈：听说十月。通车以后，就让你爸爸也坐地铁上班。其实我也不愿意他多开车。路上车水马龙，常常堵车，又慢又不

车水马龙

安全。再说，如果大家都开车，对环境也不好，污染空气。

汤姆：还有，在上海停车特别不容易。有时候，我看爸爸把车开来开去，找一个停车的地方，找半个小时也不一定能找到。要是坐公交，就没有这种麻烦了。

妈妈：你说得对。最近三十多年来，中国发展得非常快，不少人都买了房子买了车。不像我小时候，那时候大家都是坐公交车、骑自行车、或者走路去上班上学。路上很少堵车。现在马路公路造得比以前多得多，但是有车的人增加得也很快，所以一到上下班时间就堵车。

汤姆：虽然开车有开车的问题，但是我觉得有了车比较自由。特别是到了周末，要去城外玩，坐公交车会花很多时间，还要等车。自己开车方便多了。

妈妈：大家的想法都差不多，所以到了周末，公路上常常堵车，开开停停，非常慢。有时候，公路成了一个大停车场。

汤姆：等爸爸回来，我们告诉他，地铁一通车，他就别开车了。

妈妈：好主意。

对话二

玛丽娅：学校旁边的居民社区建设得很快，每天都能看到变化。

凯丽：对，昨天我们上经济课的时候，钱老师带我们去参观了建设工地，还跟负责建设这个社区的工程师举行了座谈。

玛丽娅：我看到建设工地的外面有一个牌子，说这将是一个绿色小区。绿色小区跟别的小区有什么不一样？

凯丽：这正是我们去校外考察的目的。我们的经济课正在讨论经济发展和环境的关系。大家都认为，既然经济发展是免不了的，我们应该从一开始就注意怎么保护环境，不让环境受到不好的影响。所以我们昨天去参观的时候，大家问了很多关于“绿色”的问题，特别是绿色建设和绿色材料。

玛丽娅：什么是绿色建设？

凯丽：就是在建设这个小区的时候，不污染环境，也不浪费资源。这个小区用了不少回收再生的材料，比如，回收再生的木头、塑料什么的。其他的建筑材料也都是低污染的环保材料。

玛丽娅：说到节约资源，这个小区做了些什么？

凯丽：他们用的都是节能灯泡和节能电器。同时，小区能用太阳能和风能的地方，就用太阳能和风能。这样不但保护了资源，也让居民可以少花钱。那个工程师介绍说，住在这个小区不用付很多电费。对了，那个工程师还介绍说，小区的建筑材料比较特别。冬天可以保暖，夏天可以去热，这可以让居民节约不少能源。

玛丽娅：我看过一个电视节目，说的是一个小区怎么节约用水。这个小区打算怎么节约用水呢？

凯丽：他们要重复使用生活用水。居民洗衣洗菜的水，会被小区的绿化再次使用，这样可以节约很多水。居民可以节约水费。

玛丽娅：这个小区听上去真不错。谁都可以去参观吗？

凯丽：可以，每个星期一、三、五下午都对外开放。你也可以去看看。

玛丽娅：行，这个星期五下午我就去。

建设中的居民小区

生词

	Simplified	*Traditional*	*Pinyin*	*Part of Speech*	*English*
1.	鼓励	鼓勵	gǔlì	*n./v.*	encouragement, encourage
2.	车水马龙	車水馬龍	chē shuǐ mǎ lóng	*s.p.*	heavy traffic in the street
3.	材料		cáiliào	*n.*	material
4.	木头	木頭	mùtóu	*n.*	wood
5.	电器	電器	diànqì	*n.*	electric appliance
6.	太阳能	太陽能	tàiyángnéng	*n.*	solar energy
7.	风能	風能	fēngnéng	*n.*	wind energy
8.	保暖		bǎonuǎn	*v.c.*	keep something warm

生词扩充

Many Chinese words are formed by combining two or more characters. If you know the characters in a word, you can often guess the meaning of that word. See if you understand the meaning of the following words.

发电		去湿	
风车		地平线	
平地		草原	
人来人往		开关	
环保工程		水电站	
野菜		山区	
费钱费时		再生能源	
一通百通		环保学	
茶点		河床	

SELF-ASSESSMENT

In Unit 3, you have learned to talk about economic development, globalization, localization, commercialism, and their impact on the environment. You have also learned about China's geographic environment and environmental protection. Have you reached the learning goals of Unit 3? After completing the exercises for Unit 3 in your Workbook, fill out the following self-assessment sheet.

Yes/No	*Can you do these things in Chinese?*
	Describe, in some detail, a greener way to celebrate holidays
	Describe different types of pollution
	Describe general economic development
	Describe various ways to protect the environment
	Describe, with some examples, a green life
	Compare globalization and localization
	Discuss the impact of commercialization, particularly commercial advertisements
	Describe, in some detail, an online business transaction
	Describe China's geography
	Discuss the relationship between geography and economic development

9–10	yes	excellent
6–8	yes	good
1–5	yes	need some work

第四单元：往前看

UNIT 4 Looking Forward

LEARNING GOALS OF UNIT 4

By the end of this unit, you will learn how to:

- Describe, in some detail, China's college entrance examination
- Give step-by-step instructions on filling out a university application form in China
- Describe, in some detail, the university admission process in China
- Describe, in some detail, a job in the service industry
- Describe prerequisites for finding employment
- Give instructions on preparations for study abroad
- Describe, in some detail, housing choices for study abroad programs
- Describe, in some detail, the procedures for applying to a US university
- Talk about feelings and opinions on living independently
- Talk about renting a house and finding a roommate
- Describe a senior prom in a US high school
- Talk about feelings towards friendship and plans to maintain a friendship

4.1 升学 Continuing Education at a Higher Level

对话一

（在学校的电脑房。）

丁老师：同学们，如果你们打算参加高考，就需要上网去填写高考报名表。请大家先登录高考报名网站，然后看一下表格。如果有问题，可以问我。

玛丽娅：丁老师，我还没决定要不要在中国参加高考呢。您觉得我需要报名吗？

丁老师：因为报名的时间一共只有五天，所以我建议你先报名。如果你现在不报名，到时候又想去参加高考，那时候再要报名就来不及了。

金顺爱：我想去上护理学校，不是大学，也要报名参加高考吗？

丁老师：是的，护理学校是大专，也是高等教育的一部分。在中国，一个人不管上大学还是上大专都要根据他的高考成绩，所以都需要参加高考。

汤姆：丁老师，我已经登录了，正在填表呢。这里有几个词的意思我不懂，上面问我是"应届"还是"往届"高中毕业生，这是什么意思？

丁老师：哦，应届的意思是今年从高中毕业的学生，往届是前几年毕业的。

汤姆：报名表上写的报考科目是：语文、数学、英语。我们只要考三门功课吗？

丁老师：不是的，还有一门是"综合"，就是把物理、化学、生物、历史、地理和政治这六个科目放在一起考。同时，你自己还需要在这六个科目中，再选择一门作为第五个考试科目。

玛丽娅：丁老师，我对第五个考试科目不太清楚。

丁老师：是这样的。综合考试考的是一般的常识，是每个人都要考的。另外，你还可以根据自己的特长，选择一门考试。比方说，你觉得自己的物理不错，就可以选择物理。如果你的历史课成绩很好，就可以选择历史。

汤姆：您是说，高考一共要考五个科目，对吗？

丁老师：对，四门是固定的，一门由你们自己选择。

大卫：那高考一共要考多长时间？

丁老师：每个科目要考两个小时，每天考两个科目，所以一共要考两天半。

在大学校园里

对话二

汤姆：要填高考报考志愿了，你们知道怎么填吗？

凯丽：是这样的，中国的大学分成重点和普通的大学。等高考成绩出来以后，先由重点大学根据高考成绩挑选他们打算录取的学生。等他们挑选完了以后，再由普通大学从剩下的学生中挑选。等普通大学选完了，最后由大专挑选。

汤姆：这么说，要分三批来挑选学生吗？

玛丽娅：是的。所以在填报考志愿的时候，我们都需要选十二个大学，四个是比较好的大学，四个是普通大学，还有四个是大专。这样，万一你考不上最好的大学，还有可能上普通大学，如果普通大学也不录取你，你还可能上大专。

金顺爱：要是我只想考大专，是不是只要填四个大专就可以了？

凯丽：我看，也许你可以多填几个大专，如果你选的大专都录取你了，你就可以在这几个大专学校里选你最喜欢的上。

金顺爱：好主意。

汤姆：那我们可以选多少个专业呢？

凯丽：在你报考的每个大学里，你都可以选六个专业。

汤姆：哇，太棒了！一个大学可以选六个，十二个大学可以选七十二个不同的专业了。

凯丽：恐怕只有你会选择七十二个不同的专业。多数同学一定是在不同的大学报考一样的专业。

王大明：就是啊，比方说，我父母非要我当电子工程师不可，所以我选择的都是电子工程专业。虽然每个大学都可以选六个专业，可是我六个专业选的都是电子工程。

汤姆：这么说，你只选了一个专业？为什么不选别的专业呢？

王大明：我非常喜欢电脑。为了让父母和我自己高兴，我是铁了心要当电子工程师了。

汤姆：祝你好运。

上海外贸学院

生词

Simplified	Traditional	Pinyin	Part of Speech	English
1. 升学	升學	shēngxué	*v.o.*	go to a higher-level school, matriculate
2. 登录	登錄	dēnglù	*v.o.*	log on
3. 护理	護理	hùlǐ	*n./v.*	nursing care; nurse
4. 大专	大專	dàzhuān	*n.*	junior college
5. 应届	應屆	yìngjiè	*n.*	the present graduating year
6. 往届	往屆	wǎngjiè	*n.*	previous graduating classes
7. 报考	報考	bàokǎo	*v.*	register for examination
8. 科目		kēmù	*n.*	subject (in a curriculum), course
9. 综合	綜合	zōnghé	*adj.*	comprehensive
10. 政治		zhèngzhì	*n.*	politics
11. 作为	作為	zuòwéi	*v.c.*	regard as, as
12. 常识	常識	chángshí	*n.*	common sense
13. 特长	特長	tècháng	*n.*	special skill, strong point, specialty
14. 固定		gùdìng	*adj./v.*	fixed; fix
15. 志愿	志願	zhìyuàn	*n.*	wish, aspiration, ideal
16. 普通		pǔtōng	*adj.*	general, common, ordinary
17. 挑选	挑選	tiāoxuǎn	*v.*	select, choose
18. 批		pī	*m.w.*	batch, lot, group
19. 非…不可		fēi...bùkě	*s.p.*	must, have to
20. 铁了心	鐵了心	tiě le xīn	*s.p.*	unshakable in one's determination

语言注释

1. 作为 (Regard as, as)

学生们都把王老师作为朋友。
Students all take Teacher Wang as their friends.

因为他的房子很小，所以只能把客厅作为孩子的卧室。
Because his house is very small, he has to use the living room as his children's bedroom.

2. 是这样的 (Let me explain)

This is a colloquial expression. It is usually used at the beginning of a sentence.

A: 这些苹果很小，为什么比那些大的贵呢?
B: 是这样的，这些是有机苹果，所以比较贵。
A: These apples are small. Why are they more expensive than those big ones?
B: Let me explain. These are organic applies, therefore they are more expensive.

A: 他怎么三天没来上班了?
B: 是这样的，他父亲病了，所以他回家去照顾父亲了。
A: How come he hasn't been to work for three days?
B: Let me explain. His father is sick so he has gone home to take care of his father.

3. 恐怕 (I am afraid, probably, perhaps)

恐怕 can be placed before or after the subject in a clause.

今天下大雨，恐怕他来不了了。
It's raining heavily today. Perhaps he won't be able to come.

虽然我很想报考北京大学，但是我的成绩太差了，恐怕考不进那么好的大学。
Although I'd like very much to apply to Beijing University, my grades are too poor and I probably won't be able to test into such a good university.

4. 非…不可 (Must, have to)

非…不可 is a set phrase. A verbal phrase is usually placed after the word 非. 不可 is placed at the end of a sentence.

我去中国的时候，非要去参观一下长城不可。
When I go to China, I must visit the Great Wall.

A: 你为什么每天非上网不可呢？
B: 我的朋友都在网上，不上网，我怎么跟他们联系呢？
A: Why do you have to get online every day?
B: My friends are all online. If I don't get online, how can I contact them?

学无止境

We have learned many words about the College Entrance Examination in China. Here are some additional words on the same topic. Pinyin is provided for new characters only.

考生 *test taker*	准考证 *test taker ID card*	考场 *place to take the test*
监(jiān)考老师 *teachers who administer (monitor) the test*	录取(qǔ) *admission, get admitted*	录取分数线 *cut-off scores for admission*
上榜(bǎng) *be on the admission list*	落(luò)榜 *be off the admission list*	落榜生 *student who is off the admission list*
复读 *re-study high school courses for next year's college entrance examination*	招生简章(jiǎnzhāng) *admission brochure*	招生办公室 *admission office*

温故知新 GAIN NEW INSIGHT THROUGH REVIEW

We have learned how to say some subject areas in Chinese. Let's review them. The following list also has a few new subject areas. See if you can guess their meanings.

语文	数学	物理	化学	生物
几何	电机工程学	英语	汉语	法语
日语	地理	政治	经济学	音乐
电脑工程学	语言学	美术	艺术	体育
社会学	历史	教育学	文学	民族学

中国文化一瞥

Chinese proverbs and sayings

The following proverbs either urge people to value time or to take opportunities as they come. Pinyin is only provided for those phrases with new characters.

1. zhǐ zhēng zhāo xī
只 争 朝 夕

seize the time at dawn and at dusk; seize every minute; make the best use of one's time

IN USE:

高考马上要来了。高三的学生都在只争朝夕地学习。
The college examination is coming. All seniors are making the best use their time and studying.

他这两个星期只争朝夕地写报告，为了能在月底以前写完。
In order to finish the report by the end of the month, he has been working every minute over the last two weeks.

YOUR TURN:

Answer the following questions based on your own situation:

1. 考试以前，你会只争朝夕地准备考试吗？
2. 在什么情况下，你会只争朝夕？
3. 在你的同学和朋友里，谁总是只争朝夕？请你举一个他/她只争朝夕的例子。

2. dāng jī lì duàn
当 机 立 断

make a prompt decision; prompt decision at the right moment

IN USE:

因为天气不好，去北京的飞机都不能起飞。他当机立断，决定坐火车去。

Because of bad weather, all flights to Beijing couldn't take off. He made a snap decision to take the train.

听说今天晚上有音乐会。他们当机立断，上网去买了两张票。

They heard that there would be a concert tonight. They made a prompt decision to buy two tickets online.

YOUR TURN:

Can you use 当机立断 to describe the following situations?

小丽听说上海大学也有新闻学专业，马上决定报考上海大学。	可以	不可以
那个商店夏天的衣服打五折。小周一看就买了三条裙子。	可以	不可以
黄新建的女朋友说他们应该在春节结婚。黄新建说，"我们还是先去问问父母再决定吧。"	可以	不可以

钱雪看到了她想买的书，可是那本书有点儿贵。她决定再去旧书店看看，有没有便宜一点儿的。	可以	不可以

3. jī bù kě shī, shī bù zài lái
机 不 可 失， 失 不 再 来

opportunity knocks but once; don't lose an opportunity, if you lose it, it won't come back

IN USE:

我觉得你应该马上申请那个工作。机不可失，失不再来。

I think you should apply for that job right away. Opportunity knocks but once.

YOUR TURN:

Can you give an example of 机不可失，失不再来？

The Chinese Aesthetic

Introduction:

In Unit 4 you will be reading about some common aspirations of contemporary Chinese students. You may notice that most of them aspire to become doctors, businessmen, or engineers. It was a very different case in the past, especially in ancient times, when the highest ideal of the educated elite was to become a scholar-official employed by the Imperial Court. This ideal created a unique life-style and artistic sensibility for the Chinese literati, a sensibility that is often associated with elegance, discipline, and propriety. In this section, we will be introducing some basic art forms and aesthetic ideas practiced by Chinese literati in the past. We will also present some folk arts and crafts that were not fully embraced by the literati culture, yet were highly influential in the formation of Chinese artistic taste.

Since the content is quite different from the texts you have learned so far, a loose English translation is provided to facilitate your understanding.

文人画

中国画有很多流派 (liúpài, school of thought or trend)，其中最有名的一个流派叫做“文人画”。“文人画”这个名字，来自画画儿的人：他们大多都是受过传统教育的文人(scholar-officials)；他们画画儿是为了表达自己对自然、哲学 (zhéxué, philosophy)、和宗教 (zōngjiào, religion)的理解。跟职业画家不同，中国的文人崇尚 (chóngshàng, promote and admire) 把艺术作为一种爱好而不是作为一种专业。

“文人画”这个词，是明朝的著名画家董其昌 (Dǒng Qí Chāng, personal name) 提出来的。董其昌认为，唐代诗人王维（关于王维的诗，请看《欢迎4》3.4课的中国文化一瞥）是虔诚 (qiánchéng, devout) 的佛教徒 (fójiào tú, Buddhist)、著名的诗人、和有成就(chéngjiù, accomplished) 的画家。他是中国文人画的创始人 (chuàngshǐrén, founder)，因为王维的画表现了中国文人的最高理想。他的画把有佛、道意味的诗、美丽的书法 (calligraphy)、和淡雅 (dànyǎ, simple and elegant) 的画结合在一起。虽然从表面 (appearance) 上看起来，文人画里面画的只是山水、花鸟等等自然景象 (jǐngxiàng, scenery and images)，可是，文人画不是要画现实里的自然景色，而是画家对自然景色的感受 (gǎnshòu, feeling or understanding)。文人画是传统中国文人表现自我的一种特别方式。

Literati Painting

Among the different schools of painting in China, the most famous one is “literati painting.” The term comes from the people who made these paintings: the majority of painters were scholar-officials; they painted in order to show their understanding of nature, philosophy and religion. They were different from professional painters, as these literati promoted art for art’s sake, making it a hobby rather than a profession. Dong Qichang, a well-know scholar-painter of the Ming Dynasty, first came up with the term “literati painting.” According to him, literati painting as a genre was created by the Tang Dynasty poet Wang Wei. (For a poem by Wang Wei, please see “A Glimpse into Chinese Culture” in Lesson 3.4 of this volume.) Wang Wei was a devout Buddhist, a famous poet, and an accomplished painter. He was one of the founders of the Chinese literati school of painting, as he exemplified the highest ideals of the Chinese literati class. In his paintings he could combine traces of Buddhism and Daosim as well as beautiful calligraphy with an elegant painting style. To an untrained eye, a literati painting might be no more than an exaggerated depiction of some conventional scenery such as mountains, rivers, flowers, and birds. In fact, a literati painting conveys the artist's feelings and understandings about nature. It is the artist's self-expression.

YOUR TURN:

Choose one Chinese artist from the list below. Prepare an oral presentation on this artist. Your presentation should include the biographical information of the artist, his accomplishments, and his impact on later generations.

Artists:

Dong Qichang (董其昌), Chen Zhou (沈周), Wen Zhengming (文徵明), Ni Zan (倪赞), Huang Gongwang (黄公望)

你知道吗?

我们已经知道，在中国，高中被分成“普通高中”和“重点高中”。同样，中国的大学也分成“重点大学”和“普通大学”。有些大学历史很长，教学质量也非常好，这些大学是重点大学。比较有名的重点大学有：北京大学、清华大学、交通大学、南京大学、中山大学、南开大学等等。在高考的时候，这些重点大学可以第一批挑选学生。重点大学的录取分数线比普通大学要高得多，所以能考进重点大学的学生不太多。重点大学挑选完了以后，第二批挑选学生的是普通大学。除了重点大学和普通大学以外，中国还有大学专科(大专)。大专和大学的不同是大专只要上两年，大学要上四年。第三批挑选学生的是大专。

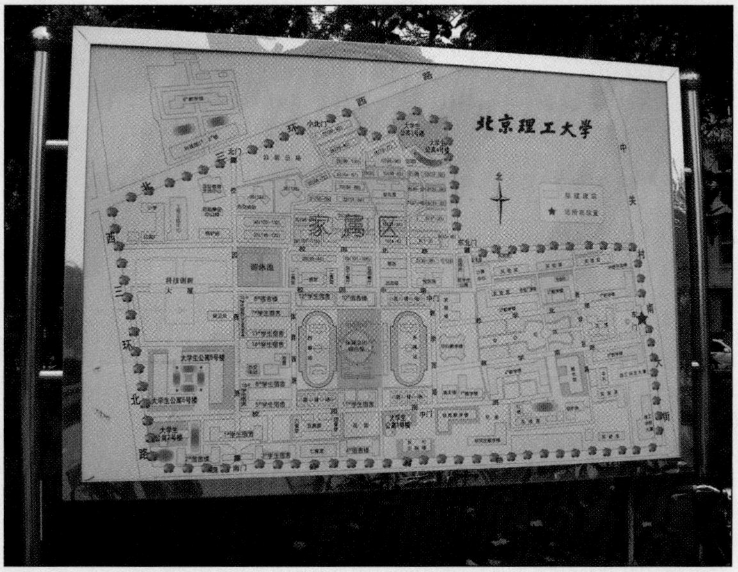

4.2 就业 Employment

对话一

玛丽娅：周英，最近你一下了课就急急忙忙地离开学校，你在忙什么呢？

周英：忙着找工作。

玛丽娅：你不打算上大学了？

周英：我念书念得不太好。一想到高考，我就很紧张，睡觉睡不好，学习也学不进去。虽然我妈妈还是希望我去考大学，但是我决定今年不考了，先去工作。以后如果还想上大学，再去考也来得及。

玛丽娅：那你想找哪方面的工作呢？

周英：当然是比较低层次、低技术的。我原来希望能去当个秘书。可是秘书的工作也不容易找。每次去申请工作，公司都要看我的工作简历。我的个人简历上除了上学以外，什么工作经验都没有，人家当然不会要我。

玛丽娅：听上去的确很困难。那你打算怎么办呢？

周英：靠亲戚朋友帮忙吧。昨天我爸爸的老朋友给我介绍了一个工作，让我去郊区的一个旅店当服务员。主要是为客人介绍旅店提供的服务，还有附近可参观的旅游景点。这个工作不是特别理想，因为工资不高，有时候还要上夜班，而且离家很远，坐公交车来回要三个小时。我妈妈不太愿意让我去，可是我爸爸说，这是一个锻炼的机会，可以先做起来，积累一些工作经验。

玛丽娅：你自己怎么想呢？

周英：我认为爸爸说得对，万事开头难。找第一个工作总是比较难，但是如果我把第一个工作做好了，积累了一些工作经验，以后再要找第二个工作就不会那么难了。再说，那个工作也有长处，福利不错，旅店每天为我们提供免费午餐和晚餐，一年还有两个星期的休假。

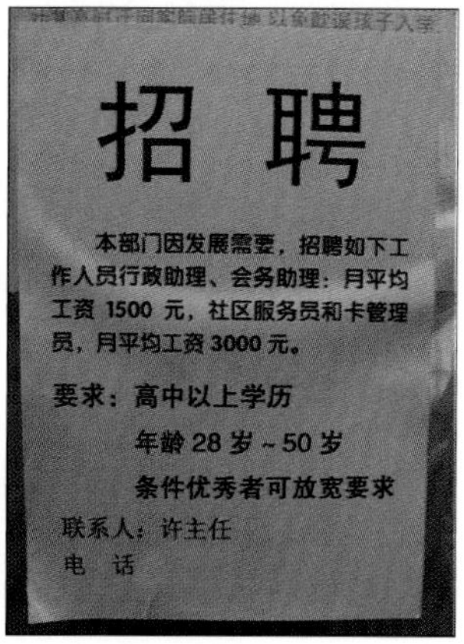

玛丽娅：那你什么时候开始工作？

周英：八月一日。第一个月是在职培训，从九月一日开始正式工作。

玛丽娅：你去工作以后，别忘了老同学。有空我们多联系。

周英：行，一言为定。

对话二

玛丽娅：听说有些同学高中毕业以后，马上就去工作。

凯丽：他们为什么不上大学？现在工作市场竞争非常厉害，连有些大学毕业生都找不到工作，高中毕业生就更难了。

大卫：那要看找什么工作。有些工作不需要大学毕业生。

凯丽：你说得也对，制造业、服务业、农业的一些体力工作，的确不需要大学生。可是那样的工作比较辛苦。

汤姆：你觉得辛苦，别人不一定觉得辛苦。有人喜欢动手，有人喜欢动脑。

玛丽娅：有道理。有人认为坐在办公室里舒服，也有人非常讨厌坐办公室。比方说我有一个邻居叫阿健，去年从高中毕业了。阿健的理想工作是每天都能跟不同的人打交道，所以他适合在商店工作。他可以跟顾客聊天，根据他们的喜爱和需要，把不同的东西卖给他们。阿健的爸爸开了一个商店，高中一毕业他就去那儿当营业员。阿健和他爸爸一样都是卖东西的天才，所以他们的生意越做越好，有时候忙到半夜才回家，可是他们总是高高兴兴的。

大卫：只要你热爱你的工作，而且努力去做，做什么都可能成功。

汤姆：听你们这么一说，我可能也不应该去上大学。我最喜欢旅游了，应该想法儿去旅行社找一个工作，当个导游，这样可以去世界各地逛逛。

玛丽娅：现在要当导游也不容易，需要从旅游学校毕业，经过正式的训练，不是谁想当就可以当的。再说，导游这个工作也挺复杂的，不只是带着游客玩，还得介绍风景点的历史文化。同时，导游还要安排游客的住、食、行，没有组织能力，不一定做得了这个工作。

凯丽：对，这个工作得跟许多不同的人打交道。要是碰到一些古怪的游客，也会让人受不了。汤姆，你没有客户服务方面的经验吧？我看你还是好好考虑一下再决定是不是要去当导游吧。

汤姆：其实当导游只是我的兴趣之一。还有不少其他的工作我也很感兴趣，比如开飞机、当警察、拍电影什么的，这些工作都挺有意思的。我们从小学到高中，在学校呆了十多年了，万一考上了大学，又得在大学呆四年。你们难道还没在学校呆够？不想出去工作工作，轻松轻松吗？

大卫：我看你把工作想得太容易了，真的要把一个工作做好，也不能随随便便。要是为了轻松一下，我劝你在暑假的时候好好休息休息，不就行了吗？

凯丽：大卫说得对。如果有两种方法解决问题，一种简单，一种复杂，一般的人都是避难就易，汤姆一定是避易就难。他喜欢戏剧化的生活。

汤姆：所以我说嘛，凯丽最理解我了。

生词

	Simplified	*Traditional*	*Pinyin*	*Part of Speech*	*English*
1.	紧张	緊張	jǐnzhāng	*adj.*	nervous, tense, intense
2.	层次	層次	céngcì	*n.*	level
3.	简历	簡歷	jiǎnlì	*n.*	resume
4.	夜班		yèbān	*n.*	night shift
5.	积累	積累	jīlěi	*n./v.*	accumulation; accumulate
6.	认为	認為	rènwéi	*v.*	think, consider
7.	万事开头难	萬事開頭難	wàn shì kāi tóu nán	*s.p.*	the first step is difficult
8.	福利		fúlì	*n.*	benefits, welfare
9.	在职	在職	zàizhí	*adj.*	on the job
10.	制造业	製造業	zhìzàoyè	*n.*	manufacturing industry
11.	服务业	服務業	fúwùyè	*n.*	service industry
12.	体力	體力	tǐlì	*n.*	physical strength
13.	动手	動手	dòngshǒu	*v.o.*	work with one's hands
14.	动脑	動腦	dòngnǎo	*v.o.*	work with one's mind
15.	热爱	熱愛	rè'ài	*v.*	love
16.	古怪		gǔguài	*adj.*	odd, eccentric
17.	呆		dāi	*v.* , adj	stay , dumb
18.	避难就易	避難就易	bì nán jiù yì	*s.p.*	avoid the difficult and choose the easy
19.	避易就难	避易就難	bì yì jiù nán	*s.p.*	avoid the easy and choose the difficult (a twist on 避难就易)
20.	戏剧化	戲劇化	xìjùhuà	*n./v.*	dramatization, dramatize

语言注释

1. 主要是 (Primarily, mainly)

他没有找到工作，主要是因为没有工作经验。
He didn't find a job mainly because he didn't have any work experience.

玩这个网上游戏的主要是一些小学生。
Those who play this online game are primarily students from elementary schools.

2. 可 + verb (Worth doing)

可 is the short form for 可以。

在北京，可参观的历史景点非常多。
In Beijing, there are many historical sites worth visiting.

那个国家可看、可玩的地方非常多。
That country has many places worth visiting and enjoying.

学无止境

Here are some Chinese words that are often used as subtitles in a resume. Pinyin is provided for new characters only.

个人信息 *personal information*	求职意向 *seeking a job in...*	教育经历 *education (experience)*
实习经历 *internship (experience)*	工作经历 *work (experience)*	语言能力 *language skills*
电脑能力 *computer skills*	其他专长 *other specialized skills*	个人爱好 *interests/hobbies*

YOUR TURN:

Create a short Chinese resume for yourself by using the following templates:

个人基本信息（姓名、地址、电话）

教育经历：

工作经历/实习经历：

义工经历：

语言能力：

电脑能力：

其他专长：

个人爱好和社团活动：

温故知新 GAIN NEW INSIGHT THROUGH REVIEW

We have learned many words related to employment. Let's review them. Group the following words into two categories and add a title for each category.

工程师	培训	工作时间	护士
医生	工资	经理	工作责任
老师	律师	上夜班	工人
福利	休假时间	翻译	导游
服务员	营业员	下班	警察
上班	农民	教练	驾驶员

中国文化一瞥

Chinese proverbs and sayings

Many Chinese proverbs and sayings give advice on how to act and speak in an appropriate way. Here are a few proverbs on behavior. Pinyin is provided only for those phrases with new characters.

1. 有 志 者，事 竟 成

Where there is a will, there is a way.

IN USE:

A: 去年马克来中国的时候还不会说汉语，现在已经说得不错了。
B: 马克每天都在学习汉语。有志者，事竟成嘛。

A: Last year when Mark came to China, he couldn't speak any Chinese. Now he can speak pretty well.
B: Mark studies Chinese every day. Where there is a will, there is a way.

YOUR TURN:

Answer the following questions based on your own situation:

1. 在你的个人经历中，有没有"有志者，事竟成"的例子？
2. 你相信"有志者，事竟成"吗？为什么？

2. 敏 于 事，慎 于 言

quick in actions and cautious in speech; alert and quick at what you do but careful in what you say

IN USE:

中国人觉得一个人应该敏于事，慎于言。做事做得好是最重要的。有些人说话说得好听，可是后来又做不到。这样会让别人不相信你。

Chinese believe one should be quick in actions and cautious in speech. It is most important to do a good job. Some people give beautiful speeches but later can't make them a reality. This behavior will make others lose their trust in you.

YOUR TURN:

Answer the following questions based on your own situation:

1. 敏于事，慎于言有哪些好处和坏处？
2. 在今天的社会里，谁最应该做到敏于事，慎于言？为什么？

3. 事 在 人 为

human effort is the decisive factor; it all depends on human effort; where there is a will, there is a way

IN USE:

虽然我的学习成绩马马虎虎，但是我相信事在人为。只要我高考以前好好准备，一定能考上大学。

Even though my grades are so-so, I believe in the power of human effort. As long as I prepare well before the college examination, I will definitely test into a college.

YOUR TURN:

Can you use 事在人为 to describe the following situations?

1. 玛丽娅希望能当班长。她努力为大家服务，最后同学们都选她当班长。	可以	不可以
2. 三姆想买一个新手机，可是没有钱。他姥姥知道以后，送了一个手机给他。	可以	不可以
3. 林达因为不打算上大学了，所以她每天在外边玩。现在她对旧金山的公园、商店、饭店、风景点什么的都非常了解。	可以	不可以
4. 凯文想兼职教英文。他在网上找了半天，终于在英文夏令营里找到了工作。	可以	不可以

The Chinese Aesthetic

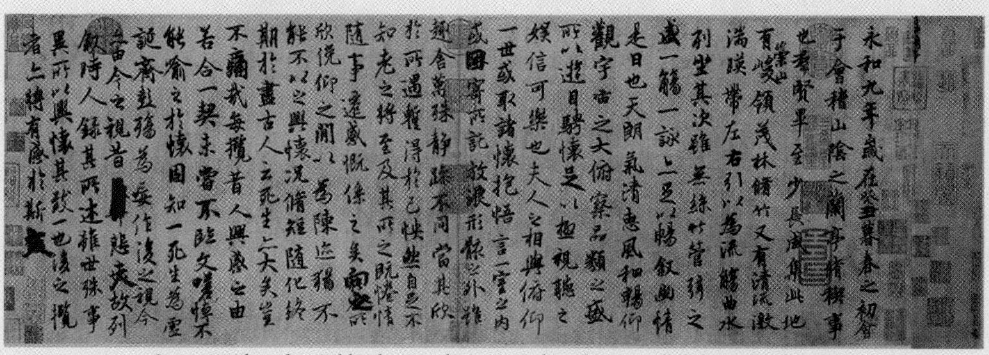

Source: Wikipedia, Public domain. http://en.wikipedia.org/wiki/File:LantingXu.jpg

王羲之和《兰亭序》

如果你问一个中国人，在两千多年的中国书法 (calligraphy) 历史上，哪一个书法作品最有名，她可能会告诉你，是晋代书法家王羲之 (Wáng Xīzhī, 303-361 A.D.) 的《兰亭序》(Lántíng Xù, the Preface to the Poems Composed at the Orchid Pavilion)。《兰亭序》是怎么写成的？为什么它这么有名呢？

公元353年的三月三日，著名士大夫 (shìdàfū, scholar-official) 王羲之和四十多个朋友在山阴 (Shān Yīn, a district in present-day Shaoxing City, Zhejiang Province) 的兰亭聚会，会上各个人都写诗赞美 (zànměi, praise) 兰亭的山水。朋友们把诗写完以后，王羲之把它们聚集起来，并为这些诗写了一个序言 (xùyán, preface)。序言中王羲之不但记录了这个聚会的欢乐，同时也感叹 (gǎntàn, reflect with awe) 好景短暂 (duǎnzàn, short)，生死无常(wúcháng, impermanent)。王羲之的序言一共有二十八行，三百二十四个字，章句 (zhāngjù, prose and rhythm)、结构 (jiégòu, structure)、笔法 (bǐfǎ, the brush work) 都很完美。在序言中，“之”字出现了二十次，可是每一个“之”字的形状 (xíngzhuàng, shape) 都不同。后人评论 (pínglùn, comment) 说，《兰亭序》的内容意味深刻 (yìwèi shēnkè, have profound meaning)，表达了作者对人生无常的领悟 (lǐngwù, understanding through contemplation)，《兰亭序》的书法好像行云流水 (floating cloud and flowing water, fluid)，可以说是“天下第一行书 (xíng shū, running script, a style of calligraphy)”。

兰亭

Wang Xizhi and *Lanting Xu*

If you ask a Chinese to name one of the most famous works of calligraphy in Chinese history, most likely she will tell you: it is the "Preface to the Poems Composed at the Orchid Pavilion" or *Lanting Xu* by Wang Xizhi, a scholar-official of the Jin Dynasty. What makes *Lanting Xu* so famous? For which occasion was it composed? Here is the story behind this famous work:

On March 3rd, 353 AD, the famous scholar Wang Xizhi and more than forty friends gathered at the Orchid Pavilion in Shan Yin (located in present-day Shaoxing, Zhejiang Province). During the celebration, each party member was asked to write a poem praising the scenery at the Orchid Pavilion. Afterwards, Wang Xizhi collected all the poems and wrote a preface for the collection. In the preface, Wang Xizhi not only described the cheerful gathering, but also reflected on the impermanence of life. The preface consists of 324 Chinese characters in 28 lines; the rhythm and structure of the prose as well as the brushwork were all masterful. For example, the character *zhi* (之) in the preface appears 20 times, but no two look the same. Generations of scholars and art connoisseurs have commented on *Lanting Xu*, praising its profound understanding of life and the fluidity of its calligraphy. It can be seen as the best example of running script calligraphy in the world.

YOUR TURN:

Choose one of the Chinese calligraphers from the list below. Prepare an oral presentation on this calligrapher. Your presentation should include the biographical information of the artist, his accomplishments, and his impact on later generations.

Artists:

Huai Su (怀素), Zhao Mengfu (赵孟頫), Wang Xianzhi (王献之), Tang Huai Zong (唐怀宗)

你知道吗?

中国城市里的高中毕业生一般都没有工作经验。中国家长认为，高中生的主要任务是学习和准备高考，不是去打工。因为没有工作经验，所以在竞争非常厉害的中国工作市场，高中毕业生要找到工作，不是一件容易的事。

可能有人认为，找一个在制造业或者服务业的体力工作应该不会很困难吧?

可是，最近二三十年来，不少农民离开农村到城市里来找工作。他们找的也都是这些体力工作。农民习惯了做体力工作，而且能吃苦，所以城市里的高中毕业生常常竞争不过他们。

那么，高中生是不是可以去做一些技术工作呢?

有些学生初中毕业以后直接去技术学校（技校）上学。上技校的学生多数都不打算报考大学。他们打算念完三年技校就去工作。技校的课程都跟工作有关，而且技校还会安排学生去实习。一般来说，技校毕业生比高中毕业生多一点儿实习经验，所以也比高中毕业生容易找到工作。

如果一个工作需要比较高的技术，多数的公司就都会找大学毕业生。最近十多年来，为了让更多的人受大学教育，中国大学增加了招生人数。因此，大学毕业生也一年比一年多。也就是说，在工作市场中，高中毕业生除了要跟农民和技校毕业生竞争以外，他们还要跟大学毕业生竞争。

虽然工作不容易找，但是“有志者，事竟成。”高中生可以去做义工，参加社区活动，或者找实习机会，慢慢地积累一点工作经验。这样就能帮助他们找到工作。

4.3 出国留学 Study Abroad

对话一

（汤姆接到了一个老同学从旧金山打来的电话。）

高乐天：喂，汤姆你好，我是高乐天。你还记得我吗？我是你的小学同学，上课的时候，我老坐在你旁边。

汤姆：乐天啊，我们好多年没见了。你是从哪儿知道我的电话号码的？

高乐天：你一搬家到上海就把这个电话号码告诉我了。只不过这么多年来，我一直没给你打电话。

汤姆：哦，对不起，我忘了。你还住在旧金山吗？高中毕业以后打算做什么？

高乐天：我们家还住在原来的地方。秋天我就要去纽约大学学习经济学了。我们还是长话短说吧，我想在暑假的时候到中国去学习汉语。有些问题想问问你。

汤姆：行啊，只要我能帮你的，一定帮你。

高乐天：如果我想去中国留学，要办哪些手续？

汤姆：先要申请入学。你找到学校了吗？

高乐天：我对一个语言大学非常感兴趣，他们的汉语课程很密集，每天要上四五个小时的汉语课。下午有文化课和个别辅导。每个星期还组织我们去不同的地方旅游参观。

汤姆：听上去不错。你报名了吗？

高乐天：还没有，因为大学的网站上说，只收大学生。我不知道他们收不收像我这样刚从高中毕业的。

汤姆：你不是已经被纽约大学录取了吗？你可以把情况跟那个大学谈一谈。我想应该不是一个大问题。

高乐天：关于住宿，这个大学的网站说，有三种选择，一是可以住在国际学生宿舍，二是跟当地的中国家庭住在一起，三是自己租房子住。我知道这三种情况都各有长处和短处。我比较想选择第二种，你看呢？

汤姆：要是我，我也会选择第二种。跟中国人吃在一起，住在一起，玩在一起，每天有许多练习中文的机会。再说，不知不觉就可以了解到许多中国人的传统和习惯了。不过，有些中国父母太喜欢管孩子，你住在他们家，他们也会把你当自己的孩子一样来管。你不会介意吧？

高乐天：应该不会，我父母也老管着我， 我习惯被人管了。他们管我，我不是正好可以练习听力吗？

汤姆：那你马上去报名吧，因为被录取以后，还要办一些手续才能到中国来。办手续也需要一定时间。

高乐天：要办哪些手续？

汤姆：你有护照吗？没有的话，需要马上去办。大学录取了你以后，会发给你录取通知。你拿到录取通知以后，就可以去中国的大使馆办留学签证。

高乐天：好，我马上就上网报名。有了消息，我再告诉你。

汤姆：行，我等你的消息。再见。

对话二

玛丽娅：真对不起，说好昨天晚上要给你打电话的，可是一个邻居来找我，我跟他谈啊谈啊，谈了两三个小时，不知不觉就十点了。因为太晚了，就没给你打电话。

凯丽：你们谈什么呢？

玛丽娅：这个邻居正在上高中，打算明年去美国留学。他选好了三个大学，昨天来向我了解一些出国的细节。

凯丽：现在想去国外留学的中国学生很多，外面有不少办出国留学手续的公司。他去那儿了解过了吗？

玛丽娅：去过了，但是因为一些有名的大学入学要求比较多，所以他虽然了解过了，还是不太清楚。于是他就东问西问，结果是有人说东，有人说西，听得他糊里糊涂的。他想我刚刚被美国的加州大学录取，一定非常了解怎么入学，所以就来问我。

凯丽： 这下他问对人了。

玛丽娅：希望如此。我告诉他，要去美国上大学，首先要通过一些标准化的考试，像美国的大学入学考试，还有英文考试。

凯丽： 除了考试成绩以外，美国的大学也需要课程的平均分。是不是有些好大学要求的课程平均分非常高?

玛丽娅：是的。对许多中国学生来说，考试成绩和课程平均分都不是问题。他们在学校里一天到晚念书，成绩非常好。可是一些美国大学对“书呆子”不感兴趣，他们比较注意学生的个性。

凯丽： 哦，所以申请入学的时候，应该把参加过的课外活动都写上。课外活动包括很多方面，比如运动、文艺、社区服务、竞赛等等。我还是不太清楚，一个大学怎么了解学生的个性。

玛丽娅：他们会看你写的个人陈述，还有老师写的推荐信。如果考试成绩、平均分和个性三方面都非常好，就容易被录取。

凯丽： 被录取只是第一步。你邻居知道在美国上大学非常贵吗?

玛丽娅：知道，他父母已经存了不少钱，到时候，他们还可以向亲戚借点儿钱。对了，他问我，可以不可以在美国一边打工一边上学。

凯丽： 外国学生好像只能在学校里打工，不能去校外打工。

玛丽娅：我还告诉他，等拿到录取通知以后，他还需要去美国大使馆办签证。

凯丽： 要出国留学需要办的手续太多了。

玛丽娅：对啊，所以我们一谈就谈了两三个小时。我对他说，如果他想到别的问题，还可以随时来问我。

生词

	Simplified	*Traditional*	*Pinyin*	*Part of Speech*	*English*
1.	留学	留學	liúxué	*v.o.*	study abroad
2.	长话短说	長話短說	cháng huà duǎn shuō	*s.p.*	make a long story short
3.	手续	手續	shǒuxù	*n.*	procedures, formalities, processes
4.	密集		mìjí	*adj.*	intensive
5.	住宿		zhùsù	*n.*	housing, lodging
6.	租		zū	*v.*	rent, lease
7.	习惯	習慣	xíguàn	*n./v.*	custom; be accustomed to
8.	介意		jièyì	*v.*	mind, take offense
9.	护照	護照	hùzhào	*n.*	passport
10.	大使馆	大使館	dàshǐguǎn	*n.*	embassy
11.	签证	簽證	qiānzhèng	*n./v.o.*	visa; issue a visa
12.	细节	細節	xìjié	*n.*	details, specifics
13.	入学	入學	rùxué	*v.o.*	enter a school, enroll
14.	如此		rúcǐ	*adv.*	such, like that, so
15.	标准化	標準化	biāozhǔnhuà	*n./v.*	standardization; standardize
16.	平均分		píngjūnfēn	*n.*	grade point average (GPA)
17.	书呆子	書呆子	shūdāizi	*n.*	nerd, bookworm
18.	个性	個性	gèxìng	*n.*	personality
19.	陈述	陳述	chénshù	*n./v.*	statement; state
20.	推荐信	推薦信	tuījiànxìn	*n.*	recommendation letter
21.	随时	隨時	suíshí	*adv.*	at any time, at all times

语言注释

1. 东 + Verb 西 + Verb (Do the same thing repeatedly)

When someone is doing the same thing at different times and places, we can use this idiomatic expression 东 + Verb 西 + Verb. Note: the verb should be the same.

我们昨天在购物中心东逛西逛。一个下午很快就过去了。
Yesterday we strolled here and there in the shopping center. The afternoon went by very fast.

他说要上网去找工作，可是每次一上网就东看西看，结果时间都浪费了。
He said he would look for a job on the Internet, but every time he got online, he looked at this and that. In the end he wasted his time.

2. 如此 (Such, like that, so)

When you agree with what is said, you can use "希望如此" (I hope so).

如此 can also be used in front of an adjective, with the meaning of 这么，这样(so, like this). 如此 is usually used in written Chinese.

数学考试怎么如此容易?
How come the math test was so easy?

我们没想到工作如此困难。
We didn't expect the work would be so difficult.

学无止境

The following is an application form for international students who would like to study in China. See if you can fill it out.

外国留学生入学申请表

1. 护照用名 ______________________
2. 中文姓名 ______________ 3. 国籍 ______________
4. 护照号码 ______________ 5. 性别 （ ）男 （ ）女
6. 婚姻 （ ）未婚 （ ）已婚
7. 出生日期 ______________ 8. 出生地点 ______________
9. 通讯地址 ______________________________
10. 在华学习学校、专业 ______________________
11. 学习期限

自 ________年________月________日

至 ________年________月________日

12. 教育经历

学校	地点	专业	时间	学历
________	________	________	________	________
________	________	________	________	________

13. 工作经历

工作单位	地点	时间	职位
________	________	________	________
________	________	________	________

14. 语言能力（很好，好，一般，初级）

语言	听	说	读	写
________	________	________	________	________
________	________	________	________	________

申请人签字 ______________________ 日期 ______________

温故知新 GAIN NEW INSIGHT THROUGH REVIEW

We have learned some words related to college admission. Let's review them. There are a few new words in the list. See if you can guess their meanings.

入学手续	入学申请	申请人	注册
注册费	推荐人	推荐信	平均分
申请表	学费	书费	经济来源
专业	科目	学位	招生
报考	标准化考试	录取	录取通知
大学	大专	应届毕业生	往届毕业生
高考	高考成绩	个人陈述	招生办公室

中国文化一瞥

Chinese proverbs and sayings

The following proverbs and sayings describe feeling anxious or at a loss. Pinyin is provided only for those phrases with new characters.

1. shǒu zú wú cuò
手 足 无 措

do not know what to do with one's hands and feet; at a loss for what to do; be bewildered; confused

IN USE:

汤姆骑车撞到丁老师以后，手足无措。

After Tom's bike collided into Teacher Ding, he was at a loss for what to do.

我的组织能力很差。每次让我组织一个活动，我都会手足无措。

I have poor organizational skills. Every time I was asked to organize an activity, I would be at a loss for what to do.

YOUR TURN:

Answer the following question based on your own situation:

在什么情况下，你会手足无措？请举一个例子。

2. tǎn tè bù ān
忐忑不安

very anxious; in a nervous state; nervous and uneasy

IN USE:

听说明天校长要来听课，张老师一天都忐忑不安。

Hearing that the principal will come tomorrow to observe his teaching, Teacher Zhang was nervous and uneasy all day.

高考马上就要来了。同学们都忐忑不安。

The college exam is coming soon. All of the students are very anxious.

YOUR TURN:

Will anyone be 忐忑不安 in the following situations? Choose those situations that apply. Then select one to make a sentence with 忐忑不安.

第一次见到校长	考试	申请学校
申请工作	见男朋友/女朋友	跟朋友出去吃饭
校长让你去谈话	做讲演	做义工
第一次一个人去旅游	出国	参加晚会

3. rú zuò zhēn zhān

如 坐 针 毡

as if sitting on a spiked rug; sit on pins and needles; in an extremely uncomfortable position; ill at ease

IN USE:

张老师的汉语口试非常难。每次他给我考试，我都如坐针毡。

Teacher Zhang's Chinese oral test is very difficult. Every time he gave me a test, it was like sitting on pins and needles.

YOUR TURN:

Xiao Wang often gets very nervous when faced with difficult situations. Check those situations that would make Xiao Wang 如坐针毡.

	在校长办公室，校长批评小王不注意安全的时候，
	小王最不喜欢上地理课。高老师让他背世界各国首都的时候，
	小王喜欢吃快餐。在快餐店吃比萨的时候，
	小王的邻居非常喜欢说话，他说的话小王都不爱听。邻居来访问小王的时候，

The Chinese Aesthetic

泥人张

中国的天津有一种民间(folk)艺术，是把泥做成小泥人，然后在上面画上颜色。本来这是给小孩子的玩具，可是因为很多人做泥人做得非常好，结果泥人就成了一种民间艺术，男女老少都喜欢。清朝的时候，在天津有一个叫张明山的人，他做的泥人非常生动(vivid)，就像真人一样。所以大家就把他叫做“泥人张”。1915年，张明山做的泥人参加了巴拿马 (Bānámǎ, Panama) 国际博览会(expo)，在民间艺术比赛中得了金牌。但是，作为民间艺术，泥人不被中国的传统艺术家看作是古典艺术的一部分。到了1949年后，民间艺术才被看成珍贵 (zhēnguì, valuable) 的艺术保护起来。现在，在中国美术学院有做泥人的专业课程。民间艺术走进了大学的教室。

Zhang the Clay Figurine Maker

In the city of Tianjin there is a type of folk art which involves molding clay into small figurines, and then painting them in vivid colors. Originally these figurines were children's toys, but because of their popularity and the skills required to make them, they eventually became an art form themselves. During the Qing Dynasty there was a figurine maker by the name of Zhang Mingshan. The clay figures he made were so vivid they almost seemed to be alive. People started to call Zhang Mingshan "Zhang the Clay Figurine Maker." In 1915, the Chinese government entered Zhang's figurines for a folk art competition at the Panama World Expo, and Zhang won the gold medal. However, as a folk art, figurine making was not considered a classical Chinese art. It was not until 1949 when Chinese folk art was systematically studied and protected. Now, figurine-making is one of the academic majors at the Chinese Institute of Fine Arts. Folk art has entered into college classrooms.

YOUR TURN:

Choose one folk art form from your own country and prepare an oral presentation on it. In your presentation, describe the art form, techniques, or characteristics particular to the art form and explain its cultural significance.

你知道吗？

如果你是从一个有名的外国大学毕业的，而且还有比较高的外语能力，这对找工作非常有好处。因为中国的工作市场竞争越来越厉害，不少高中生打算毕业以后去国外上大学。这样，他们不但可以在国外得到大学学位 (degree)，而且可以提高外语能力。

受全球化的影响，英语可以说是全世界的“商业语言”，学习英语变得很重要。中国学生最想去的国家是美国、加拿大、英国、澳大利亚、新加坡等等，因为这些国家说英语，能帮助他们提高英语水平。虽然也有一些学生去日本、德国、法国、意大利、韩国、俄国等国家留学，但是多数的中国学生还是比较愿意去说英语的国家留学。

出国留学要办不少手续。如果你去中文网站看一下，就会发现不少计划出国留学的学生在网上提问：“我想出国留学，应该怎么做准备？”网上的回答五花八门。可是简单地来说，中国学生出国留学应该做好三种准备。

第一是准备英语考试。去英国、澳大利亚留学，要考International English Language Testing System (IELTS)，中国人把这个考试叫作“雅(yǎ)思”。去美国和加拿大留学，要考Test of English as a Foreign Language (TOEFL)，中国人把这个考试叫作“托福”。如果英语考试的成绩不好，就很难被大学录取。因此，准备英语考试，并且考出一个好成绩是非常重要的。

第二是申请大学和专业。可以先决定要去哪个国家留学，然后选几个学校申请。最好先跟你打算申请的大学联系一下，问清楚申请的手续。然后可以在网上填写申请表，给学校发邮件。同时，还要准备老师的推荐信、高中课程的平均分、个人陈述等等。

第三是在被国外大学录取以后，要去大使馆办签证。拿到了签证就可以订飞机票，准备出国了。

4.4 自由啦！ Freedom at Last!

对话一

凯丽：周末回杭州，看到我妈妈已经在为我准备上大学要用的东西了。

玛丽娅：你高中还没毕业呢，现在准备是不是太早了？

汤姆：我看做父母的就是喜欢担心。我妈妈也一样，现在她一做饭就说："汤姆，你快过来学习学习怎么做饭。以后你离开了家，没有人为你做饭了。你吃什么呢？"我说，"那还不容易？我到饭店里去吃。"她一听就急了，说在外边吃饭又贵又不健康，我的钱会不够花，我还可能变得很胖。

玛丽娅：做父母的总是把一些小事情看得很严重。好像我们还是小孩子，离开大人就不会生活了。

汤姆：他们觉得要是我们遇到一点小问题，一定会像无头苍蝇，不知道东南西北。

凯丽：这是用老眼光来看新世界。现在不会做饭有什么关系？到处都是食品店，要饿死也不是那么容易的。做饭遇到难题，我们还可以上网或者打电话去求助。

大卫：你们一点都不懂得父母的心。他们这么说，是为了让你们准备得好一些，这样你们离开家以后，独立生活就会容易一些。

凯丽：大卫真是个好孩子。那么理解父母的心。说正经的，你们想过离开家以后的生活吗？

汤姆：当然想过，一想到就让我高兴。再也不用晚上十点以前回家了，要多晚回家就多晚回家，一个晚上不回家也没关系。也不用每天必须吃蔬菜了，想吃就吃，不想吃就不吃。我等了快十八年了，终于要等到自由了！

玛丽娅：汤姆，你别把现在的生活说得那么可怕，好像你被关在监狱里。

凯丽：其实这不一定是汤姆的心里话，想到要离开父母，他也免不了有点儿担心，有点儿难过。不过为了不让我们看出他的担心和难过，就像演戏一样，老说什么"自由要来啦！"

大卫：汤姆，凯丽说得对吗？你不是说她最了解你了吗？

汤姆：这要看你怎么看了。半杯水放在那儿，有人看到的是半杯满了，有人看到的是半杯空了。凯丽是两面都看到了，我只看到了一面。很难说谁对谁不对。

玛丽娅：哇塞，汤姆成外交家了。

对话二

玛丽娅：汤姆，你在看什么呢？

汤姆：我在看南京大学附近的房子出租广告。虽然我还不知道能不能上南大，但是先了解一下住宿情况也挺有帮助的。

玛丽娅：秋天你不打算住在学生宿舍吗？

汤姆：不，我打算自己租一个公寓。

房地产公司（在中国，可以去房地产公司租房）

玛丽娅：看到合适的房子了吗？

汤姆：还没有。有的太贵，有的太远，有的条件不好。要找到合适的房子还真不容易。

玛丽娅：如果房子太贵，你可能要跟别人合租。遇到负责的室友还可以，要不然，会很麻烦的。

汤姆：你说得对。所以我已经上网登过找室友的广告了，有好几个人愿意跟我合租。可是我父母看了那些人的情况以后，都觉得不理想。

玛丽娅：有哪些方面不理想？

汤姆：有几个是女生，父母不让我跟女生住。有一个男生，是在南大学体育的，还发来了他的照片。我父母一看就说，这个人长得五大三粗，一点也不像个大学生。还有一个男生也住在上海，因为我们的父母都不放心，所以就决定先在一个咖啡馆见个面，看看我们是不是合得来。我觉得那个男生挺好的，非常安静。可是我妈妈觉得那个男生一点都不成熟。

玛丽娅：你妈妈怎么知道那个人不成熟？

汤姆：我们在咖啡馆见面的时候，那个男生不是在用手机打短信，就是在手机上玩游戏，一句话也没说，都是他父母在说话。

玛丽娅：听上去的确不太理想。那你怎么认为他还不错呢？

汤姆：他做的都是我爱做的，我们的兴趣很相像。我觉得这样的室友非常好，我们俩一天到晚都忙自己的事，安安静静，客客气气，不会互相麻烦的。

玛丽娅：你说的也有道理，希望你早日找到合适的房子和室友。

汤姆：谢谢。

生词

Simplified	Traditional	Pinyin	Part of Speech	English
1. 遇到		yùdào	*v.*	encounter, run into
2. 无头苍蝇	無頭蒼蠅	wútóu cāngyíng	*n.*	headless fly
3. 眼光		yǎnguāng	*n.*	sight, view
4. 正经	正經	zhèngjīng	*adj.*	proper, serious
5. 可怕		kěpà	*adj.*	terrible, terrifying
6. 监狱	監獄	jiānyù	*n.*	prison
7. 外交家		wàijiāojiā	*n.*	diplomat
8. 出租		chūzū	*v.*	for rent
9. 合租		hézū	*v.*	co-rent, co-lease
10. 室友		shìyǒu	*n.*	roommate
11. 登		dēng	*v.*	publish, print
12. 五大三粗		wǔ dà sān cū	*s.p.*	big and tall, muscular, sturdy
13. 合得来		hédelái	*s.p.*	get along well
14. 成熟		chéngshú	*adj.*	mature

专名

15. 南大		Nándà		Nanjing University

语言注释

1. 说正经的 (Seriously speaking)

说正经的 is an idiomatic expression. It usually signals the speaker wants to change to a more serious topic.

说正经的，你真的不打算参加高考了吗？
Seriously, are you really not planning to take the college entrance examination?

我们谈天说地非常有意思。现在说正经的，你来找我有什么事吗？

We talked about everything under the sun and it was great. Now let's talk seriously—why did you come to see me?

2. 再也 + 不/没 (Never again, no longer)

再也 is usually placed before 不 or 没 to indicate the meaning of "never again."

他高中毕业以后，再也没看到过王老师。

After he graduated from high school, he never saw Teacher Wang again.

A: 我高中毕业以后，就再也不用参加考试了。

B: 不一定吧？我爷爷八十五岁还参加路考呢。

A: After I graduate from high school, I will never need to take another test again.

B: Are you sure? My 85-year-old grandfather just took a road test.

学无止境

We have learned some words about renting an apartment. Here are some additional words related to the same topic.

月租 *monthly rent*	租金 *rent*	定金 *deposit*
租房合同 *lease agreement*	出租广告 *for rent advertisement*	带家具 *furnished*
房东 *landlord*	房客 *renter*	包水电 *utilities included*
水费 *water bill*	煤气费 *gas bill*	电费 *electricity bill*
购物方便 *close to shopping*	交通方便 *close to transportation*	一室一厅一卫 *one bedroom, one living area, and one bath*

YOUR TURN:

Suppose you are going to rent a place in Beijing. Read the following "For Rent" ads. Decide which one you would like to rent. Tell a partner the reasons for your decision.

绿色家园公寓出租 • 租金：1800元/月 • 房型：一室一厅一卫 • 面积：25平方米 • 楼层：第二层，共五层 • 配置：床、热水器、洗衣机、空调、冰箱、电视机、宽带 联系人：金先生 电话：13688772345	市中心公寓 • 月租：3500元（不包水电） • 房型：二室一厅一卫 • 面积：70平方米 • 楼层：第二层，共三层 • 交通、购物方便 • 配置：热水器、洗衣机、空调、冰箱、有线电视、宽带 联系人：张小姐 电话：6354-8164
近地铁站公寓出租 • 租金：2500元/月 • 房型：一室一厅一卫 • 面积：45平方米 • 楼层：第六层，共六层 • 配置：简单家具、热水器、洗衣机、空调、冰箱、电视机 • 近国华超市、工商银行、亚洲购物中心 联系人：华先生 电话：3359-4517	大院房出租 • 月租：4500元 • 房型：三室一卫 • 面积：100平方米 • 楼层：一层，共一层 • 农民房，带100平方米大院，能养狗 • 配置：热水器、洗衣机、冰箱 • 联系人：蓝阿姨 电话：9528-3489

我打算租 ________________________________

因为 ________________________________

________________________________。

温故知新 GAIN NEW INSIGHT THROUGH REVIEW

We have learned quite a few Chinese proverbs and sayings that contain the word 三 or 五. Work with a partner to review the following phrases.

五光十色	三三两两	三言两语	三长两短
三天打鱼，两天晒网	五颜六色	五湖四海	三心二意
五花八门	再三再四	一五一十	五大三粗

中国文化一瞥

Chinese proverbs and sayings

The following proverbs describe the pleasure people get from talking to each other. Pinyin is provided only for those phrases with new characters.

1. 谈 天 说 地

talk of everything under the sun

IN USE:

朋友们在一起谈天说地，非常高兴。

Friends were very happy to get together and talk of everything under the sun.

YOUR TURN:

Answer the following questions based on your own situation:

1. 你喜欢跟别人谈天说地吗？
2. 你认为跟网友谈天说地有意思吗？
3. 在网上跟不认识的人谈天说地有没有坏处？

2. 谈 笑 风 生

talk cheerfully and humorously; speak lively and cheerfully

IN USE:

王老师上课的时候，谈笑风生。学生们都很喜欢上她的课。

Teacher Wang speaks lively and cheerfully during class. Students all like to take her class.

YOUR TURN:

Answer the following questions based on your own situation:

1. 在你的同学里，谁常常谈笑风生？
2. 你跟谁在一起说话的时候，谈笑风生？
3. 你愿意跟谈笑风生的人交朋友吗？为什么？

3. 津 津 乐 道

delight in talking about...; dwell upon ...with great enjoyment

IN USE:

我妈妈总是对健康和饮食津津乐道。

My mother is always delighted to talk about health and diet.

YOUR TURN:

Answer the following questions and write your answers in the space below. Compare your answers with a peer to see if you have the same observations.

1. 在你们班，谁对体育比赛津津乐道？

   ____

2. 在你们国家，人民对哪些事津津乐道？

   ____

3. 美国的青少年对哪些事津津乐道？

   ____

The Chinese Aesthetic

年画

每年春节的时候，家家户户都会在门窗上贴上几幅年画。有的年画里画的是一个胖娃娃 (wáwá, baby) 一手抱着一条大鲤鱼 (lǐyú, carp)，一手拿着一枝莲花 (liánhuā, lotus flower)。有的画的是三个胖娃娃，一个捧 (pěng, hold with both hands) 着石榴 (shíliú, pomegranate)，一个抱着桃子，另外一个拿着佛手 (fóshǒu, Buddha's Hand – a type of citrus fruit)。这些年画其实都有特殊的意思。

为什么在中国的年画里胖娃娃、鲤鱼、莲花、石榴等等表示吉祥 (jíxiáng, lucky)呢？原来，鲤鱼在中国人的眼里代表富贵有余，因为"鲤"和"利"声音很近，"鱼"和"余"是谐音 (xiéyīn, homophone)。莲花表示连续不断 (liánxù bùduàn, continuity)，因为"莲"和"连"是谐音。一个胖娃娃抱着鲤鱼，拿着莲花，意思是"连年有余" (having abundance every year)。

那为什么石榴、桃子和佛手这些水果也表示吉祥呢？石榴是从中亚传到中国的。中国人认为石榴多籽 (zǐ, seed)，意思就是多生儿子，所以石榴代表"多子"。桃子在中国传统中表示长寿 (chángshòu, longevity)，因为道教传说中王母娘娘 (Wáng Mǔ Niáng Niáng, the Queen of the West) 的花园里种了桃树，每九千九百九十九年才长出桃子。谁吃了这种桃子，谁就可以长生不老。至于佛手，是一种橘类 (jú lèi, citrus) 水果，因为"佛"字的发音 (fāyīn, pronunciation) 跟"福"差不多，所以中国人用佛手表示福气(blessings)。三个胖娃娃手里拿着石榴、桃子、和佛手，意思是福、寿、子三多。

中国的年画用图画、谐音字、比喻 (bǐyù, metaphor) 等等的方法表现传统中国人对人生欢乐的希望。下次你看到年画的时候，也许可以试着猜一猜画里的意思。

Chinese New Year Pictures

Most Chinese families like to paste a few New Year pictures on their doors or windows during the Chinese New Year celebration. Some New Year pictures depict a baby holding a carp in one hand and a lotus flower in the other; and other pictures have three boys holding a pomegranate, a giant peach, and a citrus fruit called "the Buddha's hand." These paintings actually have very specialized meanings.

Why would a baby holding a carp and a lotus flower symbolize blessings? Carp in Chinese is *li yu* which sounds similar to "profit" and "abundance." Lotus flower is *lian* in Chinese, a homophone of another *lian*, meaning "to continue." A picture depicting a baby with a carp and a lotus flower expresses the wish of having abundance year after year.

Now why do pomegranates, peaches and citrus fruit represent good luck? Merchants from Central Asia brought pomegranates to China. The Chinese liked the fruit because the multitude of seeds in a pomegranate makes a nice homophone for *duo zi*, "being blessed with many sons." Peaches have been used to symbolize longevity throughout Chinese history. Legend has it that the Queen of the West planted many peach trees in her garden. These trees only bear fruit once every nine thousand nine hundred and ninety nine years. Whoever is lucky enough to eat one of these peaches will become immortal. The citrus fruit "Buddha's hand" has a similar pronunciation to the Chinese word *fu*, "blessings." So, making a picture with boys holding pomegranates, peaches and Buddha's hands symbolizes blessings, longevity, and fertility.

Symbolism is abundant in Chinese New Year paintings. Next time you see such a painting during the Chinese New Year, try to see if you can interpret the visual puns in it.

YOUR TURN:

1. Go online and find a few examples of Chinese New Year's pictures to understand the symbolism described above.
2. Visual puns are not unique to the Chinese. Different religions and cultures all have visual puns or rebuses that can serve allegorical purposes. Select some common visual puns from your own culture and prepare an oral presentation on them in Chinese.

你知道吗？

对许多大学新生来说，上大学后，最大的变化是生活环境，没有了父母的照顾，许多事情需要自己去处理，独立生活开始了。因为现在多数的中国高中生都是独生子女，在家处处 (everywhere) 受到父母的照顾，所以许多大学新生的独立生活能力比较差。

为了帮助大学新生提高独立生活的能力，有些大学老生在网上为他们提供了一些建议。主要的建议有：

一、学会理财

高中生的零花钱一般不太多，只有几十元到一两百元。但是上了大学以后，情况就不一样了。每个月的生活费就需要几百元。有的家庭在学期开始的时候，就把一个学期的生活费都给学生，所以这个学生一下子就有了几千元。有些学生因为没有理财的经验，看到有那么多钱非常高兴，花钱大手大脚：逛街、旅游、聚餐… 一两个月就把钱花得差不多了，只能再向父母要钱或者只好节衣缩食。因此 (therefore)，学会理财是非常重要的。刚入学就应该做一个计划，把每个月必须花的钱留出来。平时，能不花的钱就不花。如果有剩下的钱，可以存在银行里，为紧急情况做好准备。

二、注意生活习惯

不少大学新生觉得，高中和大学的生活大不一样。在高中，每天从早到晚上课、做作业、准备高考。到了大学以后，他们有不少自由活动的时间。有些学生觉得非常自由，于是就玩到很晚才睡觉。还有些学生上了床以后还不睡觉，跟室友谈天说地到半夜两三点钟。因为睡得太晚，第二天早上起不来。这样有人上课迟到，有人上课没精神，有人没时间吃早饭，对学习和身体都没有好处。因此，进了大学以后，应该早睡早起，让自己第二天能好好学习。同时，大学生还应该注意体育锻炼。身体好，才能学习好。

三、利用好课余 (after class) 时间

在大学里，除了上课做作业以外，学生还可以参加各种不同的活动，比如听讲座、参加社团活动、体育活动、文娱活动等等。大学生可以通过参加这些活动，学一些新知识，提高自己各方面的能力。如果有机会，大学生还可以去做义工，参加社区活动，或者去校外兼职，为将来找工作积累一些工作经验。

4.5 友谊天长地久 Auld Lang Syne

对话

玛丽娅：你们去参加毕业舞会吗？

大卫：今年学校要举行毕业舞会吗？我只知道有毕业典礼。

汤姆：哦，今年的毕业舞会是由我们美国学生俱乐部举办的。如果我们在美国上高中的话，毕业前的一两个月，大家一定会去参加毕业舞会。既然我们在国际学校，就应该用各个国家的方式来庆祝我们从高中毕业，所以我们向张校长提议，除了中国式的毕业典礼以外，我们还应该举办一个美国式的毕业舞会。

玛丽娅：张校长接受了这个提议，因为国际学校不但有不少美国来的学生，而且还有不少同学秋天要去美国留学。因此，了解一些美国文化对大家都有帮助。

凯丽：太好了。毕业舞会在哪儿举行？

汤姆：还没有决定呢。有人提议在学校礼堂，可是美国俱乐部的同学认为，我们应该去国际饭店或者人民公园。

国际饭店

人民公园

玛丽娅：这也是美国的一种习惯吧？舞会一般都在一个比较特别的地方举办。对许多美国高中生来说，浪漫又盛大的毕业舞会是他们终生难忘的经历之一。

汤姆：对，高中毕业代表告别青少年时代。舞会是我们一生中一次非常重要的聚会。

大卫：听说在美国，有些高中生非常重视毕业舞会，甚至比高考还重视。他们觉得考试以后还会有，但是高中毕业舞会一生只有一次。过了这次，就没下次了。

凯丽：怎么样，你们都去吗？

汤姆：当然要去。我们不应该错过这次聚会。以后高中同学还要聚在一起就没那么容易了。

大卫：去参加舞会是不是要穿非常漂亮的晚礼服？

玛丽娅：只要穿得正式一些就行了。为了环保，我建议我们今年都不买晚礼服，去租。这样不会浪费资源。

大卫：好啊，你知道去哪里租晚礼服吗？

凯丽：我们可以上网去找。说真的，想到我们不久就要分手了，让人挺难过的。

汤姆：就是啊。我们这四年互相帮助，互相关心。以后还不知道什么时候才能再见。

大卫：这个世界不是变得越来越小了吗？虽然我们以后不在一起，可是可以打电话写电邮发短信，放寒暑假的时候，还可以聚在一起。

玛丽娅：大卫说得对，我们虽然人不在一起，但是心总是在一起的。

课文

Send	Reply	Reply All	Forward	Print	Delete

明英：你好！

高考成绩终于出来了。很幸运我们都考取了大学。首先祝贺你被北京大学录取了。你一定非常高兴吧？汤姆考上了南京大学，他的专业是海洋学。我被上海中医大学录取了。希望大学毕业以后，我可以做个中医。

南京大学

我是不是已经告诉过你了？玛丽娅和大卫就要离开中国了。玛丽娅要去美国加州大学学习亚洲艺术史；大卫决定先去欧洲工作一年再回来上大学。大卫现在会说英语、法语和汉语，这次去欧洲打算学会德语和西班牙语。他计划先去德国住半年，然后去西班牙住半年。在那里，他要一边学习外语一边打工。

在高中的四年，我跟他们三个人形影不离，现在要分手了，还真有点不习惯呢。以前我们总是一起去这儿，去那儿，做这，做那，可是到了秋天，只有我一个人还留在上海，而且还留在浦东。你知道吗？上海中医大学也在浦东，离国际学校不太远。在高中的四年，有了你们这些好朋友，生活变得快乐、有意思。我一定会想念你们的。希望我们能继续保持联系。好在现在哪儿都有网络，要联系非常方便。再说，你、我、汤姆仍然留在中国，到了寒暑假，我们可以聚一聚，你说呢？

　　我们班的同学打算在分手以前，去玛丽娅家开晚会。玛丽娅组织的晚会让人难忘，这个告别晚会一定也不例外。开晚会的那天，我一定拍许多照片，到时候寄给你。以后只要一看到这些照片，就会想起我们的高中生活，还有在高中时期的好朋友。

　　对了，你能来参加告别晚会吗？如果你来，会给大家带来一个惊喜。晚会定在下个星期四晚上七点。等着你的来信。

你永远的好朋友，

凯丽

七月二十一日

生词

Simplified	Traditional	Pinyin	Part of Speech	English
1. 天长地久	天長地久	tiān cháng dì jiǔ	*s.p.*	everlasting, enduring as long as heaven and earth
2. 舞会	舞會	wǔhuì	*n.*	ball, dancing party
3. 方式		fāngshì	*n.*	method, way
4. 提议	提議	tíyì	*n./v.*	propose; proposal
5. 因此		yīncǐ	*conj.*	therefore, hence, for this reason
6. 浪漫		làngmàn	*adj.*	romantic
7. 盛大		shèngdà	*adj.*	grand, spectacular
8. 终身	終身	zhōngshēn	*adj.*	lifelong, all one's life
9. 告别		gàobié	*v.o.*	part from, say good bye
10. 晚礼服	晚禮服	wǎnlǐfú	*n.*	formal party dress/wear
11. 分手		fēnshǒu	*v.o.*	part company, say good bye, separate
12. 祝贺	祝賀	zhùhè	*n./v.*	congratulations; congratulate
13. 海洋学	海洋學	hǎiyángxué	*n.*	oceanography

14.	形影不离	形影不離	xíng yǐng bù lí	*s.p.*	inseparable as body and shadow, always together
15.	保持		bǎochí	*v.*	keep, maintain
16.	例外		lìwài	*adj./n.*	exceptional; exception
17.	惊喜	驚喜	jīngxǐ	*n./adj.*	pleasant surprise; pleasantly surprised

语言注释

因此 (Therefore, for this reason)

A reason is usually given before 因此. 因此 introduces the result or a consequence. In meaning, 因此 is similar to 所以, but when 因此 is used, there is no need to use 因为.

一次性的产品浪费资源。因此，我们建议大家少用一次性产品。
Disposable products waste resources. Therefore, we suggest everyone use less of them.

她非常想了解美国的文化。因此她决定去美国留学。
She really wants to understand American culture. Therefore, she has decided to study in America.

学无止境

Here are more words related to dance parties. Pinyin is provided for new characters only.

主持人 *host*	灯光 *light*	舞伴 (bàn) *dance partner*
贵宾 *distinguished guest*	来宾 *guest who has arrived*	乐曲 *music*
请柬 (jiǎn) *invitation*	音乐节目主持人 *disc jockey*	茶点 *refreshments*

温故知新 GAIN NEW INSIGHT THROUGH REVIEW

We have learned some words containing the character 朋 or 友. Work with a partner to review and learn the following words.

亲朋好友	室友	网友	校友	校友会
酒肉朋友	狐朋狗党	友好	友谊	友情

中国文化一瞥

Chinese proverbs and sayings

The following proverbs describe friendship. Pinyin is provided only for those phrases with new characters.

1. yì qì xiāng tóu
意 气 相 投

have the same likes and dislikes; friends attracted to each other; be congenial with each other

IN USE:

他们俩意气相投，所以总是形影不离。

They two have the same likes and dislikes and so they are always together.

YOUR TURN:

Answer the following questions based on your own situation:

1. 在你的同学中，谁是你意气相投的好朋友？
2. 你跟家人和亲戚意气相投吗？
3. 什么样的人会跟你意气相投？

2. 志 同 道 合

have the same ideals and follow the same path; have similar ideals and beliefs

IN USE:

大卫和玛丽娅在环保方面志同道合，他们都参加了环保组织。

David and Maria have the same ideals and beliefs about environmental protection. They both joined an environmental organization.

YOUR TURN:

State your opinion:

有人认为好朋友应该志同道合。但是也有人认为要成为好朋友，最重要的是要意气相投。

你怎么看？哪个比较重要？为什么？

3. 情 投 意 合

agree in opinion; close in opinions and feelings

(can also be used to describe people falling in love with each other)

IN USE:

他们俩情投意合，所以决定结婚。

Those two fell in love and decided to get married.

在大学的时候，他有两个情投意合的朋友。现在虽然他们三人在不同的地方工作，但是每年都要聚会一次。

When in college, he had two close friends who shared his opinions and feelings. Now they work in three different places, but get together once a year.

YOUR TURN:

Use 情投意合、志同道合 or 意气相投 to describe the following situations.

1. 他们俩都喜欢流行音乐，不喜欢古典音乐。	
2. 他们都认为，经济发展太快会给环境带来不好的影响，所以他们组织了一些社区活动和讲演，请大家注意发展和环境的关系。	
3. 只要在一起，他们俩就非常高兴。因为他们的看法、感觉常常是一样的。	
4. 王老师的历史考试总是让学生背书。因为我和明明都不喜欢背书，所以都不上王老师的历史课。	
5. 他的理想是研究外星人。我对火星人非常感兴趣。所以我们打算要建立一个关于外星人的网站。	

The Chinese Aesthetic

放风筝

在《欢迎》第一册中你学了一首诗，叫做《村居》：

Cǎo zhǎng yīng fēi èr yuè tiān,
草 长 莺 飞 二 月 天，
fú tí yáng liǔ zuì chūn yān.
拂 堤 杨 柳 醉 春 烟。
Ér tóng sǎn xué guī lái zǎo,
儿 童 散 学 归 来 早，
máng chèn dōng fēng fàng zhǐ yuān.
忙 趁 东 风 放 纸 鸢。

这首诗里说的“纸鸢”就是风筝。传说风筝是中国古代哲学家墨子 (Mò Zǐ) 发明(fāmíng, invent) 的。他花了三年的时间，用木头 (mùtóu, wood) 做了一只木鸟，可是木鸟只飞了一天就坏了。风筝最开始是用来传递 (chuándì, deliver) 信息的。到了唐宋，因为中国人发明了纸，人们开始用纸做风筝，风筝也从传递信息的工具变成娱乐的玩具，成了男女老少喜爱的运动。据说，十三世纪的时候，马可波罗 (Mǎkě Bōluó, Marco Polo) 把风筝带到了西方，现在放风筝在世界上多国家都很流行。

风筝的形状 (xíngzhuàng, shape) 各种各样，但是大多是蝙蝠 (biānfú, bat)、金鱼、凤凰 (fènghuáng, phoenix) 等等。这些形状代表吉祥。因为蝙蝠的"蝠"和福气的"福"同音 (have the same sound)，金鱼的"鱼"和有余的"余"同音，而凤凰是家庭和睦 (hé mù, harmonious) 的象征 (xiàngzhēng, symbol)。把风筝做成蝙蝠、金鱼、凤凰的形状，表达了人们在运动的时候希望把欢乐带给家人的愿望。

Flying Kites

In *Huanying*, Volume 1 you learned a poem entitled "Village Life":

Grass grows, orioles fly in the early spring,
willows stroke the river banks in the spring air.
Children come home early from school,
hurrying to fly paper kites in the east wind.

Zhiyuan is the ancient name for kites. It is believed that the Chinese philosopher Mo Zi (470–391 BC) invented kites. He spent three years trying to make a wooden bird, but the bird flew only once before it broke. Originally kites were used to deliver military information. By the Tang and Song Dynasties paper had been invented in China, and so people began to use paper to make their kites. Beginning as a news delivery system, kite flying gradually became a popular leisure activity. Legend has it that in the thirteenth century Marco Polo brought kites to the West. Now kite flying has become a popular activity in many countries in the world.

Kites come in a wide variety of shapes, however the majority of them are made in the shape of bats, gold fish, or phoenixes. These shapes are auspicious symbols. This is because "bat" in Chinese contains the syllable *fu*, a homophone of "blessing;" "fish" in Chinese is *yu*, a homophone of "abundance." As for the phoenix, this bird has always been used to symbolize a harmonious family relationship. While enjoying outdoor activities like flying kites, the Chinese still remind themselves to bring happiness and harmony to their family.

YOUR TURN:

Can you think of another Chinese leisure activity that both enhances the health and has aesthetic appeal (e.g. Tai Chi, martial arts, calligraphy, etc.)? Prepare an oral presentation on this activity in Chinese. In your presentation, describe this activity (how it is done) and discuss its cultural significance.

你知道吗？

经济的全球化给中国经济带来了非常大的影响，中国经济已经成为世界经济的一部分。中国的发展越来越需要懂外语的人才，所以中国学校，特别是城市里的学校，都把外语当作很重要的课程。在中国，学习英语的学生比学习其他外语的学生要多得多。其他的外语有日语、法语、俄语、西班牙语、阿拉伯语、德语等等。

一般来说，小学生从三、四年级就开始学习英语。也有一些小学从一年级就开始教英语。在小学，英语课程不太多，一个星期只有两节课。到了初中，英语课就多一些，一个星期有四节课。高中就更多了，最少是一天一节，有时候一天两节。到了大学以后，英语专业的学生每天都有英语课。不是英语专业的学生，一个星期也要上两三个小时的英语课。

虽然中国学生在学校学习英语的时间很长，可是不少学生英语说得不好。这是因为许多学校的英语课总是让学生做语法练习、看书、背书、准备考试，学生练习口语和听力的机会不够。有人学了十年的英语，一句话也不会说。 现在越来越多的学校注意到这个问题，开始在英语课上练习口语和听力。有些大城市的中小学还从一些说英语的国家，比如美国、英国、加拿大、澳大利亚、新西兰等等请老师来。这些外国老师到了中国以后，主要负责帮助学生听说英语。

另外，中国现在有不少英语的电视节目和英语报纸。大家还可以上网去不同的英语网站。这些都让中国学生有更多的机会练习英语。因此，不少学生到高中毕业的时候已经能说流利 (fluent) 的英语了。

4.6 第四单元复习 Unit 4 Review

对话一

大卫：玛丽娅，你怎么那么高兴？

玛丽娅：告诉你一个好消息，我被美国的加州大学录取了。

大卫：太好了！祝贺你。

玛丽娅：你怎么没参加高考？你不是填了高考报名表了吗？

大卫：是的。我开始没决定到底参加不参加高考，所以就填了。可是后来我决定今年不上大学了，所以就没去参加高考。

玛丽娅：你的功课那么好，不上大学不是很可惜吗？

大卫：大学还是要上的，不过现在不上。我对外语特别感兴趣。学外语最好的办法是住在外国，跟外国人一起生活工作，这样一边学一边用，外语可以学得又好又快。所以高中毕业以后，我要花一年的时间住在国外，一边学外语，一边打工。

玛丽娅：那你以后想去哪个大学呢？

大卫：还没想好呢。到了明年再说吧。对了，汤姆也拿到录取通知书了，他要去南京大学学习海洋学。

玛丽娅：真的？他怎么想出来要学海洋学呢？

大卫：我也不知道。他填了许多报考志愿，海洋学是其中之一。希望他喜欢那个专业。凯丽怎么样？也拿到录取通知书了吗？

玛丽娅：对，她被上海中医大学录取了。我们班有三个人学医。除了凯丽以外，高明要去北京医科大学。还有金顺爱，也考上了护理学校。

大卫：哎，那个王大明呢？

玛丽娅：那还用问吗？他是铁了心要学电子工程的。他被上海大学电子工程系录取了。你还记得明英吗？

大卫：　当然记得，她在云南，考上什么大学了。
玛丽娅：北京大学。
大卫：　她一定非常高兴吧？她要去北大学习什么专业？
玛丽娅：跟她父母一样，她想研究中国少数民族的情况，所以她要去学习考古学。
大卫：　真不错。等过了几年，大家大学毕业以后，一定要聚一聚。那时候，每个人都会有非常有意思的故事和经历。
玛丽娅：对，我们五年以后在上海见吧。
大卫：　好，不见不散。

云南的少数民族

对话二

玛丽娅：汤姆，你找到室友了吗？
汤姆：　不用找了。我在南京郊区租到了一个小房子，不太贵，我可以一个人住了。
玛丽娅：郊区？那离南大是不是很远？
汤姆：　还可以，骑自行车一个小时。
玛丽娅：那么远啊？那你每天来回要两个小时。
汤姆：　没关系，正好锻炼身体。
玛丽娅：天气好没关系，刮风下雨骑那么长时间的自行车挺辛苦的。
汤姆：　现在我可以告诉你我的秘密了。你知道我租校外房子的主要原因是什么吗？我决定要养一些不同的宠物。
玛丽娅：宠物？你为什么要养宠物呢？
汤姆：　从小到大，我都非常喜欢动物，想养猫啊，狗啊，兔子啊，小鸟啊什么的；可是父母不让我养。现在我终于可以自己住了，这次是非养不可。我连宠物的名字都想好了，狗的名字叫“毛毛”。猫呢，就叫“乐乐”。兔子我要买两只，一只叫“小朋”，一只叫“小友”。

玛丽娅：你是不是想得太简单了？养那么多宠物要负很多责任。你每天上学，哪有时间跟它们玩？再说，要是宠物生病了，要看病也很贵的。

汤姆：我都想过了。我可以很节约地生活，比如每天骑自行车上学，不坐公交；自己做饭或者在学生食堂吃饭，不去饭店吃饭；我也不买不需要的东西；为了宠物，我手机也不要了。这样一来，我的钱就够了。如果还不够，我就去打工。反正不管怎么样，我一定要养这些宠物。

玛丽娅：你怎么不想想学习呢？南京大学是重点大学，能考进去的都是学习非常好的学生，学习上的竞争一定很厉害。你要养那么多宠物，还要打工，学习会不会受影响呢？

汤姆：别担心。我终于可以做自己想做的事了。养宠物的事我想了十多年了，好不容易可以独立生活了，所以我现在虽然身在上海国际学校，可是心早已经飞到南京去了。

玛丽娅：你说得对，我应该为你高兴。你跟那么多宠物生活在一起，生活一定会很有意思的。

生词

Simplified	Traditional	Pinyin	Part of Speech	English
1. 考古学	考古學	kǎogǔxué	*n.*	archaeology
2. 不见不散	不見不散	bù jiàn bù sàn	*s.p.*	not leave without seeing each other
3. 辛苦		xīnkǔ	*adj.*	hard, laborious

生词扩充

Many Chinese words are formed by combining two or more characters. If you know the characters in a word, you can often guess the meaning of that word. See if you understand the meaning of the following words.

面试		职责	
影子		高标准	
青春		高科技	
社会底层		外交	
天不怕，地不怕		合作	
大使		脑力工作	
动手动脚		宠爱	
退学		特性	

SELF-ASSESSMENT

In Unit 4, you have learned to talk about the college entrance examination in China, and the procedures to apply to a Chinese university, a US university, and a study abroad program. You have also learned to talk about different housing options while studying abroad, looking for a rental place, and a roommate. Finally, you have learned to discuss feelings and opinions on living independently and friendship. Have you reached the learning goals of Unit 4? After completing the exercises for Unit 4 in your Workbook, fill out the following self-assessment sheet.

Yes/No	*Can you do these things in Chinese?*
	Describe, in some detail, China's college entrance examination
	Give step-by-step instructions on filling out a university application form in China
	Describe, in some detail, the university admission process in China
	Describe, in some detail, a job in the service industry
	Describe prerequisites for finding employment
	Give instructions on preparations for study abroad
	Describe, in some detail, housing choices for study abroad programs
	Describe, in some detail, the procedures for applying to a US university
	Talk about feelings and opinions on living independently
	Talk about renting a house and finding a roommate
	Describe a senior prom in a US high school
	Talk about feelings towards friendship and plans to maintain a friendship

10–12	yes	excellent
7–9	yes	good
1–6	yes	need some work

附錄
APPENDIX

對話、課文（繁體字版）
Dialogues and Texts in Traditional Characters

Unit 1.1 對話一

大衛：　湯姆，暑假你去哪兒玩了？

湯姆：　我先去北京看了爺爺奶奶，然後跟他們一起參加了一個“東北五日游”的旅行團。你呢？

大衛：　我回了一次香港，還去法國看了我爺爺奶奶。

湯姆：　你在法國住了多久？

大衛：　三個星期。我原來打算在爺爺奶奶家住兩個星期，然後坐火車從法國去意大利玩一個星期，最後從意大利回香港。可是我在法國的那三個星期，差不多天天下大雨，鐵路交通受到了影響，結果我沒去成意大利。

湯姆：　從法國坐火車去意大利要很長時間嗎？

大衛：　不，十多個小時，晚上上火車，第二天上午就到了。

湯姆：　那跟從上海坐火車去北京差不多。這次，我和杰米就是坐動車去北京的。路上才用了十個小時。我們早上出發，晚上就到了。要是去的地方不太遠，我覺得坐火車旅行比坐飛機有意思。在火車上，可以看到許多不同的風景。

大衛：　我同意，所以我本來打算坐火車去意大利，可惜最後沒去成。在去北京的路上，你看到甚麼？

湯姆：　很多城市和鄉村，還有許多自然景色。在上海住久了，我特別喜歡農村的景色。

大衛：　那你去東北的時候，有沒有機會去農村參觀一下？

湯姆：　那個旅行團安排我們去參觀了兩個村子。為了讓我們了解以前中國的農民是怎麼生活的，我們坐了一個多小時的馬車，從第一個村子到第二個村子去。

大衛：　那兩個村子離得挺遠的吧？
湯姆：　不太遠，要是坐汽車大概十五分鐘。
大衛：　馬車走得那麼慢？坐飛機從香港到上海也只需要一個多小時。
湯姆：　我覺得坐坐馬車也不錯，讓我知道以前大家是怎麼旅行的。導游說，以前，那個地方沒有公路，也沒有汽車。要去別的地方，大家只能坐馬車或者走路。
大衛：　現在大不一樣了，交通越來越方便，世界也變得越來越小了。

Unit 1.1 對話二

凱麗：　上個周末你做甚麼了？
瑪麗婭：星期六在家做作業，星期天我去看張爺爺了。
凱麗：　張爺爺現在身體怎麼樣？
瑪麗婭：從找到优盤以來，他一直在寫小說，精神很好，身體也比以前好了。那天我去他家的時候，他的一個高中同學從美國來看他。他們在一起談得很高興。
凱麗：　高中同學？張爺爺是甚麼時候上高中的？
瑪麗婭：大概是四十年代吧。他的老同學林爺爺是一九四七年去美國上大學的。對了，你知道林爺爺從上海去舊金山花了多長時間嗎？
凱麗：　一兩天嗎？
瑪麗婭：不。他說花了差不多一個月。先從上海坐船去香港，這樣就花了五六天。然後再從香港坐船去舊金山，又用了三個星期。
凱麗：　這麼長時間啊？
瑪麗婭：對，我聽了也嚇了一跳。好在那是六十多年以前的情況。林爺爺說，現在他住在舊金山附近，這次他從離開家到上海，一共才用了十幾個小時。他先坐輕軌去舊金山機場，在舊金山上飛機，過了十多個小時就到上海了。下飛機以後，他坐機場專線車直接就到了旅店。林爺爺一再說，現在的交通真是太方便了。

凱麗： 從一個月減少到十幾個小時。再過六十年，大概一兩個小時就能從中國到美國了吧？
瑪麗婭： 誰知道呢？那時候也不知道我們住在哪兒。可是只要有機會，我一定會去看你的。
凱麗： 好，一言為定。

Unit 1.2 對話一

凱麗： 今天晚上，我打算去東方百貨公司逛一逛，你想去嗎？
大衛： 我好像不需要買甚麼東西。不過，反正晚上沒甚麼事，陪你去逛逛也行。你為甚麼非要去東方百貨公司呢？那兒離學校挺遠的。
凱麗： 哦，我過生日的時候，姥姥送給我一張東方百貨公司的禮品卡，所以我想去那兒看看。
大衛： 聽你一說，我想起來了，我需要買一個新錢包。我現在的錢包太小了。
凱麗： 哇，你發財了嗎？需要大錢包放很多錢？
大衛： 不是，我是需要一個大錢包放很多卡。我的錢包只放得下五六張卡，可是我有差不多二十張卡，所以我得去買一個能放得下二十張卡的錢包。
凱麗： 你怎麼會有那麼多卡呢？
大衛： 你看，這是我的學生證、學校圖書館的借書證、上海圖書館的借書證、這裏有交通卡、電話卡、信用卡、現金卡、銀行卡、學生食堂的飯卡、超市的會員卡。
凱麗： 等一等，那張是甚麼卡？
大衛： 那是健身房的會員卡。
凱麗： 要放下這麼多卡，的确需要一個大錢包。其實，我的卡也挺多的。除了那個健身房的會員卡以外，你有的卡我都有。看來，我也應該去東方百貨公司買一個大一點兒的錢包。
大衛： 那好吧，晚上我們就去買錢包。

Unit 1.2 對話二

大衛： 你看，這是我昨天買的錢包，現在我的卡都有地方放了。
瑪麗婭： 你怎麼有三張上海銀行的卡呢？

大衛：　哦，這張是銀行取款卡；這張是現金卡；這張是信用卡。
瑪麗婭：去商店買東西的時候，這些卡都能用吧？
大衛：　不能用取款卡，但是可以用現金卡和信用卡。買完了東西，只要刷一下就行了。
瑪麗婭：現金卡和信用卡有甚麼不同？
大衛：　現金卡需要你把錢先放到卡的賬戶裏才能用。信用卡是你從銀行借錢花，花完了以後，銀行會告訴你一共借了多少錢，然後你再把錢還給銀行。其實我平時不用信用卡。這是父母給我的，他們說只有在緊急情況下，我才能用。
瑪麗婭：你說你需要把錢先放在現金卡裏，這是甚麼意思？
大衛：　其實，我們用的很多卡都是一種現金卡。比如，你去買電話卡、交通卡、禮品卡甚麼的，都需要先付錢。你買了50元的電話卡，就可以打50元的電話。買了一個商店50元的禮品卡，就可以在那個商店買50元的東西。有些現金卡是銀行發的，銀行會根據你銀行賬戶裏有多少錢，來決定你可以花多少錢。如果你的賬戶裏有50元，那麼你可以用現金卡買50元的東西。
瑪麗婭：這麼說，現金卡就跟現金一樣。那你帶錢不就行了嗎？
大衛：　帶卡比帶錢方便啊，一張卡又小又輕。
瑪麗婭：聽上去方便，其實也不一定。你想，我們去借書，要帶借書證；去坐車，要帶交通卡；去醫務所，要帶學生證；去買東西，要帶現金卡；去超市，要帶超市會員卡；去鍛煉身體，要帶健身房會員卡；去銀行拿錢，要帶取款卡。這個卡那個卡的，忘了帶，或者帶錯了卡，就不能辦事了。
大衛：　你說得對，所以我買了一個大錢包，把所有的卡都放在一起，這樣去哪兒辦事都沒有問題了。
瑪麗婭：也有問題，萬一你的錢包丟了，你不就甚麼事都辦不成了嗎？

Unit 1.3 課文一

New	Reply	Reply All	Forward	Delete	Print

明英：你好！

自從你離開上海以後，兩三個星期過去了。一直沒有收到你的電郵，我們都非常想念你。

開學以後，我們都忙著學習。這是我們在高中的最後一年，老師怕我們考不上大學，所以給的作業比較多。我每天一下課就做作業，有時候要做四五個小時。大家都覺得學習壓力挺大的。

這個學期我搬到新的宿舍樓去了，新樓生活很方便，不出宿舍樓，就能上網。樓裏還有自動售貨機，可以買到飲料和點心。幸虧新樓有這些服務，要不然，我得走十五分鐘去天天超市才能買到吃的東西。學校旁邊的那個小店關門了，因為那裏要建設一個非常大的居民社區。現在工人每天24小時都在學校外邊修路，要把只有兩個車道的馬路修成有四個車道的。聽說，除了居民住房以外，還要蓋學校、醫院、社區圖書館、社區健身房、商業服務中心、科技服務中心等等。建設這個社區會用兩三年的時間。也就是說，在我們畢業以前，我們每天都要經過建設工地。

雖然上海不是一個新城市，但是常常讓人感覺到這是一個新城市，因為每天都有新的發展和新的變化。大理呢？那兒跟上海不太一樣吧？

等著你的電郵！

凱麗

Unit 1.3 課文二

New	Reply	Reply All	Forward	Delete	Print

凱麗，你好！

很高興收到你的電郵。請別怪我到今天才回信。我沒有忘了你，也沒有忘了大家，可是自從我們搬家到大理以後，一直上不了網。我們住的房子非常舊，沒有電話，更沒有寬帶了，所以就沒跟你聯系。你可能會問，為甚麼不發短信給你。我到大理的第二天，就去大理旁邊的一個大湖游泳，結果把手機放在湖邊，忘了帶回來了。因為手機丟了，又不能上網，所以就跟外邊聯系不上了。

我父母也希望我們家可以裝寬帶，這樣上網會比較快。可是在這兒裝寬帶非常麻煩。昨天，他們找到了一個公司，那個公司建議我們裝一個無線上網的設備。今天，終於又可以上網了。我馬上就給你寫信。請告訴瑪麗婭、湯姆和大衛，我也會馬上給他們寫信的。

我父母這次來云南，是要研究中國少數民族的歷史。他們覺得大理是一個非常理想的地方，因為有許多少數民族住在這兒。大理被分成古城和新城。我們現在住在古城。古城不太大，可是有六七百年的歷史。雖然古城的房子比較舊，但是我們都很喜歡這裏的文化歷史。

大理的風景非常美麗，附近有一個大湖，還有一些山。這裏的氣候也很好，一年四季都很暖和。來大理非常方便，可以坐飛機、火車和汽車。如果放寒假的時候你有空，請一定到大理來。我可以做你的導游，帶你走一走，看一看。

請問大家好！

明英

Unit 1.4 對話

瑪麗婭：湯姆，你拿的是甚麼書？

湯姆：《數學高考題指南》和《物理高考難題分析》。

瑪麗婭：你在積極準備高考吧？

湯姆：不準備也不行啊。不管是老師還是父母，見了面就對我說："高考準備得怎麼樣了？你一定要爭取上個好大學。"

聽得我都煩了。但是我想了想，覺得他們說的也有道理。在中國要上大學就得參加高考。如果想進好大學，就得好好準備考試。你看中國的高中生都在積極備考，我當然也不能馬馬虎虎。你準備得怎麼樣了？

瑪麗婭： 除了化學課以外，別的課我都不怕。現在我每個星期六上午去參加一個化學備考班。你有沒有參加備考班？

湯姆： 沒有。我現在常去一個網校，在那裏可以得到老師的幫助。

瑪麗婭： 網校是網上的學校嗎？

湯姆： 其實，網校就是遠程教育網。我現在去的那個遠程教育網，不但有網上的課程，而且有許多不同的服務，幫助老師和學生教學。那兒有從小學到高中每個年級的教學輔導材料。比如說，我們在學幾何。網上會有很多幾何的題目。你做了題以後，馬上可以知道你做得對不對。要是你做得不對，網上會告訴你哪兒做錯了。

瑪麗婭： 那麼酷啊！

湯姆： 這個網校有老師負責不同的服務，比如：常見問題、備考中心、學習方法甚麼的。你有問題可以發電郵，老師會在24小時裏給你回答。

瑪麗婭： 如果我希望馬上得到回答呢？

湯姆： 那裏也有同步課堂，你需要看一下課程表。可以在上課的時候上網，這樣就可以直接跟老師談話。

瑪麗婭： 那個網校有許多老師嗎？

湯姆： 是的。他們都是從各個學校來的，而且都是很有經驗的老師。對了，我在網上看到一個學生寫的關於學習方法的感想，還不錯。我會把那個感想發給你看看。

瑪麗婭： 好，謝謝。

Unit 1.4 課文

(這是湯姆發給瑪麗婭的電郵。)

New	Reply	Reply All	Forward	Delete	Print

瑪麗婭，

這就是我剛才告訴你的關於學習方法的文章。我覺得這些方法我們也能用。我特別喜歡他關於數學學習方法的感想。

湯姆

網校幫我找到好的學習方法

十一中初一學生 王健如

我已經在網校學習了一個學期了。網校的老師常常回答關於學習方法的問題。現在我把我學到的好的學習方法總結一下。

一、語文

第一，要把語文課上好。上課認真地聽，把老師提的問題好好想一想，認真地做作業。第二，要多看書報雜誌。只有多看書，才能了解世界，學到很多課本以外的知識。這些知識也能幫助我更好地理解語文課的內容。第三，為了能在語文考試的時候得到好成績，在看書報的時候，我應該把一些好的詞句記錄下來。這樣以後在寫作文的時候可以用。第四，要常常動動筆，可以寫日記，也可以寫周記，把聽到的看到的有意思的事情寫下來，這樣可以幫助我提高語文水平。

二、數學

我覺得學數學最好的方法是舉一反三。多做難題不一定有用。有用的方法是要理解基礎題。這樣在做難題的時候，可以根據基礎題的原理，用不同的方法去做，這樣就不會怕難題了。

三、英語

我覺得要學好英語，就要做到“四多”：多聽、多寫、多讀、多說。不但上課要聽，而且下課以後，可以多聽英語廣播，多看英語電視節目。不管一開始是不是聽得懂，最後一定會越聽懂得越多。多寫多讀是為了幫助自己記住英語。每個生詞，我都應該寫幾遍，課文也應該讀幾遍，這樣就比較容易記住了。多說，就是要在上課的時候積極說英語，不要怕說錯。

Unit 1.5 對話一

瑪麗婭：凱麗，學校的新圖書館蓋好了，你去過了嗎？
凱麗：去過了。新圖書館的條件比舊圖書館好多了。
瑪麗婭：我還沒去過呢。從外邊看，新館比舊館大得多。以前的圖書館只有三層樓，現在有六層。
凱麗：對，雖然新館比舊館高了三層，可是上上下下比以前快多了。新圖書館有六個電梯，這六個電梯在圖書館的不同地方，不管你在哪一層，不用走很多路，就能坐電梯上下樓。
瑪麗婭：借書呢？是不是也都自動化了？
凱麗：是的，所有的目錄都在電腦裏。去圖書館以前，你可以先上網查一下，你要借的書在第幾層，有沒有被別人借走。如果被別人借走了，電腦會告訴你，借的書哪一天會到期。你可以根據還書的時間，在網上預訂你想借的書。
瑪麗婭：聽上去非常方便。新圖書館裏的書是不是比以前多了？
凱麗：其實，書報雜誌沒有增加很多。現在很多人都看電子書報。新圖書館的很多地方都是給學生學習用的。那裏有網絡學習室、閱覽室、會議室甚麼的。我們可以去那裏用電腦、學習、或者開會。你為甚麼不去看一看呢？
瑪麗婭：今天下課以後，我就去。

Unit 1.5 對話二

（在圖書館裏。）

瑪麗婭：請問，參考書在幾樓？
工作人員：在一樓的參考閱覽室裏。你往左走，右邊的第一個大房間就是參考閱覽室。我們圖書館一共有六個閱覽室。參考閱覽室除外，還有社會科學閱覽室、自然科學閱覽室、外文閱覽室、多媒體報紙閱覽室和視聽閱覽室。每層樓都有一個閱覽室，都在電梯的左邊。
瑪麗婭：謝謝。聽說圖書館還有一些學習室和電腦室，也是每層都有嗎？

工作人員：是的。在五樓，還有一個大教室，那兒每個星期都有講座。你看，在一進門的地方放著一些電腦吧？那些電腦是圖書館指南。你可以去看一下。這個學期所有的講座和活動安排都在電腦裏。

瑪麗婭：我可以在那兒查圖書目錄嗎？

工作人員：當然可以。

瑪麗婭：對了，網絡學習室有沒有打印機？

工作人員：有。如果你要打印，可以到服務台買電腦服務卡，然後就可以打印了。

瑪麗婭：哦，打印貴不貴？

工作人員：跟在學校的電腦房一樣，打印一張紙五分錢。如果你要复印，每層樓都有一個小小的复印室。

瑪麗婭：我也需要先買電腦服務卡嗎？

工作人員：是的，也是五分錢一張。

瑪麗婭：那我可以用現金打印复印嗎？

工作人員：不可以。凡是要打印复印的，都得買電腦服務卡。如果你怕麻煩，可以多放一點兒錢在卡上。這個學期用不完的話，下個學期還可以用。

瑪麗婭：圖書館每天都開門嗎？

工作人員：是的，你看，那個牌子上寫得很清楚。

瑪麗婭：謝謝！我去看看那個牌子。

圖書館開放時間	
周一到周五：	8:00 – 21:00
周六：	9:00 – 18:00
周日：	13:00 – 21:00
(國定假日除外)	

Unit 1.6 對話

凱麗：昨天我經過學校旁邊的建設工地，發現工人已經蓋好很多樓了。

大衛：是嗎？我怎麼沒看到呢。

凱麗：　不是前邊的大樓，是後邊三層樓的別墅樓。
大衛：　那也夠快的。上海甚麼都快，幾個月就能蓋好一個大樓，幾個星期就能修好一條馬路。你們看，學校門口的馬路也快修好了，好像下個月就可以通車了。
湯姆：　如果要我用一個字來總結現代生活，那就是“快”。現在交通很方便，去哪兒都很快。因為有了網絡，跟別人聯系也很快。技術發達了，蓋房子修馬路也變得很快。你們說呢？
瑪麗婭：我覺得還可以用一個字：“小”。
湯姆：　小？
瑪麗婭：是啊，你不覺得世界變得越來越小了嗎？因為可以很快地從一個地方去另外一個地方，地方的遠近變得不重要了。在網上，這個國家發生的事，別的國家馬上就知道了。如果你想買點東西，不管是中國的還是美國的，都可以在網上買到。我們雖然生活在地球不同的地方，但是就象在一個地方一樣。
大衛：　我會用一個字“冷”來總結。
凱麗：　冷？天氣沒有越變越冷啊。
大衛：　我的意思是，現在大家把多數的時間都花在網絡和電視上，不像以前每天會花很多時間跟家人朋友鄰居談話，所以人跟人的關系比以前冷了，也遠了。
瑪麗婭：大衛說的也有道理。凱麗，你會用哪個字？
凱麗：　好的字都被你們用過了。要是非要我說，我就用“多”。現在甚麼都比以前多了，人、車、房子、東西、信息、新聞、技術甚麼的。
湯姆：　我們的總結都挺有意思的。我看，我們可以讓班上的每個同學都來參加這個“一字游戲”，聽聽大家對現代生活的看法。
瑪麗婭：好主意。

Unit 1.6 課文

在美國中部的一個高中裏，有一個“中國：網絡電話俱樂部”。這個俱樂部是四五年以前成立的。那時候，這個高中的校長訪問了北京附近的一個高中。這兩個校長在談話的時候，覺得現在網絡技術發展了，網上交流很方便。他們就想，能不能用網絡技術讓兩個學校的學生互相學習，互相幫助呢。

在一些電腦工程師的幫助下，這個美國高中成立了“中國：網絡電話俱樂部”。俱樂部裏有十幾個學生。每星期有兩個晚上，他們通過網絡電話跟中國高中的學生聯系，幫助中國學生學英文。

有些中國學生會把他們做好的英語作業給美國學生看。有時候，他們也會讓美國學生幫助回答英語課本裏的一些問題。但是最常見的是，中美學生會在一起討論大家都有興趣的話題，比如高中生最喜歡的課程、運動、課外活動等等。一個中國學生告訴他的美國朋友：“在你的幫助下，我的英文考試成績越來越好了。對中國學生來說，考試是非常重要的。但是你們除了幫助我們學習英文以外，還讓我們有機會了解美國。謝謝！”

這個俱樂部成立以後，有些俱樂部的學生已經去中國訪問過了。在中國，他們受到中國高中生的歡迎。這些美國學生說：“雖然我們在電視上看到過中國，也在歷史課裏學習過中國歷史，但是‘百聞不如一見’，我們到了中國，看到了許多在電視上和書上看不到的東西，讓我們更了解中國了。”現在，一些中國學生正在打算訪問美國。他們也希望能更好地了解美國。

Unit 2.1 對話一

凱麗：　這個學期你在上經濟課吧？那門課怎麽樣？

湯姆：　我原來以為經濟課會比較枯燥，可實際上不是這樣。我們正在學習中國的農業。為了讓我們了解農業的情況，老師帶我們去參觀了農業展覽館，下個星期五，我們還要去一個村子做校外考察。

凱麗：　歷史書上常常說，中國是一個農業大國。可是我們現在住在上海，看到的都是現代化的大樓、商場、公司等等。我很難想象中國是個農業大國。

湯姆：　是啊。其實，中國的現代化和工業化是最近一兩百年的事。如果我們看一下中國五千多年的歷史，就會發現五千多年來，中國的經濟主要都是農業經濟。再説，中國非常大，我們在上海，看到的只是一個城市的情況。實際上，中國的大多數地區今天還是農業區。

凱麗：　上中國地理課的時候，我們學到過，中國山地多，平原少。這樣的地理情況是不是會影響到農業發展呢？

湯姆：　當然會。總的來說，中國是人口多，耕地少。中國的人口佔世界的百分之二十，可是中國的耕地只佔世界的百分之七。要在很少的耕地上養活這麼多人非常不容易。過去的五千年來，中國一直努力發展農業，解決人民的吃飯問題。

凱麗：　我常常聽人說，中國的南方人吃米飯，北方人吃麵食，這也跟中國糧食生產有關系吧？

湯姆：　是的，糧食作物在南方主要是大米，在北方主要是小麥。

凱麗：　聽上去，中國的農業非常值得我們了解。等你考察回來，應該把結果給我們班的同學介紹一下。

Unit 2.1 對話二

湯姆：　昨天我們去做校外考察了。

凱麗：　哦，就是你說的經濟課的校外考察吧？你們去參觀了一個村子，是嗎？

湯姆：　是的。這個村子離我們學校不遠，就在浦東。

凱麗：　浦東有村子嗎？我看到的都是高樓、商店和一些居民小區。

湯姆：　這個村子看上去跟一般的居民小區差不多，有一些六層樓的公寓樓，這些公寓樓都是九十年代以後蓋的。二十多年以前，這個村子的附近都是菜地，村裏的農民主要種蔬菜。九十年代的時候，浦東開始發展了，不少工厂和公司搬到浦東來，菜地被用來蓋房子、造馬路了，不少農民去做別的工作了。有的去工厂工作，有的當建筑工人，有的做綠化工作，現在只有很少的農民還在種地。

凱麗：　他們還種蔬菜嗎？

湯姆：　對。你知道浦東有不少菜場，在那裏，大家可以買到各種各樣新鮮的蔬菜。這個村子的農民常常一大早騎著自行車去菜場賣菜。還有一些浦東的超市、飯店也跟農民定了合同。他們種的菜可以直接送到超市和飯店去。那兒的農民告訴我們，他們不但種一些上海居民喜愛吃的菜，而且還種了一些新的蔬菜品種。這些新品種的蔬菜特別受到飯店的歡迎，因為如果飯店的菜單上有一些不同一般的菜，常常可以吸引更多的顧客。

凱麗：　萬一他們生產的蔬菜太多，怎麼辦呢？
湯姆：　在這種情況下，村民就把一部分蔬菜加工以後再賣給超市。
凱麗：　你怎麼可以買到這個村子加工的食品呢？
湯姆：　他們加工的食品是"新浦東"牌的。下次我去超市，一定去找一下。如果有，我就買一些。
凱麗：　好，萬一你吃了覺得很好，別忘了告訴我。
湯姆：　行。

Unit 2.2 對話

瑪麗婭：　周末過得好嗎？
湯姆：　不錯。星期六我爸爸的一位老同學錢叔叔請我們去吃飯。我爸爸說，錢叔叔在上大學的時候，就是一位美食家，他對吃甚麼、怎麼吃特別有研究。
瑪麗婭：　他在家請你們吃飯嗎？
湯姆：　不，我們去了一個回族飯店。
瑪麗婭：　回族是少數民族吧？
湯姆：　對，回族是中國主要的少數民族之一，大概有一億人口，住在中國各地。歷史書上說，在唐朝的時候，一些中亞國家和波斯的商人就開始到中國來做生意，有些人後來就留在中國了。
瑪麗婭：　這麼說，這些人是回族的祖先。
湯姆：　是的。他們把中亞和波斯的文化帶到了中國。因為回族人信伊斯蘭教，所以都不吃豬肉。我們去的那個回族飯店只有牛肉、羊肉和雞肉。錢叔叔說，那家飯店最好吃的菜是涮羊肉。涮羊肉就是把一片一片的生羊肉先放在熱湯裏涮一下，然後拿出來吃。涮羊肉特別嫩，也特別鮮美。
瑪麗婭：　"涮羊肉"是回族的特色菜嗎？好像現在不少飯店都有這道菜。
湯姆：　涮羊肉本來是蒙古族的菜。那是元朝的時候，蒙古軍隊殺好了羊，正準備做飯，突然聽到軍隊馬上要出發。為了能馬上吃到飯，他們就把羊肉切成一片一片的放在水裏涮一下。結果大家都覺得這樣做的羊肉非常好吃，後來就有了"涮羊肉"這道菜。中國各族人民在一起生活了幾百年，飲食習慣互相影響，所以現在許多民族的人都吃涮羊肉。對了，我在回族飯店喝了一種特別的茶，是一般的飯店沒有的，叫“十二味香茶”。

瑪麗婭：你是說，那種茶有十二種味道嗎？

湯姆：從名字上看，應該有十二種味道，可是我沒喝出那麼多味道來。錢叔叔說，這種茶裏不但有茶葉，而且有菓干和糖，所以喝起來又香又甜，非常可口。

瑪麗婭：除了回族的食品，錢叔叔還給你介紹了別的地方菜嗎？

湯姆：介紹了。喲，三點二十五了，我得馬上去參加數學小組的活動。活動完了以後，我給你發電郵吧。

瑪麗婭：好，謝謝。

Unit 2.2 課文

New	Reply	Reply All	Forward	Print	Delete

瑪麗婭：

對不起，剛才我急急忙忙的，話沒說完就走了，現在我再給你介紹別的地方菜。

錢叔叔說，中國各地的飲食很不一樣，這是因為中國很大，各地的氣候、地理都會影響到農業生產，也決定了各地的飲食。

中國各地做的菜各有特點。一般來說，中國菜被分為八大菜系。總的來說，中國菜可以說是南甜、北咸、東辣、西酸。南方的主食是米飯，北方的是麵食。

江南人，就是住在長江南邊的人喜歡吃得比較清淡，還喜歡菜裏帶一點兒甜味。他們喜歡吃得好一些少一些。如果你去上海人家吃飯，他們常常用小盤子放一點兒菜，但是菜的品種會比較多。

住在中國北部和東北的人，喜歡菜的味道濃一些，所以做得菜比較油，也比較咸。而且他們認為讓大家吃飽是非常重要的。要是我們去東北飯店吃飯，就會看到都是用大盤子放菜，數量特別多。所以到了東北飯店，我們應該少點幾個菜，要不然一定會吃不完。

中國西部的菜，特別是山西菜，帶一點酸味，因為做菜的時候，山西人喜歡放一點兒醋。

湖南、四川等地的菜都比較辣。如果你喜歡吃辣的，可以選湖南飯店或者四川飯店。

廣東菜非常有特色。廣東在中國的南部，那裏氣候好，一年四季都有新鮮的蔬菜，廣東又在海邊，所以廣東菜用許多新鮮的蔬菜和海鮮。錢叔叔還說，廣東人是中國最敢吃的人，他們甚麼都願意嘗一嘗。有一句笑話說，"除了飛機以外，天上飛的東西廣東人都敢吃；除了桌子以外，有四條腿的東西廣東人都敢吃。"

錢叔叔的介紹非常有意思。我們應該向錢叔叔學習，去吃一下中國各地不同的菜，這樣我們就知道哪些是我們最愛吃的了。怎麼樣，明天下課以後，我們是不是一起去小吃街逛一逛？

湯姆

Unit 2.3 對話一

湯姆：我媽媽說，現在中國各地的飲食差別越來越小了。以前，中國南方人吃米飯，北方人吃麵食。可是現在呢？南方北方都差不多。不少南方人為了方便，常常吃麵食。北方人為了品嘗各種各樣的菜，在酒席上一定吃米飯。所以，雖然說各地都有一些特色食品，但是我們吃的多數食品已經沒有地方特色了。

凱麗：其實，現在無論在哪個國家，吃的東西都越來越相似了。比方說，意大利麵，不但意大利人在吃，世界各地的人都在吃。

大衛：拿中國飯來說，無論你去哪個國家，都找得到中國飯店。

瑪麗婭：在許多國家都有漢堡、可樂、比薩這樣的快餐食品，它們已經變成世界食品了。

凱麗：這麼說，飲食也全球化了。

大衛：我覺得飲食全球化會帶來一些別的問題。因為每個國家的飲食是由那兒的農業決定的。如果一個地方一年四季都生產新鮮的水菓蔬菜，住在那兒的人就會多吃一點兒水菓蔬菜。如果一個地方養的牛比較多，那兒的人就會多吃一點兒牛肉。現在雖然交通發達了，可以把食品很快地從一個國家運到別的國家去，可是運食品需要用能源，還要用冰箱冷凍食品。

我認為，最簡單的方法還是吃在當地生產的食品。這樣不但方便，吃的東西新鮮，而且對環境有好處，不會浪費能源。

凱麗：　哦，我在超市裏看到過一個牌子，上面寫著"種在當地，吃在當地"。我覺得這種方法有好處，也有坏處。好處是可以幫助當地的農業生產，不浪費能源，也不需要改變傳統的飲食習慣。坏處是，當地人沒有機會品嘗外國食品，這不是很可惜嗎？

湯姆：　不一定吧？如果當地的食品很好吃，吃不到外國食品也沒有關系。

瑪麗婭：可是那些能夠全球化的食品一定是比較容易得到、比較容易準備、也比較好吃的食品。要是不好吃，誰要吃啊？

Unit 2.3 對話二

大衛：　星期五下午我們有漢語考試，考完了試，我們是不是應該出去輕松一下？

瑪麗婭：好啊，我們可以一起去吃晚飯。

凱麗：　吃中餐還是西餐？

湯姆：　在學生餐廳每天吃中餐。我們去吃西餐，換換口味吧。

凱麗：　離學校不遠有幾家西餐店，那兒有漢堡、三明治、比薩、意大利麵甚麼的，你們要去哪一家？

大衛：　你說的是那幾家快餐店吧？快餐店裏的西餐不地道。我們要吃就要吃地地道道的西餐。怎麼樣，你們想吃烤肉嗎？

湯姆：　新疆烤肉嗎？哦，不對，新疆烤肉是中餐，不是西餐。我們去吃韓國燒烤嗎？

大衛：　不，聽說世紀公園附近新開了一家巴西烤肉店。我們可以去那兒嘗嘗巴西烤肉。

瑪麗婭：我吃過巴西烤肉。巴西的烤肉實在是太鮮美了!有牛肉、豬肉、羊肉和雞肉，隨便你選用。服務員把不同的肉串在一起，拿著肉串在飯店裏走來走去。誰要吃肉，只要告訴服務員，他就根據你的選擇，把肉切下來，放到你的盤子裏，你要多少，他就切多少。

湯姆：　你是說，隨便你要吃多少肉都可以嗎？

瑪麗婭：是的，只要你吃得下，三盤、五盤、十盤都沒有關系。

凱麗： 可是，吃得太多會讓人不舒服吧？
湯姆： 別擔心，雖然我很喜歡吃肉，但是為了健康，我不會暴吃的。
瑪麗婭： 我覺得生活在上海挺好的。無論要吃哪國的飯，都能吃到。
湯姆： 其實，現在住在哪兒都沒有關系。世界各國的食品差別越來越小了，尤其是那些好吃的東西，很快就會全球化。
大衛： 對，巴西烤肉也一樣。巴西是南美洲最先養牛的國家。從十六世紀開始，就開始養牛，烤肉是巴西的傳統食品，後來才慢慢地傳到了別的國家，各國的人都覺得好吃，所以今天在每個大城市，差不多都能吃到巴西烤肉。
凱麗： 那麼有名的食品，我還沒吃過！真對不起我自己。星期五，我們一定去品嘗一下。

Unit 2.4 對話一

瑪麗婭： 周末我去超市買東西，發現很多食品上都有“綠色食品”或者“健康食品”的標誌。綠色食品和健康食品的意思是一樣的吧？為甚麼要有兩個不同的名字呢？
凱麗： 這個問題很有意思。在超市我還看到過“有機食品”和“天然食品”。這些是不是也是健康食品呢？
瑪麗婭： 不知道別人怎麼看，反正我一看到這些標誌，就會覺得這樣的食品對我們的健康有好處。
大衛： 不見得吧？有些食品，像炸薯片、餅干，也被說成是“綠色食品”。多吃這些食品對我們的健康是沒有好處的。
湯姆： 食品標誌太多，容易讓人糊裏糊塗。不管怎麼說，“健康食品”的意思應該很清楚：吃這些食品對健康有好處，讓人不容易生病。
大衛： “天然食品”也不難理解，裏邊都是天然產品，沒有其他的東西。
瑪麗婭： 可是“有機食品”跟“天然食品”有甚麼不一樣呢？
湯姆： 食品生長的時候不用化學品，就是“有機食品”。
凱麗： 聽你們這麼一說，我認為“天然食品”是廢話。食品不都是天然生長的嗎？

湯姆：　那不一定。有些食品，比如香精、糖精、味精就不是天然的，是用化學品制造的。

瑪麗婭：我們越說越糊塗了。還是上網去找找信息吧。

Unit 2.4 對話二

瑪麗婭：哎，你們看，我在綠色生活網站找到關於食品標誌的回答了。

大衛：　眞的？網上說，“綠色食品”是甚麼？

凱麗：　“有機食品”呢？

瑪麗婭：別急，我們一個一個地看。“綠色食品”就是沒有受到污染的食品。在生產這些食品的時候，沒用過或者只用過很少的化學品，這些食品沒有被化學品污染。

大衛：　所以我們可以說，吃綠色食品比較安全。

凱麗：　我們再來看一下“天然食品”。天然食品常常是生的蔬菜水菓，魚肉雞鴨等等。這些食品沒有被加過工或者只經過很少的加工。這是甚麼意思？

湯姆：　加過工的食品就是買回來就能吃的東西，還有那些只要簡單做一下就能吃的東西，像點心啊、飲料啊、熟肉啊、還有那些冷凍食品。

瑪麗婭：這麼說，天然食品就是買回來以後，要我們自己洗洗、切切、燒燒以後才能吃的食品。

湯姆：　哦，就是那些我爺爺奶奶，姥爺姥姥在菜場買的食品。他們為了做飯，每天要花很多時間。

凱麗：　也就是說，天然食品和“有機食品”還不一樣。天然食品雖然是自然生長的，可是也可能用過化學品。“有機食品”在生長的時候，一定沒有用過化學品。

大衛：　我看，所有這些食品跟“健康食品”可能有關系，也可能沒有關系。“健康食品”應該是不會影響我們身體健康的。綠色食品、天然食品、有機食品只是告訴我們，在種食品和加工食品的時候，發生了甚麼情況。

瑪麗婭：大衛，你眞會總結。我們現在知道這些食品標誌有哪些不同了。

Unit 2.5 對話一

大衛： 昨天教育頻道有一個關於中國食文化的電視節目，介紹了文化傳統對飲食的影響。這個節目說，有時候，一個國家的飲食習慣是由文化傳統決定的。

凱麗： 文化傳統有那麼大的作用嗎？飲食應該是由一個國家的農業決定的吧？

大衛： 雖然吃甚麼可能主要是由農業決定的，但是文化傳統對怎麼吃一定是有影響的。那個電視節目舉了一個例子說，從古代開始，中國人就喜歡在一起吃飯，常常是一個家庭、或者親戚朋友聚在一起吃飯。這種傳統影響到中國人對吃飯的看法。他們覺得，吃飯不但是為了吃飽，也是為了培養人跟人的感情。

湯姆： 這種說法很有道理。自從搬家來中國以後，我父母差不多每個星期不是請人吃飯就是被人請去吃飯。不像我們住在美國的時候，沒有那麼多請客吃飯的情況。

大衛： 這個電視節目還介紹說，中國的文化傳統之一是好客，如果有朋友從很遠的地方來看你，這是非常讓人愉快的。所以客人來了，中國人總是要做很多菜給客人吃。在吃飯的時候，會一再讓客人多吃一點兒，并且把菜夾到客人的碗裏。

瑪麗婭： 中國人的确很喜歡請朋友吃飯，一有機會大家就在一起吃飯。為了慶祝結婚、畢業、找到工作、過生日、生孩子甚麼的，一般的中國人常常在飯店辦酒席。要是你去朋友家玩兒，他們也常常留你吃飯。

湯姆： 我有點兒怕跟中國人去吃飯，他們總是讓你多吃一點兒。哪怕客人說已經吃飽了，他們還是會把許多吃的東西夾到你的碗裏。

凱麗： 我剛到中國的時候，也覺得這樣做有點兒奇怪，別人吃不下了，為甚麼還非要別人吃呢？後來才知道，這是中國人的傳統習慣，這樣做會讓主人和客人都很愉快。

大衛： 凱麗，現在你同意了吧？文化傳統會影響一個國家的飲食方式。

Unit 2.5 對話二

瑪麗婭：我常常聽人說，中國有一句名言“民以食為天”，這是甚麼意思？

大衛：人們覺得吃飯是生活中最重要的事。

湯姆：怪不得我姥姥常常說，“開門七件事，柴米油鹽醬醋茶。”這七樣東西都跟做飯吃飯有關。

大衛：的确是這樣。我看的那個電視節目還說，文化也影響到人們怎麼吃。比方說，從古代開始，中國人就喜歡吃熱的和熟的食品，不喜歡吃冷的和生的。幾千年來，中國人用不同的方法烹調食品，一種菜可以作出幾十種不同的味道來，所以中國人的烹調技術非常高。

凱麗：而且中國人做菜的時候，很注意菜的顏色、香味和味道。一個好的菜應該有各種顏色，紅、綠、黃、白、黑等等。這樣就需要用不同的蔬菜、魚、肉，才能讓一個菜有許多不同的顏色。

瑪麗婭：要讓一個菜有香味，就需要加一些不同的香料吧？

湯姆：對，實際上，許多國家的菜都講究香味，做菜的時候加香料是很平常的事。

大衛：要讓一個菜味道好，就需要放不同的調料。中國主要的調料是油、鹽、醬、醋、糖。

瑪麗婭：現在網上電視上常常介紹“營養學”，說是通過吃，可以讓大家少生病，更健康。你們相信嗎？

大衛：當然相信。那個電視節目說，兩千多年以前，中國人就發現不同的食品裏有不同的營養，人們應該吃不同的東西。可是有些東西沒有味道不好吃，所以可以用甜、酸、苦、辣、咸這五種味道來烹調食品，讓它們變得好吃一些。同時，中國人覺得不同的季節應該吃不同的食品。他們把食品分成“熱性”、“中性”、“涼性”等等。比方說，熱性的食品，夏天天氣太熱，就應該少吃一些，冬天可以多吃一些。

凱麗：哪些食品是熱性的？

大衛：一般來說是辣的東西。中國人覺得熱性食品吃得太多了對身體不好，容易發燒，長痘子。

湯姆： 啊呀，我的臉上長了兩個痘子，是不是因為上個星期吃了兩次四川菜？

瑪麗婭： 不會吧？能那麼“立竿見影”嗎？

Unit 2.6 對話

凱麗： 大衛，你是從香港來的。有人說，“吃在香港”。這是為甚麼呢？

大衛： 我在香港的時候，也常常聽人說，香港是“美食天堂”。他們說，香港的食文化結合了東方文化和西方文化。除了各地的中國菜以外，在香港我們還能吃到世界各國的菜，歐洲、亞洲、美洲、非洲的菜都能吃到。

凱麗： 可是只要是大城市，不是都能吃到各國的菜嗎？為甚麼說香港是美食天堂，別的城市就不是呢？

大衛： 可能每個城市都認為自己是“美食天堂”吧。不過，香港人的确是非常重視吃，香港的食品種類特別多。香港的居民來自世界各國和中國各地，而且這些居民也很不同，有的非常有錢，有的沒有錢，所以他們的飲食很不一樣。在香港，你可以花很多錢，去非常高級的飯店吃飯，也可以花很少錢，去買傳統的“街頭食品”。那些街頭食品簡單、好吃、便宜，非常有特色。

凱麗： 街頭食品品種多嗎？

大衛： 非常多，冷的、熱的、干的、濕的都有，各地各國的都有。

凱麗： 香港離廣東很近。香港人和廣東人的飲食是不是很相似？

大衛： 香港的廣東餐館的确很多，因為廣東人比較多。可是香港還有許多從中國各地來的移民，他們也帶來了各地的特色菜。一般來說，廣東來的移民在家做廣東菜，上海來的在家做上海菜，山東來的在家做山東菜。

凱麗： 廣東人愛飲茶，香港也有許多可以飲茶的餐廳吧？

大衛： 對，這樣的餐廳在香港叫“茶樓”，一般的中國餐廳叫“酒樓”。為了讓食品比較衛生，現在街頭食品都放在小飯店裏賣，這樣的小飯店叫“茶餐廳”。這是因為茶餐廳不但供應點心和小吃，而且還供應咖啡、奶茶、冷飲等等。

凱麗：　奶茶？香港人喝茶放牛奶嗎？一般的中國人喝茶不放奶，也不放糖。

大衛：　香港人學習了英國的飲食文化，許多人習慣喝英國的“下午茶”，也習慣象英國人一樣，在茶裏加牛奶和糖。

凱麗：　香港的飲食文化聽上去太有意思了。希望我有機會去香港，嘗嘗各種食品。

Unit 2.6 課文

New	Reply	Reply All	Forward	Print	Delete

凱麗：你好！

我這幾天正在準備大考，你呢？寒假你有甚麼計划嗎？如果有興趣，歡迎你來大理做客。

我在大理生活差不多半年了，非常喜歡這個城市。大理的氣候好，四季如春，風景也很美麗。一年四季都有許多游客來大理。游客們到了大理，除了參觀這兒的風景以外，都想品嘗一下云南菜。我的同學告訴我，大理菜可以說代表了云南菜。

中國人常說，“靠山吃山，靠水吃水。”意思是，住在山附近的人常常吃山裏生長的東西，住在江河和大海旁邊的人常常吃水裏生長的東西。拿大理來說，這兒有高山也有大湖，所以天然的綠色食品很多。選用綠色食品是大理菜的一個特點。同時，大理菜的味道一般都比較濃，辣的很辣，酸的很酸。

到了大理，游客們也都希望參加一些少數民族的文化活動。不少人喜歡去嘗一下白族的“三道茶”。白族人家無論是過節、慶祝生日、還是結婚，都要請客人喝“一苦二甜三回味”的三道茶。三道茶就是讓客人喝三種不同的茶。第一杯是苦的，第二杯是甜的，第三杯有不同的味道，需要客人回味。這代表了人的生活，先苦後甜，給人很多可以回味的經歷。如果你來大理，我一定帶你去喝三道茶。

請問瑪麗婭、湯姆、大衛好！

明英

Unit 3.1 對話一

湯姆：　春節過得怎麼樣？

瑪麗婭：很不錯，我姥爺姥姥也來上海過年。大年夜，跟一般的中國家庭一樣，我們全家在一起吃了年夜飯，看了"春節晚會"的節目。過春節的時候，不是我們去訪問朋友，就是朋友來我們家，非常熱鬧。

湯姆：　大年夜，你們放鞭炮了嗎？

瑪麗婭：沒有。因為放鞭炮不但聲音很大，帶來噪音污染，而且煙塵很大，容易帶來空氣污染。為了過一個綠色的春節，今年我們小區的居民建議，誰都不放鞭炮。

湯姆：　這樣不影響你們睡覺了吧？以前到了半夜十二點，大家都出來放鞭炮。放幾個還沒甚麼，可是這幾年越放越多，有人一次就放幾千個，乒乒乓乓，讓人睡不了覺。過年的時候出門去，地上到處都是紙屑，看上去很髒。不放鞭炮就沒有這些問題了。可是我也擔心過年放鞭炮是中國的傳統，代表送舊迎新，要是不放鞭炮，會不會影響大家愉快地過年？

瑪麗婭：我們小區的居民討論了這個問題，大家覺得，可以用其他的方法來送舊迎新，比如，寫春聯，挂氣球，在小區各個地方放一些花，這樣慶祝春節也很好。今年過完春節以後，大家都說，不放鞭炮是個好主意。新年的時候，小區不但很安靜，也很干淨，一點也沒有影響大家高高興興過春節。你的春節過得怎麼樣？

湯姆：　春節的時候，我們一家去海南島旅游了。

瑪麗婭：海南島天氣暖和，風景又好，春節的時候，去那裏旅游的人一定很多吧？

湯姆：　是的。因為游客比較多，所以不少旅游景點都請大家要注意保護環境，不要亂丟垃圾，要保護景點的一草一木。有個牌子上寫著，"美麗的海南島，我只留下了我的腳印，帶走了你的照片。"

瑪麗婭：哦，你的意思是說，我們都要做綠色的旅游者，要保護旅游景點的環境。

湯姆：　對。要是海南島上都是垃圾，誰還想去呢？

瑪麗婭：所以每個人都應該從小事做起，從自己做起，來保護環境。

Unit 3.1 對話二

凱麗：　過年以前我去超市買年貨，看到牆上寫著：讓野生動物平平安安地過年。這是不是有點兒奇怪？野生動物跟過年有甚麼關系？

湯姆：　這有甚麼奇怪的！亂放鞭炮，不就把野生動物都嚇跑了？

凱麗：　可是城市裏本來就沒有甚麼野生動物。除了動物園裏住著一些野生動物的後代以外，城市裏哪有野生動物？

湯姆：　對，眞是莫名其妙。

大衛：　誰說的？我們先想想，超市和野生動物有甚麼關系？

湯姆：　哦，我知道了，你是說不應該吃野生動物，是不是？

大衛：　是的。因為有些人喜歡吃野味，所以超市要他們注意最好不吃野味。

凱麗：　聽說有的人，除了桌子以外，四條腿的東西都吃。怪不得超市要讓大家保護野生動物。

湯姆：　野生動物已經越來越少了，需要大家保護它們，所以最好不要吃野味。

凱麗：　除了不吃野味以外，過年的時候最好也別大吃大喝。大吃大喝不但對身體不好，而且對環境也不好。生產食品需要用資源，大吃大喝會浪費資源。今年過春節，我們家就跟平時一樣，吃得很簡單。而且今年去看朋友的時候，大家都不送禮物。

大衛：　不送禮物是不是不客氣呢？

凱麗：　我家的親戚朋友都說，過春節本來就是為了要跟家人和朋友在一起，不是為了送禮物。

湯姆：　對，我最不喜歡去買禮物了，要浪費很多時間。有時候出去逛了半天，也不知道買甚麼禮物好。

大衛：　這是因為多數的人都不需要甚麼東西。結果又浪費時間又浪費錢，而且還浪費資源。不送禮物，就可以節約錢和時間，并且還可以讓春節不受商業化的影響。

凱麗：　我覺得這樣過春節非常好。可以說，大家都過了一個綠色的春節。

Unit 3.2 對話一

（在一個美國連鎖快餐店裏。）

瑪麗婭：你想吃甚麼？

湯姆：到了美國快餐店，當然就是吃漢堡，喝可樂了。我就要一個特价套餐吧，這樣吃的喝的都有了。

瑪麗婭：等一等，這兒有好幾個特价套餐，你要哪個？第一個是：牛肉漢堡、玉米色拉、紅茶。第二個是：豬肉漢堡、黃瓜色拉、綠茶……

湯姆：我要第六個。那是地道的美國快餐：牛肉漢堡、炸薯條、可樂。

瑪麗婭：這家快餐店的不少食品都中國化了，又有中國色拉，又有紅茶綠茶。

湯姆：這家快餐店你沒來過吧？我挺喜歡這家的，中西餐都有。要是你來吃早飯，這裏早上還賣豆漿、油條、飯團。

瑪麗婭：這些不都是傳統的中國早餐嗎？

湯姆：是啊，這家美國快餐店已經入鄉隨俗了。

瑪麗婭：哦，到甚麼山上唱甚麼歌嘛。

湯姆：這句話是甚麼意思？

瑪麗婭：意思是，我們說話做事都應該根據一個地方的情況做出改變。這家快餐廳已經根據中國人的飲食習慣改變了菜單。

湯姆：我們來看看甜品菜單，上面有綠茶冰激凌、炸芋菓，的确很有中國特色。正因為是這樣，所以來這家快餐店吃飯的人特別多。

瑪麗婭：對啊，別的美國快餐店常常是年輕人多，老年人少。這家眞不一樣，你看，男女老少都有。這大概就是經濟課老師說的，一個跨國公司要想在國外發展，就需要"本土化"。比如，我去兼職的那個小公司，為了讓國外的顧客了解他們的產品，就讓我把公司的網頁翻譯成英文。這就是"本土化"，是吧？

湯姆：哎，我們是不是應該先吃飯再研究"全球化"和"本土化"啊？我快餓死了。

瑪麗婭：好吧，好吧，我們快點菜吧。

Unit 3.2 對話二

瑪麗婭：你已經吃完了？怎麼吃得那麼快？
湯姆：因為我快餓死了，所以一下子就吃完了。你慢慢吃吧。
瑪麗婭：行，我吃，你跟我說說話。上個周末你做甚麼了？
湯姆：我正要告訴你呢。上個周末，兩個舊金山的老鄰居到上海來旅游，順便來看看我們。
瑪麗婭：他們是跟旅行團來的嗎？
湯姆：不是。他們覺得，跟旅行團旅游是"走馬觀花"，看不到真正中國人的生活，所以不願意參加旅行團。到了中國，他們也不是坐著旅游車到處走，而是跟一般的中國人一樣，坐公共交通去各地旅游。因為我在上海，當然就由我當他們的導游了。
瑪麗婭：你們去哪兒了？
湯姆：上海的歷史古跡本來就不多，再說，這兩位鄰居也不怎麼喜歡去博物館，因為他們要看"活的文化"。我只能帶他們在街上走走，去市中心、外灘、和浦東看了看，還去黃浦江坐了游船。
瑪麗婭：他們玩得高興嗎？
湯姆：玩得非常高興，看到了現代的上海，也看到了中國人現在是怎麼生活的。可是，他們也有點兒失望。
瑪麗婭：失望？為甚麼呢？
湯姆：他們喜歡了解外國文化，一來就說，到了中國一定要"入鄉隨俗"。也就是說，吃飯要吃中國飯，穿衣要穿有中國特色的，買東西要買中國造的。反正一句話，在中國說話做事都要中國化。
瑪麗婭：在中國要達到中國化應該不難。
湯姆：聽上去容易，做起來難。在上海，吃中國飯不是個問題，哪兒都有中國飯店。穿有中國特色的衣服可能就有問題了。你去大街上看看，有幾個人穿傳統的中國衣服？
瑪麗婭：對啊，現在世界各國的人穿得都差不多一樣。
湯姆：我帶他們逛了市中心和購物中心。在那裏，他們看到許多外國的連鎖店。還有不少商店，不管是外國的還是中國的，都用英文名字。商店裏賣的也不都是中國商品，外國商品非常多。一句話，在美國能買到的東西在中國都買得到。我的老鄰居看了有點兒失望，覺得中國和許多別的國家一樣，都西方化了。

瑪麗婭：這有甚麼奇怪的！我們時代的特點就是全球化。各個國家的文化都在互相影響。各國的差別越來越小，吃的東西、穿的衣服、用的東西、做的活動，都越來越相似了。

湯姆：對啊，我的老鄰居也是這麼說的。他們覺得，如果到處都差不多，不就沒有必要去國外旅行了嗎？

Unit 3.3 對話一

凱麗：電視上的廣告那麼多，看一個電影，中間要放幾十個廣告，眞討厭！

瑪麗婭：我也最討厭廣告了。廣告上要賣的那些東西，多數都是我不需要的。對我來說，看廣告是浪費時間。

大衛：你不需要，不等於別人不需要。

凱麗：大衛說得也有道理。可是如果一個人眞的需要一樣東西，不看廣告也會去買的。

大衛：要是只有在需要的時候才去買東西，那百分之五十的商店都會沒有顧客了。一個人去買東西，不一定是因為他眞的需要東西，而是因為他想要最新最時髦的東西。這跟需要不需要沒有關系。

瑪麗婭：你說得對。我看，現代人的東西都太多了。拿我來說，我有十幾雙鞋子。其實，只要有三四雙就夠穿了。

大衛：那你為甚麼要買這麼多呢？

瑪麗婭：我也說不清楚，有時候是因為看到廣告說那種牌子的鞋子很好，也有時候是因為覺得鞋子很時髦，這樣不知不覺就買了十幾雙鞋子。

大衛：所以你買那麼多的鞋子是受了廣告的影響。

瑪麗婭：可以這麼說吧。雖然我知道不應該聽廣告的，但是也免不了受廣告的影響。

大衛：這不能怪你。我們都會受影響。廣告上說這個牌子的東西好，又有一些名人用這些東西，我們去買東西的時候，就會不知不覺去找那個牌子。

凱麗： 廣告常常讓人覺得，現代生活就應該買、買、買。結果，大家的東西都越來越多。舊的東西還沒有用坏，新的已經來了。

大衛： 就是。不少人家東西放不下了，就搬到大房子裏去住。到了大房子以後，又有空的地方了，又可以買很多東西，最後又放不下了，再搬更大的房子……

瑪麗婭： 我看要保護環境，節約資源，廣告公司就應該少做一些廣告。

大衛： 你們也別太理想主義了，廣告公司不做廣告，那還要廣告公司做甚麼？

Unit 3.3 對話二

瑪麗婭： 昨天發生了一件特別奇怪的事，讓我們都大吃一惊。

凱麗： 怎麼了？

瑪麗婭： 我們正在吃晚飯，一個人來敲門，說要找妮娜。那個人推著一輛自行車，車上放著一個很大的紙盒子。我們問他為甚麼要找妮娜。他說是為妮娜送貨上門。

凱麗： 你是說，妮娜在商店買了東西，讓人送回來嗎？

瑪麗婭： 問題就在這裏啊，妮娜怎麼會有錢買東西呢？我們想那個人一定是送錯地方了。可是他說，他是替一家網上公司來送貨的。妮娜在那兒買了一輛自行車，現在應該一手交錢，一手交貨。

凱麗： 妮娜才七八歲，怎麼可以去網上買東西呢？

瑪麗婭： 我們開始也不相信，可是送貨的人把打印出來的訂單給我們看，上面的确寫著妮娜的名字。於是，我們就問妮娜，“這是你買的嗎？”她說，“我沒有買這個大盒子，我買的是紅色的自行車，車上畫著一只白貓。”那個送貨的人聽了就說，“你們聽到了吧？是這個小朋友買的東西。一手交錢一手交貨吧。”我媽媽向他解釋了半天，雖然家長也有責任，不應該讓孩子上網買東西，可是這件事主要應該由公司負責，他們的網頁有問題，那麼小的孩子怎麼可以隨便上網訂貨呢？

凱麗： 一般公司的網頁上不是都寫著嗎？如果你不到十八歲，不能訂貨。這家公司怎麼沒寫？

瑪麗婭： 那個送貨的人告訴我媽媽，他不太清楚公司網頁的情況，他只管送貨。既然我們不要，他就把貨拿回去。

瑪麗婭： 他走了以後，我媽媽一再對妮娜說，沒有經過爸爸媽媽的同意，她不可以上網去買東西。再說，她已經有自行車了，為甚麼還要再買一輛？

凱麗： 妮娜一定是看到了廣告，覺得自行車很好看吧？

瑪麗婭： 是的，她說她的自行車上沒畫著可愛的白貓，所以要買新的。我對她說，如果她要白貓，我可以幫她畫。可是不能因為她要白貓就要買新的自行車，要是她喜歡黑貓了，看到有黑貓的自行車，難道也要買一輛嗎？一個人要那麼多自行車做甚麼？不需要的東西，就不應該買，這樣對環保有好處，不浪費資源，也不會增加垃圾。

凱麗： 你說得對。那你幫她畫貓了嗎？

瑪麗婭： 畫了，可是畫得不太像。我把貓的耳朵畫得太長了，看上去像一隻兔子。妮娜說沒關系，兔子也挺可愛的。

Unit 3.4 對話一

湯姆： 昨天我去天天超市買完了東西，營業員問我要不要塑料袋。如果要的話，我得付六毛錢。以前天天超市的塑料袋都是免費的，怎麼現在要顧客付錢了呢？

凱麗： 你大概很久沒去超市了吧？為了保護環境，超市讓顧客自己帶袋子，不用或少用一次性的塑料袋。

湯姆： 哦，是這樣。

凱麗： 昨天你買塑料袋了嗎？

湯姆： 沒有，我把東西放在書包裏。有一包餅干放不下，我就拿在手裏。

凱麗： 我們可以在書包裏放一個購物袋，買了東西以後可以拿出來用。要不然，手裏拿著一大堆東西，走路坐車都不方便。

湯姆： 你說得也是。還好我昨天買的是餅干，如果是牛奶、蔬菜甚麼的，抱著一瓶牛奶或者一大堆蔬菜坐地鐵，看上去一定很可笑。

凱麗： 對啊，這太影響你的形象了。抱著蔬菜坐車一點兒都不酷。
湯姆： 別開我的玩笑了。不過，說到一次性的塑料袋，這的确對環境不好。用過一次就扔，一定會增加垃圾。再說，生產塑料袋需要用各種資源，這樣也會浪費資源，所以一次性的產品都應該少用。
凱麗： 在我們學校的餐廳，有不少一次性的餐巾、筷子、盤子、杯子甚麼的。這些一次性產品不是都在增加垃圾、浪費資源嗎？
湯姆： 你說得對。我們應該建議少用一次性產品，大家可以自己帶筷子和碗，吃過飯以後洗一洗，不就可以再用了嗎？我們可以寫一個標語，"再見了！一次性產品。"對了，還可以寫一個"減少，重复，回收"的標語。
凱麗： 這是甚麼意思啊？
湯姆： 不就是三個R嗎？Reduce, Reuse 和 Recycle。
凱麗： 你這麼翻譯，意思不太清楚。我看應該翻譯成："減少污染，重复使用，回收再生。"
湯姆： 行啊，你的翻譯可真是畫龍點睛。
凱麗： 哪裏哪裏。

Unit 3.4 對話二

瑪麗婭： 環保日馬上要來了。學校要組織一些活動，我們班負責宣傳節約能源。
大衛： 這不難做，我們可以提一些節約能源的建議，并且把這些建議做成幻燈片，在環保日放給大家看。
瑪麗婭： 行啊。我們先計划一下，節能大概有哪些方面，這樣我們可以去找些圖片照片，把幻燈片做得比較吸引人。
凱麗： 我看，交通是一個方面。應該請大家少開車，多用公共交通，或者走路騎自行車，這樣不但可以節約能源，而且可以減少空氣污染。
湯姆： 對。如果大家都不開車，就不會有堵車的問題了，這樣可以少造一些公路，不會影響農業發展。
瑪麗婭： 讓大家都不開車是不可能的，我們應該建議大家最好少開車。如果一定要開，最好拼車。

大衛： 我們也應該說一下不開車對健康的好處。現在不少人一天到晚都坐在電腦前，如果騎自行車或走路上班，不是對環保和大家的健康都有好處嗎？
瑪麗婭： 除了交通以外，我們可以讓大家注意節約用電。冬天的時候，暖氣不要開得太高，夏天的時候，空調不要開得太低。
大衛： 還有，能不坐電梯，就不坐或少坐電梯。
湯姆： 我們還可以建議大家用節能燈泡。在買冰箱、電腦、洗衣機的時候，最好都買節能產品。
瑪麗婭： 別忘了，我們還應該節約用水。
大衛： 行，我們要請大家注意，在生活中有許多地方可以節約能源。
凱麗： 另外，我們要建議大家最好別買太多的東西，因為造東西都要用能源。
瑪麗婭： 如果可能，就去二手店買東西。讓每一樣東西都物盡其用。
凱麗： 可是，有些人不喜歡二手店的東西。
大衛： 那我們可以建議，如果一個東西坏了，修一下再用。
湯姆： 最後我看還應該加一條建議，不用或者少用一次性產品。去超市買東西，別用一次性塑料袋。
凱麗： 對了，我們可以在幻燈片裏，放一張湯姆的照片，他從超市出來，手裏抱著牛奶和一大堆蔬菜，旁邊寫著："環保第一，形象第二。"
大衛： 或者我們可以寫："誰說他不酷？環保才最酷。"
湯姆： 行啊，隨便你們寫甚麼，只要保護環境就行。

Unit 3.5 對話一

凱麗： 大衛，你在忙甚麼呢？
大衛： 我在準備報告呢。這個星期五，我要去紅紅的幼兒園參加"大哥哥大姐姐"活動。每個大哥哥大姐姐都要教小朋友做一件事。我覺得學會看地圖非常有用，所以我要給他們介紹一下怎麼看地圖。
凱麗： 那你帶幾張地圖不就行了嗎？為甚麼還要做幻燈片呢？
大衛： 我打算一邊教他們用地圖，一邊介紹中國地理。你看，這是我要用的地圖。幼兒園的孩子認識的字不多，所以我還做了一些幻燈片，把各地的風景照片放在上邊。這樣，他們在聽我介紹的時候，還能看到那個地方的風景。

凱麗：這張是甚麼地圖？跟我們平時看到的地圖不太一樣。

大衛：這是中國的地形圖。棕色代表高原，淺綠色代表山地，深綠色代表平原。

凱麗：中國的地形圖很有意思。中西部都是棕色的。難道說那兒有很多高原和山地嗎？

大衛：是的。你看，中國雖然很大，可是多半都是高原和山地。你看，我這樣寫可以嗎？"中國地形的第一個特點是：山地多，平原少。"

凱麗：當然可以。這些藍色的線代表江河吧？

大衛：對，你看，中國有兩條主要的大河，一條是長江，另一條是黃河，都從西往東流。

凱麗：為甚麼中國的大河都從西往東流呢？

大衛：這個問題問得好。我可以寫第二個特點了，"西部高，東部低"。你看，中國的高原和山地都在中部和西部，平原在東部。黃河和長江都是從西部的高山往東流。

凱麗：那你還可以寫第三個特點，就是"越往西，山越高。"

大衛：對，對。還有別的特點嗎？

凱麗：你是不是應該告訴大家，中國只有一面靠海，其他的三面都是陸地？

大衛：不錯，我把這個特點也寫上去。謝謝你幫我做幻燈片。

凱麗：謝甚麼呀，你太客氣了。

Unit 3.5 對話二

瑪麗婭：凱麗，在經濟課討論的時候，你說了地理環境和經濟發展的關系。我覺得你說得很有道理。

凱麗：是嗎？其實，我是受到了大衛的啓發。前幾天他給我看了中國的地形圖，我突然發現中國的地形非常有特點，這對中國各地的經濟發展一定有影響。後來我上網做了一些研究，今天就把我了解到的情況告訴了大家。

瑪麗婭：原來我不太清楚為甚麼中國東西部的發展會有那麼大的差別，現在知道因為地形的關系，西部有些地區發展經濟非常困難。

凱麗：　是的。比方說，西部有些高原平均海拔在4000米以上，有些地區一年四季都有雪，這樣的地區很難發展農業。

瑪麗婭：不光是農業，發展工業也有困難。山那麼高，要造一條公路或者鐵路都很不容易。這樣，交通一定不方便。

凱麗：　交通不方便，經濟不發達，地理條件又不好，那些地區的人口就比較少。相比之下，中國東部的地形就比較適合人口居住和經濟發展。

瑪麗婭：怪不得中國多數的人都住在東部和中部。

凱麗：　再說，東部有平原，可以種糧食。東部的交通也比西部發達，而且又靠海，跟國外交流方便。這些都對經濟發展有好處。

瑪麗婭：所以中國的大城市都在東部吧？

凱麗：　對，主要的大城市都在東部，比方說，北京、上海、天津、廣州。但是中部也有一些大城市，比如重慶。

瑪麗婭：那是因為中國的中部有一些盆地嗎？

凱麗：　是的。中部有四川盆地，四川盆地的面積很大，四面都是高山，那裏的氣候很好，不常下雪，非常適合農業生產。四川盆地的人口也很多。重慶就在四川盆地，是中國中部的一個經濟中心。

瑪麗婭：我覺得你還提到一個很重要的方面。那就是，因為地形的不同，各地可以發展各種經濟。

凱麗：　對，在高原和山地，因為風景美麗，可以建設旅游區。

瑪麗婭：希望我在中國的時候，有機會去看看高原的美麗風景。

凱麗：　我也是。這樣吧，可能的話，我們倆一起去旅游。

瑪麗婭：太好了。

Unit 3.6 對話一

（在湯姆家。）

媽媽：　爸爸回來了嗎？

湯姆：　還沒有。平時他六點就到家了，現在快六點半了，他怎麼還沒回來？也許因為路上堵車吧。

媽媽：　哦，我想起來了，今天是“環保日”，鼓勵大家都不開車，只用公共交通，走路，或者騎自行車上班。

湯姆：　原來是這樣。我們家除了爸爸以外，大家都挺注意環保的。我和杰米每天都坐地鐵去學校。您每天都騎自行車去上班。

媽媽：　你爸爸因為上班的地方比較遠，公司附近沒有公交車，所以他只好開車。要是公共交通比較方便，他一定也會坐公交車的。

湯姆：　不是說離他們公司不遠，正在蓋地鐵站嗎？地鐵要甚麼時候才能通車？

媽媽：　聽說十月。通車以後，就讓你爸爸也坐地鐵上班。其實我也不願意他多開車。路上車水馬龍，常常堵車，又慢又不安全。再說，如果大家都開車，對環境也不好，污染空氣。

湯姆：　還有，在上海停車特別不容易。有時候，我看爸爸把車開來開去，找一個停車的地方，找半個小時也不一定能找到。要是坐公交，就沒有這種麻煩了。

媽媽：　你說得對。最近三十多年來，中國發展得非常快，不少人都買了房子買了車。不像我小時候，那時候大家都是坐公交車、騎自行車、或者走路去上班上學。路上很少堵車。現在馬路公路造得比以前多得多，但是有車的人增加得也很快，所以一到上下班時間就堵車。

湯姆：　雖然開車有開車的問題，但是我覺得有了車比較自由。特別是到了周末，要去城外玩，坐公交車會花很多時間，還要等車。自己開車方便多了。

媽媽：　大家的想法都差不多，所以到了周末，公路上常常堵車，開開停停，非常慢。有時候，公路成了一個大停車場。

湯姆：　等爸爸回來，我們告訴他，地鐵一通車，他就別開車了。

媽媽：　好主意。

Unit 3.6 對話二

瑪麗婭：學校旁邊的居民社區建設得很快，每天都能看到變化。

凱麗：　對，昨天我們上經濟課的時候，錢老師帶我們去參觀了建設工地，還跟負責建設這個社區的工程師舉行了座談。

瑪麗婭：我看到建設工地的外面有一個牌子，說這將是一個綠色小區。綠色小區跟別的小區有甚麼不一樣？

凱麗：　這正是我們去校外考察的目的。我們的經濟課正在討論經濟發展和環境的關系。大家都認為，既然經濟發展是免不了的，我們應該從一開始就注意怎麼保護環境，不讓環境受到不好的影響。所以我們昨天去參觀的時候，大家問了很多關於"綠色"的問題，特別是綠色建設和綠色材料。

瑪麗婭：甚麼是綠色建設？

凱麗：　就是在建設這個小區的時候，不污染環境，也不浪費資源。這個小區用了不少回收再生的材料，比如，回收再生的木頭、塑料甚麼的。其他的建筑材料也都是低污染的環保材料。

瑪麗婭：說到節約資源，這個小區做了些甚麼？

凱麗：　他們用的都是節能燈泡和節能電器。同時，小區能用太陽能和風能的地方，就用太陽能和風能。這樣不但保護了資源，也讓居民可以少花錢。那個工程師介紹說，住在這個小區不用付很多電費。對了，那個工程師還介紹說，小區的建筑材料比較特別。冬天可以保暖，夏天可以去熱，這可以讓居民節約不少能源。

瑪麗婭：我看過一個電視節目，說的是一個小區怎麼節約用水。這個小區打算怎麼節約用水呢？

凱麗：　他們要重复使用生活用水。居民洗衣洗菜的水，會被小區的綠化再次使用，這樣可以節約很多水。居民可以節約水費。

瑪麗婭：這個小區聽上去真不錯。誰都可以去參觀嗎？

凱麗：　可以，每個星期一、三、五下午都對外開放。你也可以去看看。

瑪麗婭：行，這個星期五下午我就去。

Unit 4.1 對話一

（在學校的電腦房。）

丁老師：同學們，如果你們打算參加高考，就需要上網去填寫高考報名表。請大家先登錄高考報名網站，然後看一下表格。如果有問題，可以問我。

瑪麗婭：丁老師，我還沒決定要不要在中國參加高考呢。您覺得我需要報名嗎？

丁老師：因為報名的時間一共只有五天，所以我建議你先報名。如果你現在不報名，到時候又想去參加高考，那時候再要報名就來不及了。

金順愛：我想去上護理學校，不是大學，也要報名參加高考嗎？

丁老師：是的，護理學校是大專，也是高等教育的一部分。在中國，一個人不管上大學還是上大專都要根據他的高考成績，所以都需要參加高考。

湯姆：丁老師，我已經登錄了，正在填表呢。這裏有幾個詞的意思我不懂，上面問我是"應屆"還是"往屆"高中畢業生，這是甚麼意思？

丁老師：哦，應屆的意思是今年從高中畢業的學生，往屆是前幾年畢業的。

湯姆：報名表上寫的報考科目是：語文、數學、英語。我們只要考三門功課嗎？

丁老師：不是的，還有一門是"綜合"，就是把物理、化學、生物、歷史、地理和政治這六個科目放在一起考。同時，你自己還需要在這六個科目中，再選擇一門作為第五個考試科目。

瑪麗婭：丁老師，我對第五個考試科目不太清楚。

丁老師：是這樣的。綜合考試考的是一般的常識，是每個人都要考的。另外，你還可以根據自己的特長，選擇一門考試。比方說，你覺得自己的物理不錯，就可以選擇物理。如果你的歷史課成績很好，就可以選擇歷史。

湯姆：您是說，高考一共要考五個科目，對嗎？

丁老師：對，四門是固定的，一門由你們自己選擇。

大衛：那高考一共要考多長時間？

丁老師：每個科目要考兩個小時，每天考兩個科目，所以一共要考兩天半。

Unit 4.1 對話二

湯姆：要填高考報考志愿了，你們知道怎麼填嗎？

凱麗：是這樣的，中國的大學分成重點和普通的大學。等高考成績出來以後，先由重點大學根據高考成績挑選他們打算錄取的學生。等他們挑選完了以後，再由普通大學從剩下的學生中挑選。等普通大學選完了，最後由大專挑選。

湯姆： 這麼說，要分三批來挑選學生嗎？

瑪麗婭： 是的。所以在填報考志愿的時候，我們都需要選十二個大學，四個是比較好的大學，四個是普通大學，還有四個是大專。這樣，萬一你考不上最好的大學，還有可能上普通大學，如果普通大學也不錄取你，你還可能上大專。

金順愛： 要是我只想考大專，是不是只要填四個大專就可以了？

凱麗： 我看，也許你可以多填幾個大專，如果你選的大專都錄取你了，你就可以在這幾個大專學校裏選你最喜歡的上。

金順愛： 好主意。

湯姆： 那我們可以選多少個專業呢？

凱麗： 在你報考的每個大學裏，你都可以選六個專業。

湯姆： 哇，太棒了！一個大學可以選六個，十二個大學可以選七十二個不同的專業了。

凱麗： 恐怕只有你會選擇七十二個不同的專業。多數同學一定是在不同的大學報考一樣的專業。

王大明： 就是啊，比方說，我父母非要我當電子工程師不可，所以我選擇的都是電子工程專業。雖然每個大學都可以選六個專業，可是我六個專業選的都是電子工程。

湯姆： 這麼說，你只選了一個專業？為甚麼不選別的專業呢？

王大明： 我非常喜歡電腦。為了讓父母和我自己高興，我是鐵了心要當電子工程師了。

湯姆： 祝你好運。

Unit 4.2 對話一

瑪麗婭： 周英，最近你一下了課就急急忙忙地離開學校，你在忙甚麼呢？

周英： 忙著找工作。

瑪麗婭： 你不打算上大學了？

周英： 我念書念得不太好。一想到高考，我就很緊張，睡覺睡不好，學習也學不進去。雖然我媽媽還是希望我去考大學，但是我決定今年不考了，先去工作。以後如果還想上大學，再去考也來得及。

瑪麗婭： 那你想找哪方面的工作呢？

周英：　當然是比較低層次、低技術的。我原來希望能去當個秘書。可是秘書的工作也不容易找。每次去申請工作，公司都要看我的工作簡歷。我的個人簡歷上除了上學以外，甚麼工作經驗都沒有，人家當然不會要我。

瑪麗婭：聽上去的确很困難。那你打算怎麼辦呢？

周英：　靠親戚朋友幫忙吧。昨天我爸爸的老朋友給我介紹了一個工作，讓我去郊區的一個旅店當服務員。主要是為客人介紹旅店提供的服務，還有附近可參觀的旅游景點。這個工作不是特別理想，因為工資不高，有時候還要上夜班，而且離家很遠，坐公交車來回要三個小時。我媽媽不太愿意讓我去，可是我爸爸說，這是一個鍛煉的機會，可以先做起來，積纍一些工作經驗。

瑪麗婭：你自己怎麼想呢？

周英：　我認為爸爸說得對，萬事開頭難。找第一個工作總是比較難，但是如果我把第一個工作做好了，積纍了一些工作經驗，以後再要找第二個工作就不會那麼難了。再說，那個工作也有長處，福利不錯，旅店每天為我們提供免費午餐和晚餐，一年還有兩個星期的休假。

瑪麗婭：那你甚麼時候開始工作？

周英：　八月一日。第一個月是在職培訓，從九月一日開始正式工作。

瑪麗婭：你去工作以後，別忘了老同學。有空我們多聯系。

周英：　行，一言為定。

Unit 4.2 對話二

瑪麗婭：聽說有些同學高中畢業以後，馬上就去工作。

凱麗：　他們為甚麼不上大學？現在工作市場競爭非常厲害，連有些大學畢業生都找不到工作，高中畢業生就更難了。

大衛：　那要看找甚麼工作。有些工作不需要大學畢業生。

凱麗：　你說得也對，制造業、服務業、農業的一些體力工作，的确不需要大學生。可是那樣的工作比較辛苦。

湯姆：　你覺得辛苦，別人不一定覺得辛苦。有人喜歡動手，有人喜歡動腦。

瑪麗婭：有道理。有人認為坐在辦公室裏舒服，也有人非常討厭坐辦公室。比方說我有一個鄰居叫阿健，去年從高中畢業了。阿健的理想工作是每天都能跟不同的人打交道，所以他適合在商店工作。他可以跟顧客聊天，根據他們的喜愛和需要，把不同的東西賣給他們。阿健的爸爸開了一個商店，高中一畢業他就去那兒當營業員。阿健和他爸爸一樣都是賣東西的天才，所以他們的生意越做越好，有時候忙到半夜才回家，可是他們總是高高興興的。

大衛：只要你熱愛你 的工作，而且努力去做，做甚麼都可能成功。

湯姆：聽你們這麼一說，我可能也不應該去上大學。我最喜歡旅游了，應該想法兒去旅行社找一個工作，當個導游，這樣可以去世界各地逛逛。

瑪麗婭：現在要當導游也不容易，需要從旅游學校畢業，經過正式的訓練，不是誰想當就可以當的。再說，導游這個工作也挺复雜的，不只是帶著游客玩，還得介紹風景點的歷史文化。同時，導游還要安排游客的住、食、行，沒有組織能力，不一定做得了這個工作。

凱麗：對，這個工作得跟許多不同的人打交道。要是碰到一些古怪的游客，也會讓人受不了。湯姆，你沒有客戶服務方面的經驗吧？我看你還是好好考慮一下再決定是不是要去當導游吧。

湯姆：其實當導游只是我的興趣之一。還有不少其他的工作我也很感興趣，比如開飛機、當警察、拍電影甚麼的，這些工作都挺有意思的。我們從小學到高中，在學校呆了十多年了，萬一考上了大學，又得在大學呆四年。你們難道還沒在學校呆夠？不想出去工作工作，輕松輕松嗎？

大衛：我看你把工作想得太容易了，眞的要把一個工作做好，也不能隨隨便便。要是為了輕松一下，我勸你在暑假的時候好好休息休息，不就行了嗎？

凱麗：大衛說得對。如果有兩種方法解決問題，一種簡單，一種复雜，一般的人都是避難就易，湯姆一定是避易就難。他喜歡戲劇化的生活。

湯姆：所以我說嘛，凱麗最理解我了。

Unit 4.3 對話一

(湯姆接到了一個老同學從舊金山打來的電話。)

高樂天：喂，湯姆你好，我是高樂天。你還記得我嗎？我是你的小學同學，上課的時候，我老坐在你旁邊。

湯姆：樂天啊，我們好多年沒見了。你是從哪兒知道我的電話號碼的？

高樂天：你一搬家到上海就把這個電話號碼告訴我了。只不過這麼多年來，我一直沒給你打電話。

湯姆：哦，對不起，我忘了。你還住在舊金山嗎？高中畢業以後打算做甚麼？

高樂天：我們家還住在原來的地方。秋天我就要去紐約大學學習經濟學了。我們還是長話短說吧，我想在暑假的時候到中國去學習漢語。有些問題想問問你。

湯姆：行啊，只要我能幫你的，一定幫你。

高樂天：如果我想去中國留學，要辦哪些手續？

湯姆：先要申請入學。你找到學校了嗎？

高樂天：我對一個語言大學非常感興趣，他們的漢語課程很密集，每天要上四五個小時的漢語課。下午有文化課和個別輔導。每個星期還組織我們去不同的地方旅游參觀。

湯姆：聽上去不錯。你報名了嗎？

高樂天：還沒有，因為大學的網站上說，只收大學生。我不知道他們收不收像我這樣剛從高中畢業的。

湯姆：你不是已經被紐約大學錄取了嗎？你可以把情況跟那個大學談一談。我想應該不是一個大問題。

高樂天：關於住宿，這個大學的網站說，有三種選擇，一是可以住在國際學生宿舍，二是跟當地的中國家庭住在一起，三是自己租房子住。我知道這三種情況都各有長處和短處。我比較想選擇第二種，你看呢？

湯姆：要是我，我也會選擇第二種。跟中國人吃在一起，住在一起，玩在一起，每天有許多練習中文的機會。再說，不知不覺就可以了解到許多中國人的傳統和習慣了。不過，有些中國父母太喜歡管孩子，你住在他們家，他們也會把你當自己的孩子一樣來管。你不會介意吧？

高樂天：應該不會，我父母也老管著我，我習慣被人管了。他們管我，我不是正好可以練習聽力嗎？

湯姆：那你馬上去報名吧，因為被錄取以後，還要辦一些手續才能到中國來。辦手續也需要一定時間。

高樂天：要辦哪些手續？

湯姆：你有護照嗎？沒有的話，需要馬上去辦。大學錄取了你以後，會發給你錄取通知。你拿到錄取通知以後，就可以去中國的大使館辦留學簽證。

高樂天：好，我馬上就上網報名。有了消息，我再告訴你。

湯姆：行，我等你的消息。再見。

Unit 4.3 對話二

瑪麗婭：真對不起，說好昨天晚上要給你打電話的，可是一個鄰居來找我，我跟他談啊談啊，談了兩三個小時，不知不覺就十點了。因為太晚了，就沒給你打電話。

凱麗：你們談甚麼呢？

瑪麗婭：這個鄰居正在上高中，打算明年去美國留學。他選好了三個大學，昨天來向我了解一些出國的細節。

凱麗：現在想去國外留學的中國學生很多，外面有不少辦出國留學手續的公司。他去那兒了解過了嗎？

瑪麗婭：去過了，但是因為一些有名的大學入學要求比較多，所以他雖然了解過了，還是不太清楚。於是他就東問西問，結果是有人說東，有人說西，聽得他糊裏糊塗的。他想我剛剛被美國的加州大學錄取，一定非常了解怎麼入學，所以就來問我。

凱麗：這下他問對人了。

瑪麗婭：希望如此。我告訴他，要去美國上大學，首先要通過一些標準化的考試，像美國的大學入學考試，還有英文考試。

凱麗：除了考試成績以外，美國的大學也需要課程的平均分。是不是有些好大學要求的課程平均分非常高？

瑪麗婭：是的。對許多中國學生來說，考試成績和課程平均分都不是問題。他們在學校裏一天到晚念書，成績非常好。可是一些美國大學對“書呆子”不感興趣，他們比較注意學生的個性。

凱麗：哦，所以申請入學的時候，應該把參加過的課外活動都寫上。課外活動包括很多方面，比如運動、文藝、社區服務、競賽等等。我還是不太清楚，一個大學怎麼了解學生的個性。

瑪麗婭：他們會看你寫的個人陳述，還有老師寫的推荐信。如果考試成績、平均分和個性三方面都非常好，就容易被錄取。

凱麗：被錄取只是第一步。你鄰居知道在美國上大學非常貴嗎？

瑪麗婭：知道，他父母已經存了不少錢，到時候，他們還可以向親戚借點兒錢。對了，他問我，可以不可以在美國一邊打工一邊上學。

凱麗：外國學生好像只能在學校裏打工，不能去校外打工。

瑪麗婭：我還告訴他，等拿到錄取通知以後，他還需要去美國大使館辦簽證。

凱麗：要出國留學需要辦的手續太多了。

瑪麗婭：對啊，所以我們一談就談了兩三個小時。我對他說，如果他想到別的問題，還可以隨時來問我。

Unit 4.4 對話一

凱麗：周末回杭州，看到我媽媽已經在為我準備上大學要用的東西了。

瑪麗婭：你高中還沒畢業呢，現在準備是不是太早了？

湯姆：我看做父母的就是喜歡擔心。我媽媽也一樣，現在她一做飯就說：“湯姆，你快過來學習學習怎麼做飯。以後你離開了家，沒有人為你做飯了。你吃甚麼呢？”我說，“那還不容易？我到飯店裏去吃。”她一聽就急了，說在外邊吃飯又貴又不健康，我的錢會不夠花，我還可能變得很胖。

瑪麗婭：做父母的總是把一些小事情看得很嚴重。好像我們還是小孩子，離開大人就不會生活了。

湯姆： 他們覺得要是我們遇到一點小問題，一定會像無頭蒼蠅，不知道東南西北。

凱麗： 這是用老眼光來看新世界。現在不會做飯有甚麼關系？到處都是食品店，要餓死也不是那麼容易的。做飯遇到難題，我們還可以上網或者打電話去求助。

大衛： 你們一點都不懂得父母的心。他們這麼說，是為了讓你們準備得好一些，這樣你們離開家以後，獨立生活就會容易一些。

凱麗： 大衛眞是個好孩子。那麼理解父母的心。說正經的，你們想過離開家以後的生活嗎？

湯姆： 當然想過，一想到就讓我高興。再也不用晚上十點以前回家了，要多晚回家就多晚回家，一個晚上不回家也沒關系。也不用每天必須吃蔬菜了，想吃就吃，不想吃就不吃。我等了快十八年了，終於要等到自由了！

瑪麗婭： 湯姆，你別把現在的生活說得那麼可怕，好像你被關在監獄裏。

凱麗： 其實這不一定是湯姆的心裏話，想到要離開父母，他也免不了有點兒擔心，有點兒難過。不過為了不讓我們看出他的擔心和難過，就像演戲一樣，老說甚麼“自由要來啦！”

大衛： 湯姆，凱麗說得對嗎？你不是說她最了解你了嗎？

湯姆： 這要看你怎麼看了。半杯水放在那兒，有人看到的是半杯滿了，有人看到的是半杯空了。凱麗是兩面都看到了，我只看到了一面。很難說誰對誰不對。

瑪麗婭： 哇塞，湯姆成外交家了。

Unit 4.4 對話二

瑪麗婭： 湯姆，你在看甚麼呢？

湯姆： 我在看南京大學附近的房子出租廣告。雖然我還不知道能不能上南大，但是先了解一下住宿情況也挺有幫助的。

瑪麗婭： 秋天你不打算住在學生宿舍嗎？

湯姆： 不，我打算自己租一個公寓。

瑪麗婭： 看到合適的房子了嗎？

湯姆：　還沒有。有的太貴，有的太遠，有的條件不好。要找到合適的房子還眞不容易。
瑪麗婭：如果房子太貴，你可能要跟別人合租。遇到負責的室友還可以，要不然，會很麻煩的。
湯姆：　你說得對。所以我已經上網登過找室友的廣告了，有好幾個人愿意跟我合租。可是我父母看了那些人的情況以後，都覺得不理想。
瑪麗婭：有哪些方面不理想？
湯姆：　有幾個是女生，父母不讓我跟女生住。有一個男生，是在南大學體育的，還發來了他的照片。我父母一看就說，這個人長得五大三粗，一點也不像個大學生。還有一個男生也住在上海，因為我們的父母都不放心，所以就決定先在一個咖啡館見個面，看看我們是不是合得來。我覺得那個男生挺好的，非常安靜。可是我媽媽覺得那個男生一點都不成熟。
瑪麗婭：你媽媽怎麼知道那個人不成熟？
湯姆：　我們在咖啡館見面的時候，那個男生不是在用手機打短信，就是在手機上玩游戲，一句話也沒說，都是他父母在說話。
瑪麗婭：聽上去的确不太理想。那你怎麼認為他還不錯呢？
湯姆：　他做的都是我愛做的，我們的興趣很相像。我覺得這樣的室友非常好，我們倆一天到晚都忙自己的事，安安靜靜，客客氣氣，不會互相麻煩的。
瑪麗婭：你說的也有道理，希望你早日找到合適的房子和室友。
湯姆：　謝謝。

Unit 4.5 對話

瑪麗婭：你們去參加畢業舞會嗎？
大衛：　今年學校要舉行畢業舞會嗎？我只知道有畢業典禮。
湯姆：　哦，今年的畢業舞會是由我們美國學生俱樂部舉辦的。如果我們在美國上高中的話，畢業前的一兩個月，大家一定會去參加畢業舞會。既然我們在國際學校，就應該用各個國家的方式來慶祝我們從高中畢業，所以我們向張校長提議，除了中國式的畢業典禮以外，我們還應該舉辦一個美國式的畢業舞會。

瑪麗婭：張校長接受了這個提議，因為國際學校不但有不少美國來的學生，而且還有不少同學秋天要去美國留學。因此，了解一些美國文化對大家都有幫助。

凱麗：太好了。畢業舞會在哪兒舉行？

湯姆：還沒有決定呢。有人提議在學校禮堂，可是美國俱樂部的同學認為，我們應該去國際飯店或者人民公園。

瑪麗婭：這也是美國的一種習慣吧？舞會一般都在一個比較特別的地方舉辦。對許多美國高中生來說，浪漫又盛大的畢業舞會是他們終生難忘的經歷之一。

湯姆：對，高中畢業代表告別青少年時代。舞會是我們一生中一次非常重要的聚會。

大衛：聽說在美國，有些高中生非常重視畢業舞會，甚至比高考還重視。他們覺得考試以後還會有，但是高中畢業舞會一生只有一次。過了這次，就沒下次了。

凱麗：怎麼樣，你們都去嗎？

湯姆：當然要去。我們不應該錯過這次聚會。以後高中同學還要聚在一起就沒那麼容易了。

大衛：去參加舞會是不是要穿非常漂亮的晚禮服？

瑪麗婭：只要穿得正式一些就行了。為了環保，我建議我們今年都不買晚禮服，去租。這樣不會浪費資源。

大衛：好啊，你知道去哪裏租晚禮服嗎？

凱麗：我們可以上網去找。說真的，想到我們不久就要分手了，讓人挺難過的。

湯姆：就是啊。我們這四年互相幫助，互相關心。以後還不知道甚麼時候才能再見。

大衛：這個世界不是變得越來越小了嗎？雖然我們以後不在一起，可是可以打電話寫電郵發短信，放寒暑假的時候，還可以聚在一起。

瑪麗婭：大衛說得對，我們雖然人不在一起，但是心總是在一起的。

Unit 4.5 課文

New	Reply	Reply All	Forward	Print	Delete

明英：你好！

高考成績終於出來了。很幸運我們都考取了大學。首先祝賀你被北京大學錄取了。你一定非常高興吧？湯姆考上了南京大學，他的專業是海洋學。我被上海中醫大學錄取了。希望大學畢業以後，我可以做個中醫。

我是不是已經告訴過你了？瑪麗婭和大衛就要離開中國了。瑪麗婭要去美國加州大學學習亞洲藝術史；大衛決定先去歐洲工作一年再回來上大學。大衛現在會說英語、法語和漢語，這次去歐洲打算學會德語和西班牙語。他計划先去德國住半年，然後去西班牙住半年。在那裏，他要一邊學習外語一邊打工。

在高中的四年，我跟他們三個人形影不離，現在要分手了，還眞有點不習慣呢。以前我們總是一起去這兒，去那兒，做這，做那，可是到了秋天，只有我一個人還留在上海，而且還留在浦東。你知道嗎？上海中醫大學也在浦東，離國際學校不太遠。

在高中的四年，有了你們這些好朋友，生活變得快樂、有意思。我一定會想念你們的。希望我們能繼續保持聯系。好在現在哪兒都有網絡，要聯系非常方便。再說，你、我、湯姆仍然留在中國，到了寒暑假，我們可以聚一聚，你說呢？

我們班的同學打算在分手以前，去瑪麗婭家開晚會。瑪麗婭組織的晚會讓人難忘，這個告別晚會一定也不例外。開晚會的那天，我一定拍許多照片，到時候寄給你。以後只要一看到這些照片，就會想起我們的高中生活，還有在高中時期的好朋友。

對了，你能來參加告別晚會嗎？如果你來，會給大家帶來一個惊喜。晚會定在下個星期四晚上七點。等著你的來信。

你永遠的好朋友，

凱麗

七月二十一日

Unit 4.6 對話一

大衛：　瑪麗婭，你怎麼那麼高興？
瑪麗婭：告訴你一個好消息，我被美國的加州大學錄取了。
大衛：　太好了！祝賀你。
瑪麗婭：你怎麼沒參加高考？你不是填了高考報名表了嗎？
大衛：　是的。我開始沒決定到底參加不參加高考，所以就填了。可是後來我決定今年不上大學了，所以就沒去參加高考。
瑪麗婭：你的功課那麼好，不上大學不是很可惜嗎？
大衛：　大學還是要上的，不過現在不上。我對外語特別感興趣。學外語最好的辦法是住在外國，跟外國人一起生活工作，這樣一邊學一邊用，外語可以學得又好又快。所以高中畢業以後，我要花一年的時間住在國外，一邊學外語，一邊打工。
瑪麗婭：那你以後想去哪個大學呢？
大衛：　還沒想好呢。到了明年再說吧。對了，湯姆也拿到錄取通知書了，他要去南京大學學習海洋學。
瑪麗婭：眞的？他怎麼想出來要學海洋學呢？
大衛：　我也不知道。他填了許多報考志愿，海洋學是其中之一。希望他喜歡那個專業。凱麗怎麼樣？也拿到錄取通知書了嗎？
瑪麗婭：對，她被上海中醫大學錄取了。我們班有三個人學醫。除了凱麗以外，高明要去北京醫科大學。還有金順愛，也考上了護理學校。
大衛：　哎，那個王大明呢？
瑪麗婭：那還用問嗎？他是鐵了心要學電子工程的。他被上海大學電子工程系錄取了。你還記得明英嗎？
大衛：　當然記得，她在云南，考上甚麼大學了。
瑪麗婭：北京大學。
大衛：　她一定非常高興吧？她要去北大學習甚麼專業？
瑪麗婭：跟她父母一樣，她想研究中國少數民族的情況，所以她要去學習考古學。
大衛：　眞不錯。等過了幾年，大家大學畢業以後，一定要聚一聚。那時候，每個人都會有非常有意思的故事和經歷。
瑪麗婭：對，我們五年以後在上海見吧。
大衛：　好，不見不散。

Unit 4.6 對話二

瑪麗婭：湯姆，你找到室友了嗎？

湯姆：不用找了。我在南京郊區租到了一個小房子，不太貴，我可以一個人住了。

瑪麗婭：郊區？那離南大是不是很遠？

湯姆：還可以，騎自行車一個小時。

瑪麗婭：那麼遠啊？那你每天來回要兩個小時。

湯姆：沒關系，正好鍛煉身體。

瑪麗婭：天氣好沒關系，刮風下雨騎那麼長時間的自行車挺辛苦的。

湯姆：現在我可以告訴你我的秘密了。你知道我租校外房子的主要原因是甚麼嗎？我決定要養一些不同的寵物。

瑪麗婭：寵物？你為甚麼要養寵物呢？

湯姆：從小到大，我都非常喜歡動物，想養貓啊，狗啊，兔子啊，小鳥啊甚麼的；可是父母不讓我養。現在我終於可以自己住了，這次是非養不可。我連寵物的名字都想好了，狗的名字叫"毛毛"。貓呢，就叫"樂樂"。兔子我要買兩只，一只叫"小朋"，一只叫"小友"。

瑪麗婭：你是不是想得太簡單了？養那麼多寵物要負很多責任。你每天上學，哪有時間跟它們玩？再說，要是寵物生病了，要看病也很貴的。

湯姆：我都想過了。我可以很節約地生活，比如每天騎自行車上學，不坐公交；自己做飯或者在學生食堂吃飯，不去飯店吃飯；我也不買不需要的東西；為了寵物，我手機也不要了。這樣一來，我的錢就夠了。如果還不夠，我就去打工。反正不管怎麼樣，我一定要養這些寵物。

瑪麗婭：你怎麼不想想學習呢？南京大學是重點大學，能考進去的都是學習非常好的學生，學習上的競爭一定很厲害。你要養那麼多寵物，還要打工，學習會不會受影響呢？

湯姆：別擔心。我終於可以做自己想做的事了。養寵物的事我想了十多年了，好不容易可以獨立生活了，所以我現在雖然身在上海國際學校，可是心早已經飛到南京去了。

瑪麗婭：你說得對，我應該為你高興。你跟那麼多寵物生活在一起，生活一定會很有意思的。

生词索引
Vocabulary Index (Chinese–English)

This list contains vocabulary found in each lesson's New Words and Extend Your Knowledge (EYK) sections. Words from Extend Your Knowledge are shown in color because they are supplementary and not required for students to memorize. For proper nouns, see the Proper Nouns Index.

Simplified	Traditional	Pinyin	Part of Speech	English	Lesson
B					
百闻不如一见	百聞不如一見	bǎi wén bù rú yī jiàn	s.p.	seeing is believing	1.6
百分之		bǎifēnzhī	n.	per cent, percentage	2.1
办	辦	bàn	v.	do, handle	1.2
抱		bào	v.	embrace, hold with arms	3.4
暴		bào	adv.	excessively	2.3
保持		bǎochí	v.	keep, maintain	4.5
保存方法		bǎocúnfāngfǎ	n.	storage (method)	2.4EYK
报告	報告	bàogào	n./v.	report	3.5
报考	報考	bàokǎo	v.	register for examination	4.1
保暖		bǎonuǎn	v.c.	keep something warm	3.6
包水电	包水電	bāoshuǐdiàn	v.o.	utilities included	4.4EYK
保险卡	保險卡	bǎoxiǎnkǎ	n.	medical insurance card (in Taiwan)	1.2EYK
保质期	保質期	bǎozhìqī	n.	good until	2.4EYK
备考	備考	bèikǎo	v.o.	prepare for a test	1.4
本土化		běntǔhuà	n./v.	localization, localize	3.2

Simplified	Traditional	Pinyin	Part of Speech	English	Lesson
避难就易	避難就易	bì nán jiù yì	s.p.	avoid the difficult and choose the easy	4.2
避易就难	避易就難	bì yì jiù nán	s.p.	avoid the easy and choose the difficult	4.2
标语	標語	biāoyǔ	n.	poster, slogan	3.4
标志	標誌	biāozhì	n.	label	2.4
标准化	標準化	biāozhǔnhuà	n./v.	standardization; standardize	4.3
饼干	餅乾	bǐnggān	n.	cookies, crackers	2.4
并且	並且	bìngqiě	conj.	moreover, furthermore	2.5
不见不散	不見不散	bù jiàn bù sàn	s.p.	not leave without seeing each other	4.6
不知不觉	不知不覺	bù zhī bù jué	s.p.	unconsciously, unknowingly	3.3
布丁蛋糕		bùdīngdàngāo	n.	muffin	2.3EYK
不管		bùguǎn	conj.	regardless of, no matter (what, when, where, how…)	1.4
不光		bùguāng	conj.	not only	3.5
不见得	不見得	bùjiàndé	s.f.	not necessarily	2.4
不同一般		bùtóngyībān	s.p.	extraordinary, special	2.1

C

Simplified	Traditional	Pinyin	Part of Speech	English	Lesson
材料		cáiliào	n.	material	3.6
菜系		càixì	n.	cuisine	2.2
参考	參考	cānkǎo	n./v.	reference, consult, refer to	1.5
层次	層次	céngcì	n.	level	4.2
查		chá	v.	check, look up, look into	1.5
差别		chàbié	n.	difference, discrepancy	2.3

Simplified	Traditional	Pinyin	Part of Speech	English	Lesson
茶点	茶點	chádiǎn	n.	refreshments	4.5EYK
柴		chái	n.	firewood	2.5
尝	嘗	cháng	v.	taste	2.2
长话	長話	cháng huà	s.p.	make a long story short	4.3
短说	短說	duǎn shuō			
常识	常識	chángshí	n.	common sense	4.1
产量	產量	chǎnliàng	n.	yield, output	2.1EYK
车水马龙	車水馬龍	chē shuǐ mǎ lóng	s.p.	heavy traffic in the street	3.6
车道	車道	chēdào	n.	(driving) lane	1.3
城		chéng	n.	city	1.3
城市化		chéngshìhuà	v.	urbanize	1.5EYK
城市建筑	城市建築	chéngshìjiànzhù	n.	city building	1.3EYK
成熟		chéngshú	adj.	mature	4.4
陈皮鸡	陳皮雞	chénpíjī	n.	Mandarin chicken	2.5EYK
陈述	陳述	chénshù	n./v.	statement; state	4.3
豉汁鸡	豉汁雞	chǐzhījī	n.	chicken in black bean sauce	2.5EYK
重复		chóngfù	v.	repeat	3.4
串		chuàn	n./v.	string, string together	2.3
创业	創業	chuàngyè	v.o.	start a business	2.2EYK
川酱鸡	川醬雞	Chuānjiàngjī	n.	chicken in Sichuan spicy sauce	2.5EYK
出发城市	出發城市	chūfāchéngshì	n.	starting city	1.1EYK
出发日期	出發日期	chūfārìqī	n.	starting date	1.1EYK
春联	春聯	chūnlián	n.	Spring Festival couplets	3.1
除外		chúwài	v.	except, with the exception of	1.5
出行天数	出行天數	chūxíngtiānshù	n.	number of days on tour	1.1EYK
出租		chūzū	v.	for rent	4.4
出租广告	出租廣告	chūzūguǎnggào	n.	for rent advertisement	4.4EYK
葱油鸡	蔥油雞	cōngyóujī	n.	steamed chicken with onion	2.5EYK

Simplified	Traditional	Pinyin	Part of Speech	English	Lesson
村子		cūnzi	n.	village	1.1
促销	促銷	cùxiāo	v.o.	(promote) sales	3.3EYK

D

Simplified	Traditional	Pinyin	Part of Speech	English	Lesson
达到	達到	dádào	v.	reach	3.2
大概	大概	dàgài	adj./adv.	about, approximately, probably	1.1
呆		dāi	v.	stay	4.2
袋（子）		dài (zi)	n.	bag, pocket	3.4
代表		dàibiǎo	v.	represent	3.5
带家具	帶傢具	dàijiājù	v.o.	furnished	4.4EYK
蛋白质	蛋白質	dànbáizhì	n.	protein	2.4EYK
当地	當地	dāngdì	adj.	local	2.3
到处	到處	dàochù	adv.	everywhere, in all places	3.3
道理		dàolǐ	n.	reason, sense	1.4
道路		dàolù	n.	road	1.3EYK
到期		dàoqī	v.o.	become due, mature, expire	1.5
导游服务	導遊服務	dǎoyóufúwù	n.	tour guide services	1.1EYK
大气层	大氣層	dàqìcéng	n.	atmosphere	3.4EYK
大使馆	大使館	dàshǐguǎn	n.	embassy	4.3
打印		dǎyìn	v.	print	1.5
打印机	打印機	dǎyìnjī	n.	printer	1.5
大众化	大衆化	dàzhònghuà	v.	popularize (make something accessible for ordinary people)	1.5EYK
大专	大專	dàzhuān	n.	junior college	4.1
登		dēng	v.	publish, print	4.4
灯光	燈光	dēngguāng	n.	light	4.5EYK
登录	登錄	dēnglù	v.o.	log on	4.1
灯泡	燈泡	dēngpào	n.	light bulb	3.4

Simplified	Traditional	Pinyin	Part of Speech	English	Lesson
等于	等於	děngyú	v.	equal to, be equivalent to	3.3
电费	電費	diànfèi	n.	electricity bill	4.4EYK
电脑能力	電腦能力	diànnǎonénglì	n.	computer skills	4.2EYK
电器	電器	diànqì	n.	electric appliance	3.6
电气化	電氣化	diànqìhuà	v.	electrify	1.5EYK
电梯	電梯	diàntī	n.	elevator	1.5
电子垃圾	電子垃圾	diànzilājī	n.	electronic waste, e-waste	3.4EYK
电子商业	電子商業	diànzishāngyè	n.	e-commerce	3.3EYK
地道		dìdào	adj.	authentic, real	2.3
订单	訂單	dìngdān	n.	order (form)	3.3
订货	訂貨	dìnghuò	v.o.	order goods	3.3
定金		dìngjīn	n.	deposit	4.4EYK
地球		dìqiú	n.	the earth, the globe	1.6
的确		díquè	adv.	indeed, really	1.2
地下水		dìxiàshuǐ	n.	underground water	3.4EYK
地形		dìxíng	n.	topography, landform	3.5
动笔	動筆	dòngbǐ	v.o.	start writing	1.4
动脑	動腦	dòngnǎo	v.o.	work with mind	4.2
动手	動手	dòngshǒu	v.o.	work with hands	4.2
动物	動物	dòngwù	n.	animal	3.1
豆浆	豆漿	dòujiāng	n.	soy milk	3.2
痘子		dòuzi	n.	pimple	2.5
对…有研究	對…有研究	duì... yǒu yánjiū	v.p.	knowledgeable, well learned	2.2
多媒体	多媒體	duōméitǐ	n.	multimedia	1.5

E

Simplified	Traditional	Pinyin	Part of Speech	English	Lesson
二手店		èrshǒudiàn	n.	second-hand store	3.4

Simplified	Traditional	Pinyin	Part of Speech	English	Lesson
F					
烦	煩	fán	adj.	be tired of	1.4
放鞭炮		fàng biānpào	v.o.	light firecracker	3.1
房东	房東	fángdōng	n.	landlord	4.4EYK
房客		fángkè	n.	renter	4.4EYK
方式		fāngshì	n.	method, way	4.5
凡是		fánshì	adj./adv.	every, any, all	1.5
饭团	飯糰	fàntuán	n.	rice ball (usu. w/stuffing)	3.2
发票	發票	fāpiào	n.	sales receipt	3.3EYK
发生	發生	fāshēng	n./v.	occurrence, occur, happen	3.3
发现	發現	fāxiàn	n./v.	discovery, discover	3.5
非…不可		fēi...bùkě	s.p.	must, have to	4.1
废话	廢話	fèihuà	n.	nonsense, rubbish	2.4
废气	廢氣	fèiqì	n.	exhaust gas, tail gas	3.4EYK
风能	風能	fēngnéng	n.	wind energy	3.6
分手		fēnshǒu	v.o.	part company, say good bye, separate	4.5
复读	複讀	fùdú	v.	re-study high school courses for next year's college entrance examination	4.1EYK
福利		fúlì	n.	benefits, welfare	4.2
服务业	服務業	fúwùyè	n.	service industry	4.2
复印	復印	fùyìn	v.	make a photocopy, duplicate	1.5
G					
盖	蓋	gài	v.	build	1.3
改变	改變	gǎibiàn	n./v.	change	3.2
咖喱鸡	咖喱雞	gālíjī	n.	curry chicken	2.3EYK

Simplified	Traditional	Pinyin	Part of Speech	English	Lesson
敢		gǎn	v.	dare, venture	2.2
感想		gǎnxiǎng	n.	reflections, impressions	1.4
告别		gàobié	v.o.	part from, say good bye	4.5
高级	高級	gāojí	adj.	high-class, high-ranking	2.6
高原		gāoyuán	n.	plateau	3.5
耕地		gēngdì	n.	arable land, farm land	2.1
耕种	耕種	gēngzhòng	v.	plough and sow, cultivate	2.1EYK
个人爱好	個人愛好	gèrénàihào	n.	interests/hobbies	4.2EYK
个人化	個人化	gèrénhuà	v.	individualize	1.5EYK
个人信息	個人信息	gèrénxìnxī	n.	personal information	4.2EYK
个性	個性	gèxìng	n.	personality	4.3
个性化	個性化	gèxìnghuà	v.	personalize	1.5EYK
宫保鸡	宮保雞	gōngbǎojī	n.	Kung Pao chicken	2.5EYK
工地		gōngdì	n.	construction site	1.3
供电系统	供電系統	gòngdiànxìtǒng	n.	electricity supply system	1.3EYK
公费医疗证	公費醫療證	gōngfèiyīliáokǎ	n.	medical care ID card	1.2EYK
公路		gōnglù	n.	highway	1.1
供煤气系统	供煤氣系統	gòngméiqìxìtǒng	n.	gas supply system	1.3EYK
供水系统	供水系統	gòngshuǐxìtǒng	n.	water supply system	1.3EYK
工业化	工業化	gōngyèhuà	n./v.	industrialization, industrialize	2.1
供应商	供應商	gòngyìngshāng	n.	supplier	3.3EYK
工资卡	工資卡	gōngzīkǎ	n.	salary card (Similar to an ATM card)	1.2EYK
工作经历	工作經歷	gōngzuòjīnglì	n.	work (experience)	4.2EYK
工作证	工作證	gōngzuòzhèng	n.	employee ID card	1.2EYK
购物方便	購物方便	gòuwùfāngbiàn		close to shopping	4.4EYK
古		gǔ	adj.	ancient	1.3

Simplified	Traditional	Pinyin	Part of Speech	English	Lesson
关	關	guān	v.	close, shut, turn off	1.3
广播	廣播	guǎngbō	n./v.	broadcast, be on the air	1.4
广告	廣告	guǎnggào	n.	advertisement	3.3
古代		gǔdài	n.	ancient time	2.5
固定		gùdìng	adj./v.	fixed; fix	4.1
古怪		gǔguài	adj.	odd, eccentric	4.2
贵宾	貴賓	guìbīn	n.	distinguished guest	4.5EYK
古迹	古跡	gǔjī	n.	ancient site	3.2
顾客	顧客	gùkè	n.	customer	2.1
鼓励	鼓勵	gǔlì	n./v.	encouragement, encourage	3.6
国定假日	國定假日	guódìng jiàrì	n.	national holidays	1.5
果干	菓乾	guǒgān	n.	dried fruit	2.2

H

Simplified	Traditional	Pinyin	Part of Speech	English	Lesson
海拔		hǎibá	n.	height above sea level	3.5
海洋学	海洋學	hǎiyángxué	n.	ocean studies	4.5
好处	好處	hǎochù	n.	advantage, benefit	2.3
豪华游	豪華游	háohuáyóu	n.	luxurious tour	1.1EYK
好客		hàokè	adj.	hospitable	2.5
合得来		hédelái	s.p.	get along well	4.4
合同		hétóng	n.	contract	2.1
合租		hézū	v.	co-rent, co-lease	4.4
后代	後代	hòudài	n.	descendant	3.1
画龙点睛	畫龍點睛	huà long diǎn jīng	s.f.	add the final touch	3.4
坏处	壞處	huàichù	n.	disadvantage, harm	2.3
幻灯片	幻燈片	huàndēngpiàn	n.	slide	3.4
黄瓜		huángguā	n.	cucumber	3.2
换货	換貨	huànhuò	v.o.	exchange (goods)	3.3EYK
化学品	化學品	huàxuépǐn	n.	chemical product	2.4
回收		huíshōu	v.	recycle, recover	3.4

Simplified	Traditional	Pinyin	Part of Speech	English	Lesson
回味		huíwèi	n./v.	aftertaste, retrospect	2.6
会议	會議	huìyì	n.	meeting, conference	1.5
会员	會員	huìyuán	n.	membership, member	1.2
会员证	會員證	huìyuánzhèng	n.	membership card	1.2EYK
护理	護理	hùlǐ	n./v.	nursing care; nurse	4.1
糊里糊涂	糊裡糊塗	húlihútu	s.p.	muddle-headed, puzzled, mixed up	2.4
货到付款	貨到付款	huòdàofùkuǎn	s.p.	cash on delivery	3.3EYK
货运	貨運	huòyùn	n.	shipping	2.2EYK
糊涂	糊塗	hútu	n.	muddle-headed, puzzled, mixed up	2.4
护照	護照	hùzhào	n.	passport	4.3

J

Simplified	Traditional	Pinyin	Part of Speech	English	Lesson
夹		jiā	v.	press from both sides (pick up food with chopsticks)	2.5
加工		jiāgōng	v.	process	2.1
简单	簡單	jiǎndān	adj.	simple	2.3
酱		jiàng	n.	sauce	2.5
监考老师	監考老師	jiānkǎolǎoshī	n.	teachers who administer (monitor) the test	4.1EYK
简历	簡歷	jiǎnlì	n.	resume	4.2
减少		jiǎnshǎo	v.	decrease, reduce	1.1
监狱	監獄	jiānyù	n.	prison	4.4
交流		jiāoliú	n./v.	exchange, interchange	3.5
交通方便		jiāotōngfāngbiàn		close to transportation	4.4EYK
脚印		jiǎoyìn	n.	footprint	3.1
教育经历	教育經歷	jiàoyùjīnglì	n.	education (experience)	4.2EYK
家庭聚会	家庭聚會	jiātíngjùhuì		family gathering	3.1EYK
基础	基礎	jīchǔ	n.	base, foundation	1.4

Simplified	Traditional	Pinyin	Part of Speech	English	Lesson
结合	結合	jiéhé	n./v.	combination, combine	2.6
解决		jiějué	v.	solve	2.1
节能	節能	jiénéng	v.o.	save energy	3.4
借书证	借書証	jièshū zhèng	n.	library card	1.2
街头食品	街頭食品	jiētóu shípǐn	n.	street food, food sold on street	2.6
介意		jièyì	v.	mind, take offense	4.3
节约	節約	jiéyuē	v.	save, practice thrift	3.1
几何	幾何	jǐhé	n.	geometry	1.4
积极	積極	jījí	adj.	active, positive, vigorous	1.4
积累	積累	jīlěi	n./v.	accumulation; accumulate	4.2
景点	景點	jǐngdiǎn	n.	scenic point, scenic spot	3.1
经过	經過	jīngguò	v.	pass, go by	1.3
净含量	淨含量	jìnghánliàng	n.	net weight	2.4EYK
景区	景區	jǐngqū	n.	scenic area	1.1EYK
景色		jǐngsè	n.	scenery, scene	1.1
经商	經商	jīngshāng	v.o.	do business (formal)	2.2EYK
惊喜	驚喜	jīngxǐ	n./adj.	pleasant surprise; pleasantly surprised	4.5
紧张	緊張	jǐnzhāng	adj.	nervous, tense, intense	4.2
既然		jìrán	conj.	now that, since, as	3.3
聚		jù	v.	gather	2.5
举一反三	舉一反三	jǔ yī fǎn sān	s.p.	draw inferences	1.4
举例子	舉例子	jǔlìzi	v.o.	give an example, cite an example	2.5
军队	軍隊	jūnduì	n.	army, troops	2.2
军人证	軍人證	jūnrénzhèng	n.	military ID	1.2EYK
居留证	居留證	jūliú zhèng	n.	resident card	1.2EYK

K

开联欢会	開聯歡會	kāiliánhuānhuì	v.o.	have a get-together	3.1EYK

Simplified	Traditional	Pinyin	Part of Speech	English	Lesson
看灯	看燈	kàndēng	v.o.	look at lights	3.1EYK
看体育比赛	看體育比賽	kàntǐyù bǐsài	v.o.	watch sports competition	3.1EYK
看文娱表演		kànwényù biǎoyǎn	v.o.	watch entertainment shows	3.1EYK
看焰火		kànyànhuǒ	v.o.	watch fireworks	3.1EYK
考场	考場	kǎochǎng	n.	place to take the test	4.1EYK
考古学	考古學	kǎogǔxué	n.	archaeology	4.6
考生		kǎoshēng	n.	test taker	4.1EYK
客户		kèhù	n.	client	2.2EYK
科目		kēmù	n.	subject (in a curriculum), course	4.1
可怕		kěpà	adj.	terrible, terrifying	4.4
可惜		kěxī	adj	it's a pity, it's too bad, unfortunate	1.1
可笑		kěxiào	adj.	laughable, ridiculous, funny	3.4
空调旅游车	空調旅遊車	kōngtiáo lǚyóuchē	n.	air-conditioned coach	1.1EYK
枯燥		kūzào	adj.	dry, boring, uninteresting	2.1
L					
来宾	來賓	láibīn	n.	guest who comes	4.5EYK
垃圾		lājī	n.	trash, rubbish	3.1
垃圾分类	垃圾分類	lājīfēnlèi	n./v.	categorize waste (trash)	3.4EYK
浪费	浪費	làngfèi	n./v.	waste	3.3
浪漫		làngmàn	adj.	romantic	4.5
老同学聚会	老同學聚會	lǎotóngxué jùhuì		re-union with former classmates	3.1EYK
辣子鸡	辣子雞	làzijī	n.	spicy chicken	2.5EYK
冷冻	冷凍	lěngdòng	adj.	frozen	2.3

Simplified	Traditional	Pinyin	Part of Speech	English	Lesson
立竿见影	立竿見影	lì gān jiàn yǐng	s.p.	set up a pole and see its shadow – get instant results	2.5
粮食		liángshí	n.	grain	2.1
凉性		liángxìng	n.	cool type (of food or medicine)	2.5
连锁(店)	連鎖(店)	liánsuǒ(diàn)	n.	chain store	3.2
礼品卡	禮品卡	lǐpǐn kǎ	n.	gift card	1.2
留		liú	v.	ask someone to stay	2.5
留学	留學	liúxué	v.o.	study abroad	4.3
例外		lìwài	adj./n.	exceptional; exception	4.5
理想		lǐxiǎng	adj./n.	ideal	1.3
理想主义	理想主義	lǐxiǎngzhǔyì	n.	idealism	3.3
陆地	陸地	lùdì	n.	land	3.5
绿化	綠化	lǜhuà	v.	make an area green	1.5EYK
绿化地带	綠化地帶	lǜhuàdìdài	n.	green area	1.3EYK
落榜		luòbǎng	v.o.	be off the admission list	4.1EYK
落榜生		luòbǎngshēng	n.	student who is off the admission list	4.1EYK
录取	錄取	lùqǔ	n.	admission	4.1EYK
录取 分数线	錄取 分數線	lùqǔ fēnshùxiàn	n.	cut-off scores for admission	4.1EYK
绿色生产	綠色生產	lǜsèshēngchǎn	n.	green production	3.4EYK
绿色消费	綠色消費	lǜsèxiāofèi	n.	green consumption	3.4EYK
旅游网	旅遊網	lǚyóuwǎng	n.	tourism website	1.1EYK
旅游线路	旅遊線路	lǚyóuxiànlù	n.	tour route	1.1EYK

M

马车	馬車	mǎchē	n.	horse cart, horse carriage	1.1
美化		měihuà	v.	beautify	1.5EYK

Simplified	Traditional	Pinyin	Part of Speech	English	Lesson
煤气费	煤氣費	méiqìfèi	n.	gas bill	4.4EYK
美食		měishí	n.	delicious food	2.6
美食家		měishíjiā	n.	food connoisseur	2.2
门票自理	門票自理	ménpiàozìlǐ		entrance ticket not included	1.1EYK
米		mǐ	n.	rice (uncooked)	2.5
免不了		miǎnbùliǎo	s.p.	can't help, be unavoidable	3.3
免费运货	免費運貨	miǎnfèiyùnhuò	n.	free shipping	3.3EYK
面食	麵食	miànshí	n.	food made of wheat	2.1
密集		mìjí	adj.	intensive	4.3
民以食为天	民以食為天	mín yǐ shí wéi tiān	s.p.	bread is the staff of life	2.1
名言		míngyán	n.	well-known saying	2.5
莫名其妙		mò míng qí miào	s.p.	baffling, absurd, be baffled	3.1
目录	目錄	mùlù	n.	catalog	1.5
木头	木頭	mùtóu	n.	wood	3.6

N

Simplified	Traditional	Pinyin	Part of Speech	English	Lesson
难题	難題	nántí	n.	difficult problem, headache	1.4
哪怕		nǎpà	conj.	even, even if, even though	2.5
嫩		nèn	adj.	tender, delicate	2.2
能源		néngyuán	n.	energy	2.3
柠檬鸡	檸檬雞	níngméngjī	n.	lemon chicken	2.5EYK
浓	濃	nóng	adj.	strong, dense, thick	2.2
农场	農場	nóngchǎng	n.	farm	2.1EYK
农产品	農產品	nóngchǎnpǐn	n.	agricultural produce	2.1EYK
农地	農地	nóngdì	n.	farmland	2.1EYK

Simplified	Traditional	Pinyin	Part of Speech	English	Lesson
农民	農民	nóngmín	n.	farmer	1.1
农田	農田	nóngtián	n.	farmland	2.1EYK
农业技术	農業技術	nóngyèjìshù	n.	farming techniques	2.1EYK
农业科学	農業科學	nóngyèkēxué	n.	agricultural science	2.1EYK
农业生产	農業生產	nóngyèshēngchǎn	n.	agricultural production	2.1EYK
农作物	農作物	nóngzuòwù	n.	agricultural crops	2.1EYK
暖气	暖氣	nuǎnqì	n.	heater, warm air	3.4

P

Simplified	Traditional	Pinyin	Part of Speech	English	Lesson
泡菜		pàocài	n.	pickled vegetables	2.3EYK
配料		pèiliào	n.	ingredients	2.4EYK
盆地		péndì	n.	basin	3.5
批		pī	m.w.	batch, lot, group	4.1
品尝	品嘗	pǐncháng	v.	taste	2.3
拼车	拼車	pīnchē	v.o.	share a ride	3.4
平均		píngjūn	n.	mean, average	3.5
平均分		píngjūnfēn	n.	grade point average (GPA)	4.3
平平安安		píngpíng'ān'ān	adv.	safely, quietly	3.1
乒乒乓乓		pīngpīngpāngpāng	ono.	bang, ping	3.1
平原		píngyuán	n.	plain	2.1
普通		pǔtōng	adj.	general, common, ordinary	4.1

Q

Simplified	Traditional	Pinyin	Part of Speech	English	Lesson
浅	淺	qiǎn	adj.	light (color), shallow	3.5
钱包	錢包	qiánbāo	n.	wallet	1.2
签证	簽證	qiānzhèng	n./v.o.	visa; issue a visa	4.3
敲门	敲門	qiāomén	v.o.	knock on the door	3.3
启发	啓發	qǐfā	n./v.	enlightenment, enlighten, illuminate	3.5
清淡		qīngdàn	adj.	light (food)	2.2

Simplified	Traditional	Pinyin	Part of Speech	English	Lesson
轻轨	輕軌	qīngguǐ	n.	light rail	1.1
请柬	請柬	qǐngjiǎn	n.	invitation	4.5EYK
气球	氣球	qìqiú	n.	balloon	3.1
其他专长	其他專長	qítāzhuāncháng	n.	other special skills	4.2EYK
求职意向	求職意向	qiúzhíyìxiàng	n.	seeking a job in…	4.2EYK
全程导游	全程導遊	quánchéngdǎoyóu	n.	tour guide throughout the trip	1.1EYK
全球化		quánqiúhuà	n./v.	globalization, globalize	2.3
取款		qǔkuǎn	v.o.	withdraw money	1.2

R

Simplified	Traditional	Pinyin	Part of Speech	English	Lesson
热爱	熱愛	rè'ài	v.	love	4.2
热量	熱量	rèliàng	n.	calories	2.4EYK
扔		rēng	v.	throw, toss, cast	3.4
认为	認為	rènwéi	v.	think, consider	4.2
热性	熱性	rèxìng	n.	hot type (of food or medicine)	2.5
日新月异	日新月異	rì xīn yuè yì	s.p.	change rapidly, change day by day	1.3
日记	日記	rìjì	n.	diary	1.4
肉串		ròuchuàn	n.	kabobs	2.3EYK
入乡随俗	入鄉隨俗	rù xiāng suí sú	s.p.	when in Rome, do as the Romans do	3.2
如此		rúcǐ	s.f.	such, like that, so	4.3
入学	入學	rùxué	v.o.	enter a school, enroll	4.3

S

Simplified	Traditional	Pinyin	Part of Speech	English	Lesson
杀	殺	shā	v.	kill	2.2
山地		shāndì	n.	hilly area	2.1
上榜		shàngbǎng	v.o.	be on the admission list	4.1EYK
商城		shāngchéng	n.	shopping center, big store	3.3EYK

Simplified	Traditional	Pinyin	Part of Speech	English	Lesson
商法		shāngfǎ	n.	business law	2.2EYK
商机	商機	shāngjī	n.	business opportunity	2.2EYK
商家		shāngjiā	n.	business (company, store)	3.3EYK
商品		shāngpǐn	n.	commodity	2.2EYK
商人		shāngrén	n.	businessman	2.2
上网卡	上網卡	shàngwǎngkǎ	n.	Internet card	1.2EYK
商务	商務	shāngwù	n.	business	2.2EYK
商业化	商業化	shāngyèhuà	n./v.	commercialization, commercialize	3.1
烧	燒	shāo	v.	cook, burn	2.4
烧烤	燒烤	shāokǎo	n.	barbecue, roast	2.3
设备	設備	shèbèi	n.	device, equipment	1.3
社会化	社會化	shèhuìhuà	v.	socialize	1.5EYK
深		shēn	adj.	deep (color), deep	3.5
身份证	身份證	shēnfènzhèng	n.	ID card	1.2EYK
生		shēng	adj.	raw, uncooked	2.2
生产	生產	shēngchǎn	n./v.	production, produce	3.1
生产厂家	生產廠家	shēngchǎnchǎngjiā	n.	manufacturer	2.4EYK
生产日期	生產日期	shēngchǎnrìqī	n.	manufacturing date	2.4EYK
盛大		shèngdà	adj.	grand, spectacular	4.5
生态环境	生態環境	shēngtàihuánjìng	n.	ecological environment	3.4EYK
升学	升學	shēngxué	v.o.	go to a higher-level school, matriculate	4.1
生意		shēngyì	n.	business, business transaction	2.2
生长	生長	shēngzhǎng	v.	grow	2.6
湿		shī	adj.	wet	2.6
市场	市場	shìchǎng	n.	market	2.2EYK
适合	適合	shìhé	v.	suit, fit, be appropriate for	3.5
实际上	實際上	shíjìshàng	conj.	actually, as a matter of fact, in fact	2.1

Simplified	Traditional	Pinyin	Part of Speech	English	Lesson
时髦	時髦	shímáo	adj.	fashionable	3.3
视听	視聽	shìtīng	n.	audio-video	1.5
失望		shīwàng	n./v.o.	disappointment, lose hope	3.2
实习经历	實習經歷	shíxíjīnglì	n.	internship (experience)	4.2EYK
使用		shǐyòng	v.	use	3.4
室友		shìyǒu	n.	roommate	4.4
收成		shōuchéng	n.	crop harvest	2.1EYK
售货机	售貨機	shòuhuòjī	n.	vending machine	1.3
寿司	壽司	shòuī	n.	sushi	2.3EYK
手续	手續	shǒuxù	n.	procedures, formalities, processes	4.3
熟		shú	adj.	cooked	2.4
薯条	薯條	shǔtiáo	n.	French fries	2.3EYK
刷（卡）		shuā (kǎ)	v.(o.)	swipe the card	1.2
涮		shuàn	v.	dip in boiling water, rinse	2.2
书呆子	書呆子	shūdāizi	n.	nerd, bookworm	4.3
水费	水費	shuǐfèi	n.	water bill	4.4EYK
水平		shuǐpíng	n.	level	1.4
水源		shuǐyuán	n.	water resource	3.4EYK
数量	數量	shùliàng	n.	quantity	2.2
数码化	數碼化	shùmǎhuà	v.	digitize	1.5EYK
顺便	順便	shùnbiàn	adv.	in passing, conveniently	3.2
死		sǐ	v.	die	3.2
私有化		sīyǒuhuà	v.	privatize	1.5EYK
送旧迎新	送舊迎新	sòng jiù yíng xīn	s.p.	greet the new year	3.1
酸雨		suānyǔ	n.	acid rain	3.4EYK
随时	隨時	suíshí	adv.	at any time, at all times	4.3
塑料		sùliào	n.	plastic	3.4

Simplified	Traditional	Pinyin	Part of Speech	English	Lesson
T					
太阳能	太陽能	tàiyángnéng	n.	solar energy	3.6
糖精		tángjīng	n.	artificial sugar	2.4
套餐		tàocān	n.	set meal, set menu	3.2
讨厌	討厭	tǎoyàn	adj./v.	disgusting, dislike, be disgusted with	3.3
特长	特長	tècháng	n.	special skill, strong point, specialty	4.1
特价游	特價游	tèjiàyóu	n.	tour special	1.1EYK
特色		tèsè	n.	special characteristics/ feature	2.2
天长地久	天長地久	tiān cháng dì jiǔ	s.p.	everlasting, enduring as long as the heaven and the earth	4.5
天然		tiānrán	adj.	natural	2.4
甜酸鸡	甜酸雞	tiánsuānjī	n.	sweet and sour chicken	2.5EYK
天堂		tiāntáng	n.	paradise, heaven	2.6
甜甜圈		tiántiánquān	n.	donut	2.3EYK
条件	條件	tiáojiàn	n.	condition, qualification	1.5
调料	調料	tiáoliào	n.	seasoning	2.5
挑选	挑選	tiāoxuǎn	v.	select, choose	4.1
提到		tídào	v.	mention	3.5
铁了心	鐵了心	tiě le xīn	s.p.	unshakable in one's determination	4.1
铁板鸡	鐵板雞	tiěbǎnjī	n.	sizzling chicken	2.5EYK
铁路	鐵路	tiělù	n.	railway, rail	1.1
体力	體力	tǐlì	n.	physical strength	4.2
提议	提議	tíyì	n./v.	propose; proposal	4.5
同步		tóngbù	adj./n.	synchronous, synchronization	1.4
同步教学	同步教學	tóngbùjiàoxué	n.	synchronous education	1.4EYK

Simplified	Traditional	Pinyin	Part of Speech	English	Lesson
通车	通車	tōngchē	v.o.	be open to traffic	1.6
通信网络	通信網絡	tōngxìnxìtǒng	n.	communication network	1.3EYK
土地		tǔdì	n.	land	2.1EYK
推	推	tuī	v.	push	3.3
退货	退貨	tuìhuò	v.o.	return (goods)	3.3EYK
推荐信	推薦信	tuījiànxìn	n.	recommendation letter	4.3
兔子		tùzi	n.	rabbit	3.3

W

Simplified	Traditional	Pinyin	Part of Speech	English	Lesson
外交家		wàijiāojiā	n.	diplomat	4.4
万事开头难	萬事開頭難	wàn shì kāi tóu nán	s.p.	the first step is difficult	4.2
网店	網店	wǎngdiàn	n.	online store	3.3EYK
往届	往屆	wǎngjiè	n.	previous graduating classes	4.1
网路	網路	wǎnglù	n.	net, network *(in Taiwan)*	1.6
网络	網絡	wǎngluò	n.	net, network *(in mainland China)*	1.6
网络大学	網絡大學	wǎngluòdàxué	n.	cyber university	1.4EYK
网络教育	網絡教育	wǎngluòjiàoyù	n.	online (cyber) education	1.4EYK
网络教育学院	網絡教育學院	wǎngluòjiàoyù xuéyuàn	n.	online educational institution	1.4EYK
网上教学	網上教學	wǎngshàngjiàoxué	n.	E-learning	1.4EYK
网上课程	網上課程	wǎngshàngkèchéng	n.	online course	1.4EYK
网校	網校	wǎngxiào	n.	online school, school on the web	1.4
晚礼服	晚禮服	wǎnlǐfú	n.	formal party dress/wear	4.5
万一	萬一	wànyī	conj.	in case, if by any chance	1.2
味精		wèijīng	n.	monosodium glutamate (MSG)	2.4
五大三粗		wǔ dà sān cū	s.p.	big and tall, muscular, sturdy	4.4

Simplified	Traditional	Pinyin	Part of Speech	English	Lesson
物尽其用	物盡其用	wù jǐn qí yòng	n.	make the best use of everything	3.4
舞伴		wǔbàn	n.	dance partner	4.5EYK
午餐自理		wǔcānzìlǐ		lunch excluded	1.1EYK
舞会	舞會	wǔhuì	n.	ball, dancing party	4.5
无论	無論	wúlùn	conj.	regardless of, no matter (what, whether…)	2.3
污染		wūrǎn	n./v.	pollution, pollute	2.4
污水		wūshuǐ	n.	wastewater	3.4EYK
无头苍蝇	無頭蒼蠅	wútóu cāngyíng	n.	headless fly	4.4
无线	無線	wúxiàn	adj.	wireless	1.3
无线上网卡	無線上網卡	wúxiàn shàngwǎngkǎ	n.	wireless card	1.2EYK

X

Simplified	Traditional	Pinyin	Part of Speech	English	Lesson
馅饼	餡餅	xiànbǐng	n.	pie (sweet or salty)	2.3EYK
相比之下		xiāng bǐ zhī xià	s.p.	in comparison	3.5
香精		xiāngjīng	n.	artificial flavor	2.4
香料		xiāngliào	n.	spice	2.5
想念		xiǎngniàn	v.	miss, think about	1.3
相似		xiāngsì	adj.	similar	2.3
想像		xiǎngxiàng	v.	imagine	2.1
相信		xiāngxìn	v.	believe	3.3
香叶鸡	香葉雞	xiāngyèjī	n.	basil chicken	2.5EYK
现金	現金	xiànjīn	n.	cash	1.2
鲜美	鮮美	xiānměi	adj.	delicious, fresh and tasty	2.2
消防		xiāofáng	n.	fire fighting	1.3EYK
消费者	消費者	xiāofèizhě	n.	consumer	3.3EYK
小麦	小麥	xiǎomài	n.	wheat	2.1
销售	銷售	xiāoshòu	n./v.	sell/sales	2.2EYK
下水道		xiàshuǐdào	n.	sewer	1.3EYK

Simplified	Traditional	Pinyin	Part of Speech	English	Lesson
西方化		Xīfānghuà	n./v.	Westernization, Westernize	3.2
习惯	習慣	xíguàn	n./v.	custom; be accustomed to	4.3
细节	細節	xìjié	n.	details, specifics	4.3
戏剧化	戲劇化	xìjùhuà	n./v.	dramatization, dramatize	4.2
形影不离	形影不離	xíng yǐng bù lí	s.p.	inseparable as body and shadow, always together	4.5
幸亏	幸虧	xìngkuī	adv.	fortunately, luckily	1.3
形象		xíngxiàng	n.	image	3.4
信息		xìnī	n.	information	2.4
辛苦		xīnkǔ	adj.	hard, laborious	4.6
信用		xìnyòng	n.	credit	1.2
休闲	休閒	xiūxián	v.	lie fallow	3.1EYK
吸引		xīyǐn	v.	attract	2.1
宣传	宣傳	xuānchuán	v.	give publicity to	3.4
选择	選擇	xuǎnzé	n./v.	choice, choose, select	2.3
学生证	學生証	xuéshēng zhèng	n.	student ID card	1.2
虚拟大学	虛擬大學	xūnǐdàxué	n.	cyber learning community that simulates a university	1.4EYK
虚拟教室	虛擬教室	xūnǐjiàoshì	n.	cyber learning community that simulates a classroom	1.4EYK

Y

Simplified	Traditional	Pinyin	Part of Speech	English	Lesson
烟尘	煙塵	yānchén	n.	smoke dust	3.1
养活	養活	yǎnghuó	v.c.	support, feed	2.1
羊肉		yángròu	n.	lamb	2.2
眼光		yǎnguāng	n.	sight, view	4.4

Simplified	Traditional	Pinyin	Part of Speech	English	Lesson
盐水鸡	鹽水雞	yánshuǐjī	n.	boiled salted chicken	2.5EYK
夜班		yèbān	n.	night shift	4.2
野生		yěshēng	adj.	wild	3.1
野味		yěwèi	n.	game (as food)	3.1
业务	業務	yèwù	n.	business, professional work	2.2EYK
业务员	業務員	yèwùyuán	n.	sales person	2.2EYK
亿	億	yì	n.	a hundred million	2.2
一草一木		yī cǎo yī mù	s.p.	all plants, every plant	3.1
一言为定	一言為定	yī yán wéi dìng	s.p.	it's a deal, a promise is a promise	1.1
医保卡	醫保卡	yībǎokǎ	n.	medical insurance card	1.2EYK
异步教学	異步教學	yìbùjiàoxué	n.	asynchronous education	1.4EYK
医疗	醫療	yīliáo	n.	medical care	1.3EYK
因此		yīncǐ	conj.	therefore, hence, for this reason	4.5
应届	應屆	yìngjiè	n.	the present graduating year	4.1
应急系统	應急系統	yìngjíxìtǒng	n.	emergency system	1.3EYK
营销	營銷	yíngxiāo	n./v.	sales	2.2EYK
营养成分表	營養成份表	yíngyǎngchénfèn biǎo	n.	nutrition facts	2.4EYK
营养学	營養學	yíngyǎngxué	n.	nutriology, nutrition	2.5
音乐节目主持人	音樂節目主持人	yīnyuèjiémù zhǔchírén	n.	disc jockey	4.5EYK
一日游	一日遊	yīrìyóu	n.	one-day tour	1.1EYK
一室一厅一卫	一室一廳一衛	yīshìyītīng yīwèi		one bedroom, one living area, and one bath	4.4EYK
一再		yīzài	adv.	repeatedly, time and again	1.1
游	遊	yóu	v.	tour	1.1

Simplified	Traditional	Pinyin	Part of Speech	English	Lesson
邮电	郵電	yóudiàn	n.	postal service	1.3EYK
邮购	郵購	yóugòu	v.	mail order	3.3EYK
有机	有機	yǒujī	adj.	organic	2.4
尤其		yóuqí	adv.	particularly, especially	2.3
游山玩水	遊山玩水	yóushānwánshuǐ	s.p.	go to scenic spots	3.1EYK
油条	油條	yóutiáo	n.	fried bread stick	3.2
游行	遊行	yóuxíng	v.	parade	3.1EYK
远程	遠程	yuǎnchéng	adj.	long-distance, remote	1.4
远程教育	遠程教育	yuǎnchéngjiàoyù	n.	distance learning	1.4EYK
原理		yuánlǐ	n.	principle, theory	1.4
遇到		yùdào	v.	encounter, run into	4.4
预订	預訂	yùdìng	v.	reserve, make a reservation	1.5
乐曲	樂曲	yuèqǔ	n.	music	4.5EYK
月租		yuèzū	n.	monthly rent	4.4EYK
愉快		yúkuài	adj.	pleasant, happy	2.5
玉米		yùmǐ	n.	corn	3.2
玉米饼	玉米餅	yùmǐbǐng	n.	taco, tortilla	2.3EYK
运	運	yùn	v.	ship, transport	2.3
运费	運費	yùnfèi	n.	shipping cost	3.3EYK
于是	於是	yúshì	conj.	hence, consequently, as a result	3.3
语文	語文	yǔwén	n.	language	1.4
语言能力	語言能力	yǔyánnénglì	n.	language skills	4.2EYK

Z

再生		zàishēng	v.	regenerate, revive	3.4
再生能源		zàishēngnéngyuán	n.	regenerated energy	3.4EYK
在线教育	在線教育	zàixiànjiàoyù	n.	online education	1.4EYK
在职	在職	zàizhí	adj.	on the job	4.2
噪音		zàoyīn	n.	noise	3.1

Simplified	Traditional	Pinyin	Part of Speech	English	Lesson
杂志	雜誌	zázhì	n.	magazine	1.5
增加		zēngjiā	n./v.	increase	1.5
占	佔	zhàn	v.	take up, occupy	2.1
账户	賬戶	zhànghù	n.	account	1.2
招生办公室	招生辦公室	zhāoshēng bàngōngshì	n.	admission office	4.1EYK
招生简章	招生簡章	zhāoshēngjiǎnzhāng	n.	admission (information) brochure	4.1EYK
炸薯片		zháshǔpiàn	n.	friend potato chips	2.4
炸鱼	炸魚	zháyú	n.	fried fish	2.3EYK
正经	正經	zhèngjīng	adj.	proper, serious	4.4
争取	爭取	zhēngqǔ	v.	strive for, fight for	1.4
政治		zhèngzhì	n.	politics	4.1
值得	值得	zhídé	adj.	worthwhile	2.1
脂肪		zhīfáng	n.	fat	2.4EYK
直销店	直銷店	zhíxiāodiàn	n.	outlet store	3.3EYK
纸屑	紙屑	zhǐxiè	n.	shredded paper	3.1
志愿	志願	zhìyuàn	n.	wish, aspiration, ideal	4.1
制造	製造	zhìzào	v.	make, manufacture	2.4
制造商	製造商	zhìzàoshāng	n.	manufacturer	2.4EYK
制造业	製造業	zhìzàoyè	n.	manufacturing industry	4.2
种	種	zhòng	v.	plant, grow	2.3
中东口袋面包	中東口袋麵包	Zhōngdōngkǒudài miànbāo	n.	pita bread	2.3EYK
中国化	中國化	Zhōngguóhuà	v.	make it Chinese	3.2
终身	終身	zhōngshēn	adj.	lifelong, all one's life	4.5
中性		zhōngxìng	n.	neutral type (of food or medicine)	2.5
终于	終於	zhōngyú	adv.	finally, in the end, at last	1.3
周记	週記	zhōujì	n.	weekly journal	1.4
装		zhuāng	v.	install	1.3

Simplified	Traditional	Pinyin	Part of Speech	English	Lesson
主持人		zhǔchírén	n.	host	4.5EYK
住房		zhùfáng	n.	housing, house	1.3
祝贺	祝賀	zhùhè	n./v.	congratulation; congratulate	4.5
准考证	准考證	zhǔnkǎozhèng	n.	test taker ID card	4.1EYK
猪肉	豬肉	zhūròu	n.	pork	3.2
住宿		zhùsù	n.	housing, lodging	4.3
自从	自從	zìcóng	prep.	since	1.3
自动	自動	zìdòng	adj.	automatic	1.3
自动化	自動化	zìdònghuà	n./v.	automation, make something automated	1.5
自然		zìrán	adj./n.	natural, nature	1.1
资源	資源	zīyuán	n.	resource	3.1
自助游	自助遊	zìzhùyóu	n.	self-guided tour	1.1EYK
总的来说	總的來說	zǒngdeláishuō	s.p.	in summary, in the final analysis	2.1
综合	綜合	zōnghé	adj.	comprehensive	4.1
总结	總結	zǒngjié	n./v.	summary, summarize	1.4
棕色		zōngsè	n.	brown	3.5
走马观花	走馬觀花	zǒu mǎ guān huā	s.f.	glance over things in a hurry	3.2
走亲访友	走親訪友	zǒuqīnfángyǒu	s.p.	visit relatives and friends	3.1EYK
租		zū	v.	rent, lease	4.3
租房合同		zūfánghétóng	n.	lease agreement	4.4EYK
租金		zūjīn	n.	rent	4.4EYK
做买卖	做買賣	zuòmǎimài	v.o.	do business (informal)	2.2EYK
作为	作為	zuòwéi	v.c.	regard as, as	4.1
作物		zuòwù	n.	crop	2.1
祖先		zǔxiān	n.	ancestor	2.2

生词索引
Vocabulary Index (English–Chinese)

This list contains vocabulary found in each lesson's New Words and Extend Your Knowledge (EYK) sections. Words from Extend Your Knowledge are shown in color because they are supplementary and not required for students to memorize. For proper nouns, see the Proper Nouns Index.

English	Simplified	Traditional	Pinyin	Lesson
A				
about, approximately, probably	大概	大概	dàgài	1.1
account	账户	賬戶	zhànghù	1.2
accumulation; accumulate	积累	積累	jīlěi	4.2
acid rain	酸雨		suānyǔ	3.4EYK
active, positive, vigorous	积极	積極	jījí	1.4
actually, as a matter of fact, in fact	实际上	實際上	shíjìshàng	2.1
add the final touch	画龙点睛	畫龍點睛	huà long diǎn jīng	3.4
admission	录取	錄取	lùqǔ	4.1EYK
admission (information) brochure	招生简章	招生簡章	zhāoshēng jiǎnzhāng	4.1EYK
admission office	招生办公室	招生辦公室	zhāoshēng bàngōngshì	4.1EYK
advantage, benefit	好处	好處	hǎochù	2.3
advertisement	广告	廣告	guǎnggào	3.3
aftertaste, retrospect	回味		huíwèi	2.6

English	Simplified	Traditional	Pinyin	Lesson
agricultural crops	农作物	農作物	nóngzuòwù	2.1EYK
agricultural produce	农产品	農產品	nóngchǎnpǐn	2.1EYK
agricultural production	农业生产	農業生產	nóngyèshēngchǎn	2.1EYK
agricultural science	农业科学	農業科學	nóngyèkēxué	2.1EYK
air-conditioned coach	空调旅游车	空調旅遊車	kōngtiáolǚyóuchē	1.1EYK
all plants, every plant	一草一木		yī cǎo yī mù	3.1
ancestor	祖先		zǔxiān	2.2
ancient	古		gǔ	1.3
ancient site	古迹	古跡	gǔjī	3.2
ancient time	古代		gǔdài	2.5
animal	动物	動物	dòngwù	3.1
arable land, farm land	耕地		gēngdì	2.1
archaeology	考古学	考古學	kǎogǔxué	4.6
army, troops	军队	軍隊	jūnduì	2.2
artificial flavor	香精		xiāngjīng	2.4
artificial sugar	糖精		tángjīng	2.4
ask someone to stay	留		liú	2.5
asynchronous education	异步教学	異步教學	yìbùjiàoxué	1.4EYK
at any time, at all times	随时	隨時	suíshí	4.3
atmosphere	大气层	大氣層	dàqìcéng	3.4EYK
attract	吸引		xīyǐn	2.1
audio-video	视听	視聽	shìtīng	1.5
authentic, real	地道		dìdào	2.3
automatic	自动	自動	zìdòng	1.3
automation, make something automated	自动化	自動化	zìdònghuà	1.5
avoid the difficult and choose the easy	避难就易	避難就易	bì nán jiù yì	4.2
avoid the easy and choose the difficult	避易就难	避易就難	bì yì jiù nán	4.2

English	Simplified	Traditional	Pinyin	Lesson
B				
baffling, absurd, be baffled	莫名其妙		mò míng qí miào	3.1
bag, pocket	袋（子）		dài (zi)	3.4
ball, dancing party	舞会	舞會	wǔhuì	4.5
balloon	气球	氣球	qìqiú	3.1
bang, ping	乒乒乓乓		pīngpīngpāngpāng	3.1
barbecue, roast	烧烤	燒烤	shāokǎo	2.3
base, foundation	基础	基礎	jīchǔ	1.4
basil chicken	香叶鸡	香葉雞	xiāngyèjī	2.5EYK
basin	盆地		péndì	3.5
batch, lot, group	批		pī	4.1
be off the admission list	落榜		luòbǎng	4.1EYK
be on the admission list	上榜		shàngbǎng	4.1EYK
be open to traffic	通车	通車	tōngchē	1.6
be tired of	烦	煩	fán	1.4
beautify	美化		měihuà	1.5EYK
become due, mature, expire	到期		dàoqī	1.5
believe	相信		xiāngxìn	3.3
benefits, welfare	福利		fúlì	4.2
big and tall, muscular, sturdy	五大三粗		wǔ dà sān cū	4.4
boiled salted chicken	盐水鸡	鹽水雞	yánshuǐjī	2.5EYK
bread is the staff of life	民以食为天	民以食為天	mín yǐ shí wéi tiān	2.1
broadcast, be on the air	广播	廣播	guǎngbō	1.4
brown	棕色		zōngsè	3.5
build	盖	蓋	gài	1.3
business	商务	商務	shāngwù	2.2EYK
business (company, store)	商家		shāngjiā	3.3EYK
business law	商法		shāngfǎ	2.2EYK
business opportunity	商机	商機	shāngjī	2.2EYK
business, business transaction	生意		shēngyì	2.2
business, professional work	业务	業務	yèwù	2.2EYK

English	Simplified	Traditional	Pinyin	Lesson
businessman	商人		shāngrén	2.2

C

English	Simplified	Traditional	Pinyin	Lesson
calories	热量	熱量	rèliàng	2.4EYK
can't help, be unavoidable	免不了		miǎnbùliǎo	3.3
cash	现金	現金	xiànjīn	1.2
cash on delivery	货到付款	貨到付款	huòdàofùkuǎn	3.3EYK
catalog	目录	目錄	mùlù	1.5
categorize waste (trash)	垃圾分类	垃圾分類	lājīfēnlèi	3.4EYK
chain store	连锁(店)	連鎖(店)	liánsuǒ(diàn)	3.2
change	改变	改變	gǎibiàn	3.2
change rapidly, change day by day	日新月异	日新月異	rì xīn yuè yì	1.3
check, look up, look into	查		chá	1.5
chemical product	化学品	化學品	huàxuépǐn	2.4
chicken in black bean sauce	豉汁鸡	豉汁雞	chǐzhījī	2.5EYK
chicken in Sichuan spicy sauce	川酱鸡	川醬雞	Chuānjiàngjī	2.5EYK
choice, choose, select	选择	選擇	xuǎnzé	2.3
city	城		chéng	1.3
city building	城市建筑	城市建築	chéngshìjiànzhù	1.3EYK
client	客户		kèhù	2.2EYK
close to shopping	购物方便	購物方便	gòuwùfāngbiàn	4.4EYK
close to transportation	交通方便		jiāotōngfāngbiàn	4.4EYK
close, shut, turn off	关	關	guān	1.3
combination, combine	结合	結合	jiéhé	2.6
commercialization, commercialize	商业化	商業化	shāngyèhuà	3.1
commodity	商品		shāngpǐn	2.2EYK
common sense	常识	常識	chángshí	4.1
communication network	通信网络	通信網絡	tōngxìnxìtōng	1.3EYK
comprehensive	综合	綜合	zōnghé	4.1
computer skills	电脑能力	電腦能力	diànnǎonénglì	4.2EYK

English	Simplified	Traditional	Pinyin	Lesson
condition, qualification	条件	條件	tiáojiàn	1.5
congratulation; congratulate	祝贺	祝賀	zhùhè	4.5
construction site	工地		gōngdì	1.3
consumer	消费者	消費者	xiāofèizhě	3.3EYK
contract	合同		hétóng	2.1
cook, burn	烧	燒	shāo	2.4
cooked	熟		shú	2.4
cookies, crackers	饼干	餅乾	bǐnggān	2.4
cool type (of food or medicine)	凉性		liángxìng	2.5
co-rent, co-lease	合租		hézū	4.4
corn	玉米		yùmǐ	3.2
credit	信用		xìnyòng	1.2
crop	作物		zuòwù	2.1
crop harvest	收成		shōuchéng	2.1EYK
cucumber	黄瓜		huángguā	3.2
cuisine	菜系		càixì	2.2
curry chicken	咖喱鸡	咖喱雞	gālìjī	2.3EYK
custom; be accustomed to	习惯	習慣	xíguàn	4.3
customer	顾客	顧客	gùkè	2.1
cut-off scores for admission	录取分数线	錄取分數線	lùqǔfēnshùxiàn	4.1EYK
cyber learning community that simulates a classroom	虚拟教室	虛擬教室	xūnǐjiàoshì	1.4EYK
cyber learning community that simulates a university	虚拟大学	虛擬大學	xūnǐdàxué	1.4EYK
cyber university	网络大学	網絡大學	wǎngluòdàxué	1.4EYK

D

English	Simplified	Traditional	Pinyin	Lesson
dance partner	舞伴		wǔbàn	4.5EYK
dare, venture	敢		gǎn	2.2

English	Simplified	Traditional	Pinyin	Lesson
decrease, reduce	减少		jiǎnshǎo	1.1
deep (color), deep	深		shēn	3.5
delicious food	美食		měishí	2.6
delicious, fresh and tasty	鲜美	鮮美	xiānměi	2.2
deposit	定金		dìngjīn	4.4EYK
descendant	后代	後代	hòudài	3.1
details, specifics	细节	細節	xìjié	4.3
device, equipment	设备	設備	shèbèi	1.3
diary	日记	日記	rìjì	1.4
difference, discrepancy	差别		chàbié	2.3
difficult problem, headache	难题	難題	nántí	1.4
digitize	数码化	數碼化	shùmǎhuà	1.5EYK
dip in boiling water, rinse	涮		shuàn	2.2
diplomat	外交家		wàijiāojiā	4.4
disadvantage, harm	坏处	壞處	huàichù	2.3
disappointment, lose hope	失望		shīwàng	3.2
disc jockey	音乐节目主持人	音樂節目主持人	yīnyuèjiémù zhǔchírén	4.5EYK
discovery, discover	发现	發現	fāxiàn	3.5
disgusting, dislike, be disgusted with	讨厌	討厭	tǎoyàn	3.3
distance learning	远程教育	遠程教育	yuǎnchéngjiàoyù	1.4EYK
distinguished guest	贵宾	貴賓	guìbīn	4.5EYK
do business (formal)	经商	經商	jīngshāng	2.2EYK
do business (informal)	做买卖	做買賣	zuòmǎimài	2.2EYK
do, handle	办	辦	bàn	1.2
donut	甜甜圈		tiántiánquān	2.3EYK
dramatization, dramatize	戏剧化	戲劇化	xìjùhuà	4.2
draw inferences	举一反三	舉一反三	jǔ yī fǎn sān	1.4
dried fruit	果干	菓乾	guǒgān	2.2
(driving) lane	车道	車道	chēdào	1.3
dry, boring, uninteresting	枯燥		kūzào	2.1

English	Simplified	Traditional	Pinyin	Lesson
E				
ecological environment	生态环境	生態環境	shēngtàihuánjìng	3.4EYK
e-commerce	电子商业	電子商業	diànzishāngyè	3.3EYK
education (experience)	教育经历	教育經歷	jiàoyùjīnglì	4.2EYK
E-learning	网上教学	網上教學	wǎngshàngjiàoxué	1.4EYK
electric appliance	电器	電器	diànqì	3.6
electricity bill	电费	電費	diànfèi	4.4EYK
electricity supply system	供电系统	供電系統	gòngdiànxìtǒng	1.3EYK
electrify	电气化	電氣化	diànqìhuà	1.5EYK
elevator	电梯	電梯	diàntī	1.5
embassy	大使馆	大使館	dàshǐguǎn	4.3
embrace, hold with arms	抱		bào	3.4
emergency system	应急系统	應急系統	yìngjíxìtǒng	1.3EYK
employee ID card	工作证	工作證	gōngzuòzhèng	1.2EYK
encounter, run into	遇到		yùdào	4.4
encouragement, encourage	鼓励	鼓勵	gǔlì	3.6
energy	能源		néngyuán	2.3
enlightenment, enlighten, illuminate	启发	啓發	qǐfā	3.5
enter a school, enroll	入学	入學	rùxué	4.3
entrance ticket not included	门票自理	門票自理	ménpiàozìlǐ	1.1EYK
equal to, be equivalent to	等于	等於	děngyú	3.3
even, even if, even though	哪怕		nǎpà	2.5
everlasting, enduring as long as the heaven and the earth	天长地久	天長地久	tiān cháng dì jiǔ	4.5
every, any, all	凡是		fánshì	1.5
everywhere, in all places	到处	到處	dàochù	3.3
e-waste	电子垃圾	電子垃圾	diànzilājī	3.4EYK
except, with the exception of	除外		chúwài	1.5
exceptional; exception	例外		lìwài	4.5
excessively	暴		bào	2.3
exchange (goods)	换货	換貨	huànhuò	3.3EYK

English	Simplified	Traditional	Pinyin	Lesson
exchange, interchange	交流		jiāoliú	3.5
exhaust gas, tail gas	废气	廢氣	fèiqì	3.4EYK
extraordinary, special	不同一般		bùtóngyībān	2.1
extremely, die	死		sǐ	3.2

F

English	Simplified	Traditional	Pinyin	Lesson
family gathering	家庭聚会	家庭聚會	jiātíngjùhuì	3.1EYK
farm	农场	農場	nóngchǎng	2.1EYK
farmer	农民	農民	nóngmín	1.1
farming techniques	农业技术	農業技術	nóngyèjìshù	2.1EYK
farmland	农地	農地	nóngdì	2.1EYK
farmland	农田	農田	nóngtián	2.1EYK
fashionable	时髦	時髦	shímáo	3.3
fat	脂肪		zhīfáng	2.4EYK
finally, in the end, at last	终于	終於	zhōngyú	1.3
fire fighting	消防		xiāofáng	1.3EYK
firewood	柴		chái	2.5
fixed; fix	固定		gùdìng	4.1
food connoisseur	美食家		měishíjiā	2.2
food made of wheat	面食	麵食	miànshí	2.1
footprint	脚印		jiǎoyìn	3.1
for rent	出租		chūzū	4.4
for rent advertisement	出租广告	出租廣告	chūzūguǎnggào	4.4EYK
formal party dress/wear	晚礼服	晚禮服	wǎnlǐfú	4.5
fortunately, luckily	幸亏	幸虧	xìngkuī	1.3
free shipping	免费运货	免費運貨	miǎnfèiyùnhuò	3.3EYK
French fries	薯条	薯條	shǔtiáo	2.3EYK
fried bread stick	油条	油條	yóutiáo	3.2
fried fish	炸鱼	炸魚	zháyú	2.3EYK
friend potato chips	炸薯片		zháshǔpiàn	2.4
frozen	冷冻	冷凍	lěngdòng	2.3
furnished	带家具	帶傢具	dàijiājù	4.4EYK

English	Simplified	Traditional	Pinyin	Lesson
G				
game (as food)	野味		yěwèi	3.1
gas bill	煤气费	煤氣費	méiqìfèi	4.4EYK
gas supply system	供煤气系统	供煤氣系統	gòngméiqìxìtǒng	1.3EYK
gather	聚		jù	2.5
general, common, ordinary	普通		pǔtōng	4.1
geometry	几何	幾何	jǐhé	1.4
get along well	合得来		hédelái	4.4
gift card	礼品卡	禮品卡	lǐpǐn kǎ	1.2
give an example, cite an example	举例子	舉例子	jǔlìzi	2.5
give publicity to	宣传	宣傳	xuānchuán	3.4
glance over things in a hurry	走马观花	走馬觀花	zǒu mǎ guān huā	3.2
globalization, globalize	全球化		quánqiúhuà	2.3
go to a higher-level school, matriculate	升学	升學	shēngxué	4.1
go to scenic spots	游山玩水	遊山玩水	yóushānwánshuǐ	3.1EYK
good until	保质期	保質期	bǎozhìqī	2.4EYK
grade point average (GPA)	平均分		píngjūnfēn	4.3
grain	粮食		liángshí	2.1
grand, spectacular	盛大		shèngdà	4.5
green area	绿化地带	綠化地帶	lǜhuàdìdài	1.3EYK
green consumption	绿色消费	綠色消費	lǜsèxiāofèi	3.4EYK
green production	绿色生产	綠色生產	lǜsèshēngchǎn	3.4EYK
greet the new year	送旧迎新	送舊迎新	sòng jiù yíng xīn	3.1
grow	生长	生長	shēngzhǎng	2.6
guest who comes	来宾	來賓	láibīn	4.5EYK
H				
hard, laborious	辛苦		xīnkǔ	4.6
have a get-together	开联欢会	開聯歡會	kāiliánhuānhuì	3.1EYK
headless fly	无头苍蝇	無頭蒼蠅	wútóu cāngyíng	4.4

English	Simplified	Traditional	Pinyin	Lesson
heater, warm air	暖气	暖氣	nuǎnqì	3.4
heavy traffic in the street	车水马龙	車水馬龍	chē shuǐ mǎ lóng	3.6
height above sea level	海拔		hǎibá	3.5
hence, consequently, as a result	于是	於是	yúshì	3.3
high-class, high-ranking	高级	高級	gāojí	2.6
highway	公路		gōnglù	1.1
hilly area	山地		shāndì	2.1
horse cart, horse carriage	马车	馬車	mǎchē	1.1
hospitable	好客		hàokè	2.5
host	主持人		zhǔchírén	4.5EYK
hot type (of food or medicine)	热性	熱性	rèxìng	2.5
housing, house	住房		zhùfáng	1.3
housing, lodging	住宿		zhùsù	4.3
hundred million	亿	億	yì	2.2

I

English	Simplified	Traditional	Pinyin	Lesson
ID card	身份证	身份證	shēnfènzhèng	1.2EYK
ideal	理想		lǐxiǎng	1.3
idealism	理想主义	理想主義	lǐxiǎngzhǔyì	3.3
image	形象		xíngxiàng	3.4
imagine	想像		xiǎngxiàng	2.1
in case, if by any chance	万一	萬一	wànyī	1.2
in comparison	相比之下		xiāng bǐ zhī xià	3.5
in passing, conveniently	顺便	順便	shùnbiàn	3.2
in summary, in the final analysis	总的来说	總的來說	zǒngdeláishuō	2.1
increase	增加		zēngjiā	1.5
indeed, really	的确		díquè	1.2
individualize	个人化	個人化	gèrénhuà	1.5EYK
industrialization, industrialize	工业化	工業化	gōngyèhuà	2.1
information	信息		xìnī	2.4
ingredients	配料		pèiliào	2.4EYK

English	Simplified	Traditional	Pinyin	Lesson
inseparable as body and shadow, always together	形影不离	形影不離	xíng yǐng bù lí	4.5
install	装		zhuāng	1.3
intensive	密集		mìjí	4.3
interests/hobbies	个人爱好	個人愛好	gèrénàihào	4.2EYK
Internet card	上网卡	上網卡	shàngwǎngkǎ	1.2EYK
internship (experience)	实习经历	實習經歷	shíxíjīnglì	4.2EYK
invitation	请柬	請柬	qǐngjiǎn	4.5EYK
it's a deal, a promise is a promise	一言为定	一言為定	yī yán wéi dìng	1.1
it's a pity, it's too bad, unfortunate	可惜		kěxī	1.1

J

junior college	大专	大專	dàzhuān	4.1

K

kabobs	肉串		ròuchuàn	2.3EYK
keep something warm	保暖		bǎonuǎn	3.6
keep, maintain	保持		bǎochí	4.5
kill	杀	殺	shā	2.2
knock on the door	敲门	敲門	qiāomén	3.3
knowledgeable, well learned	对…有研究	對…有研究	duì...yǒu yánjiū	2.2
Kung Pao chicken	宫保鸡	宮保雞	gōngbǎojī	2.5EYK

L

label	标志	標誌	biāozhì	2.4
lamb	羊肉		yángròu	2.2
land	陆地	陸地	lùdì	3.5
land	土地		tǔdì	2.1EYK
landlord	房东	房東	fángdōng	4.4EYK
language	语文	語文	yǔwén	1.4

English	Simplified	Traditional	Pinyin	Lesson
language skills	语言能力	語言能力	yǔyánnénglì	4.2EYK
laughable, ridiculous, funny	可笑		kěxiào	3.4
lease agreement	租房合同		zūfánghétóng	4.4EYK
lemon chicken	柠檬鸡	檸檬雞	níngméngjī	2.5EYK
level	层次	層次	céngcì	4.2
level	水平		shuǐpíng	1.4
library card	借书证	借書証	jièshū zhèng	1.2
lie fallow	休闲	休閒	xiūxián	3.1EYK
lifelong, all one's life	终身	終身	zhōngshēn	4.5
light	灯光	燈光	dēngguāng	4.5EYK
light (color), shallow	浅	淺	qiǎn	3.5
light (food)	清淡		qīngdàn	2.2
light bulb	灯泡	燈泡	dēngpào	3.4
light firecracker	放鞭炮		fàng biānpào	3.1
light rail	轻轨	輕軌	qīngguǐ	1.1
local	当地	當地	dāngdì	2.3
localization, localize	本土化		běntǔhuà	3.2
log on	登录	登錄	dēnglù	4.1
long-distance, remote	远程	遠程	yuǎnchéng	1.4
look at lights	看灯	看燈	kàndēng	3.1EYK
love	热爱	熱愛	rè'ài	4.2
lunch excluded	午餐自理		wǔcānzìlǐ	1.1EYK
luxurious tour	豪华游	豪華游	háohuáyóu	1.1EYK

M

English	Simplified	Traditional	Pinyin	Lesson
magazine	杂志	雜誌	zázhì	1.5
mail order	邮购	郵購	yóugòu	3.3EYK
make a long story short	长话	長話	cháng huà	4.3
	短说	短說	duǎn shuō	
make a photocopy, duplicate	复印	復印	fùyìn	1.5
make an area green	绿化	綠化	lǜhuà	1.5EYK
make it Chinese	中国化	中國化	Zhōngguóhuà	3.2

English	Simplified	Traditional	Pinyin	Lesson
make the best use of everything	物尽其用	物盡其用	wù jǐn qí yòng	3.4
make, manufacture	制造	製造	zhìzào	2.4
Mandarin chicken	陈皮鸡	陳皮雞	chénpíjī	2.5EYK
manufacturer	生产厂家	生產廠家	shēngchǎnchǎngjiā	2.4EYK
manufacturer	制造商	製造商	zhìzàoshāng	2.4EYK
manufacturing date	生产日期	生產日期	shēngchǎnrìqī	2.4EYK
manufacturing industry	制造业	製造業	zhìzàoyè	4.2
market	市场	市場	shìchǎng	2.2EYK
material	材料		cáiliào	3.6
mature	成熟		chéngshú	4.4
mean, average	平均		píngjūn	3.5
medical care	医疗	醫療	yīliáo	1.3EYK
medical care ID card	公费医疗证	公費醫療證	gōngfèiyīliáokǎ	1.2EYK
medical insurance card	医保卡	醫保卡	yībǎokǎ	1.2EYK
medical insurance card (in Taiwan)	保险卡	保險卡	bǎoxiǎnkǎ	1.2EYK
meeting, conference	会议	會議	huìyì	1.5
membership card	会员证	會員證	huìyuánzhèng	1.2EYK
membership, member	会员	會員	huìyuán	1.2
mention	提到		tídào	3.5
method, way	方式		fāngshì	4.5
military ID	军人证	軍人證	jūnrénzhèng	1.2EYK
mind, take offense	介意		jièyì	4.3
miss, think about	想念		xiǎngniàn	1.3
monosodium glutamate (MSG)	味精		wèijīng	2.4
monthly rent	月租		yuèzū	4.4EYK
moreover, furthermore	并且	並且	bìngqiě	2.5
muddle-headed, puzzled, mixed up	糊里糊涂	糊裡糊塗	húlihútu	2.4

English	Simplified	Traditional	Pinyin	Lesson
muddle-headed, puzzled, mixed up	糊涂	糊塗	hútu	2.4
muffin	布丁蛋糕		bùdīngdàngāo	2.3EYK
multimedia	多媒体	多媒體	duōméitǐ	1.5
music	乐曲	樂曲	yuèqǔ	4.5EYK
must, have to	非…不可		fēi...bùkě	4.1

N

English	Simplified	Traditional	Pinyin	Lesson
national holidays	国定假日	國定假日	guódìng jiàrì	1.5
natural	天然		tiānrán	2.4
natural, nature	自然		zìrán	1.1
nerd, bookworm	书呆子	書呆子	shūdāizi	4.3
nervous, tense, intense	紧张	緊張	jǐnzhāng	4.2
net weight	净含量	淨含量	jìnghánliàng	2.4EYK
net, network *(in mainland China)*	网络	網絡	wǎngluò	1.6
net, network *(in Taiwan)*	网路	網路	wǎnglù	1.6
neutral type (of food or medicine)	中性		zhōngxìng	2.5
night shift	夜班		yèbān	4.2
noise	噪音		zàoyīn	3.1
nonsense, rubbish	废话	廢話	fèihuà	2.4
not leave without seeing each other	不见不散	不見不散	bù jiàn bù sàn	4.6
not necessarily	不见得	不見得	bùjiàndé	2.4
not only	不光		bùguāng	3.5
now that, since, as	既然		jìrán	3.3
number of days on tour	出行天数	出行天數	chūxíngtiānshù	1.1EYK
nursing care; nurse	护理	護理	hùlǐ	4.1
nutriology, nutrition	营养学	營養學	yíngyǎngxué	2.5
nutrition facts	营养成分表	營養成份表	yíngyǎngchénfèn biǎo	2.4EYK

English	Simplified	Traditional	Pinyin	Lesson
O				
occurrence, occur, happen	发生	發生	fāshēng	3.3
ocean studies	海洋学	海洋學	hǎiyángxué	4.5
odd, eccentric	古怪		gǔguài	4.2
on the job	在职	在職	zàizhí	4.2
one bedroom, one living area, and one bath	一室一厅一卫	一室一廳一衛	yīshìyītīng yīwèi	4.4EYK
one-day tour	一日游	一日遊	yīrìyóu	1.1EYK
online (cyber) education	网络教育	網絡教育	wǎngluòjiàoyù	1.4EYK
online course	网上课程	網上課程	wǎngshàngkèchéng	1.4EYK
online education	在线教育	在線教育	zàixiànjiàoyù	1.4EYK
online educational institution	网络教育学院	網絡教育學院	wǎngluòjiàoyù xuéyuàn	1.4EYK
online school, school on the web	网校	網校	wǎngxiào	1.4
online store	网店	網店	wǎngdiàn	3.3EYK
order (form)	订单	訂單	dìngdān	3.3
order goods	订货	訂貨	dìnghuò	3.3
organic	有机	有機	yǒujī	2.4
other special skills	其他专长	其他專長	qítāzhuāncháng	4.2EYK
outlet store	直销店	直銷店	zhíxiāodiàn	3.3EYK
P				
parade	游行	遊行	yóuxíng	3.1EYK
paradise, heaven	天堂		tiāntáng	2.6
part company, say good bye, separate	分手		fēnshǒu	4.5
part from, say good bye	告别		gàobié	4.5
particularly, especially	尤其		yóuqí	2.3
pass, go by	经过	經過	jīngguò	1.3
passport	护照	護照	hùzhào	4.3
per cent, percentage	百分之		bǎifēnzhī	2.1

English	Simplified	Traditional	Pinyin	Lesson
personal information	个人信息	個人信息	gèrénxìnxī	4.2EYK
personality	个性	個性	gèxìng	4.3
personalize	个性化	個性化	gèxìnghuà	1.5EYK
physical strength	体力	體力	tǐlì	4.2
pickled vegetables	泡菜		pàocài	2.3EYK
pie (sweet or salty)	馅饼	餡餅	xiànbǐng	2.3EYK
pimple	痘子		dòuzi	2.5
pita bread	中东口袋面包	中東口袋麵包	Zhōngdōngkǒudài miànbāo	2.3EYK
place to take the test	考场	考場	kǎochǎng	4.1EYK
plain	平原		píngyuán	2.1
plant, grow	种	種	zhòng	2.3
plastic	塑料		sùliào	3.4
plateau	高原		gāoyuán	3.5
pleasant surprise; pleasantly surprised	惊喜	驚喜	jīngxǐ	4.5
pleasant, happy	愉快		yúkuài	2.5
plough and sow, cultivate	耕种	耕種	gēngzhòng	2.1EYK
politics	政治		zhèngzhì	4.1
pollution, pollute	污染		wūrǎn	2.4
popularize (accessible for ordinary people)	大众化	大衆化	dàzhònghuà	1.5EYK
pork	猪肉	豬肉	zhūròu	3.2
postal service	邮电	郵電	yóudiàn	1.3EYK
poster, slogan	标语	標語	biāoyǔ	3.4
prepare for a test	备考	備考	bèikǎo	1.4
press from both sides (pick up food with chopsticks)	夹		jiā	2.5
previous graduating classes	往届	往屆	wǎngjiè	4.1
principle, theory	原理		yuánlǐ	1.4
print	打印		dǎyìn	1.5
printer	打印机	打印機	dǎyìnjī	1.5

English	Simplified	Traditional	Pinyin	Lesson
prison	监狱	監獄	jiānyù	4.4
privatize	私有化		sīyǒuhuà	1.5EYK
procedures, formalities, processes	手续	手續	shǒuxù	4.3
process	加工		jiāgōng	2.1
production, produce	生产	生產	shēngchǎn	3.1
(promote) sales	促销	促銷	cùxiāo	3.3EYK
proper, serious	正经	正經	zhèngjīng	4.4
propose; proposal	提议	提議	tíyì	4.5
protein	蛋白质	蛋白質	dànbáizhì	2.4EYK
publish, print	登		dēng	4.4
push	推	推	tuī	3.3

Q

English	Simplified	Traditional	Pinyin	Lesson
quantity	数量	數量	shùliàng	2.2

R

English	Simplified	Traditional	Pinyin	Lesson
rabbit	兔子		tùzi	3.3
railway, rail	铁路	鐵路	tiělù	1.1
raw, uncooked	生		shēng	2.2
reach	达到	達到	dádào	3.2
reason, sense	道理		dàolǐ	1.4
recommendation letter	推荐信	推薦信	tuījiànxìn	4.3
recycle, recover	回收		huíshōu	3.4
reference, consult, refer to	参考	參考	cānkǎo	1.5
reflections, impressions	感想		gǎnxiǎng	1.4
refreshments	茶点	茶點	chádiǎn	4.5EYK
regard as, as	作为	作為	zuòwéi	4.1
regardless of, no matter (what, when, where, how…)	不管		bùguǎn	1.4
regardless of, no matter (what, whether…)	无论	無論	wúlùn	2.3

English	Simplified	Traditional	Pinyin	Lesson
regenerate, revive	再生		zàishēng	3.4
regenerated energy	再生能源		zàishēngnéngyuán	3.4EYK
register for examination	报考	報考	bàokǎo	4.1
rent	租金		zūjīn	4.4EYK
rent, lease	租		zū	4.3
renter	房客		fángkè	4.4EYK
repeat	重复		chóngfù	3.4
repeatedly, time and again	一再		yīzài	1.1
report	报告	報告	bàogào	3.5
represent	代表		dàibiǎo	3.5
reserve, make a reservation	预订	預訂	yùdìng	1.5
resident card	居留证	居留證	jūliú zhèng	1.2EYK
resource	资源	資源	zīyuán	3.1
re-study high school courses for next year's college entrance examination	复读	複讀	fùdú	4.1EYK
resume	简历	簡歷	jiǎnlì	4.2
return (goods)	退货	退貨	tuìhuò	3.3EYK
re-union with former classmates	老同学聚会	老同學聚會	lǎotóngxuéjùhuì	3.1EYK
rice (uncooked)	米		mǐ	2.5
rice ball (usu. w/stuffing)	饭团	飯糰	fàntuán	3.2
road	道路		dàolù	1.3EYK
romantic	浪漫		làngmàn	4.5
roommate	室友		shìyǒu	4.4

S

English	Simplified	Traditional	Pinyin	Lesson
safely, quietly	平平安安		píngpíng'ān'ān	3.1
salary card (Similar to an ATM card)	工资卡	工資卡	gōngzīkǎ	1.2EYK
sales	营销	營銷	yíngxiāo	2.2EYK
sales person	业务员	業務員	yèwùyuán	2.2EYK

English	Simplified	Traditional	Pinyin	Lesson
sales receipt	发票	發票	fāpiào	3.3EYK
sauce	酱		jiàng	2.5
save energy	节能	節能	jiénéng	3.4
save, practice thrift	节约	節約	jiéyuē	3.1
scenery, scene	景色		jǐngsè	1.1
scenic area	景区	景區	jǐngqū	1.1EYK
scenic point, scenic spot	景点	景點	jǐngdiǎn	3.1
seasoning	调料	調料	tiáoliào	2.5
second-hand store	二手店		èrshǒudiàn	3.4
seeing is believing	百闻不如一见	百聞不如一見	bǎi wén bù rú yī jiàn	1.6
seeking a job in…	求职意向	求職意向	qiúzhíyìxiàng	4.2EYK
select, choose	挑选	挑選	tiāoxuǎn	4.1
self-guided tour	自助游	自助遊	zìzhùyóu	1.1EYK
sell/sales	销售	銷售	xiāoshòu	2.2EYK
service industry	服务业	服務業	fúwùyè	4.2
set meal, set menu	套餐		tàocān	3.2
set up a pole and see its shadow – get instant results	立竿见影	立竿見影	lì gān jiàn yǐng	2.5
sewer	下水道		xiàshuǐdào	1.3EYK
share a ride	拼车	拼車	pīnchē	3.4
ship, transport	运	運	yùn	2.3
shipping	货运	貨運	huòyùn	2.2EYK
shipping cost	运费	運費	yùnfèi	3.3EYK
shopping center, big store	商城		shāngchéng	3.3EYK
shredded paper	纸屑	紙屑	zhǐxiè	3.1
sight, view	眼光		yǎnguāng	4.4
similar	相似		xiāngsì	2.3
simple	简单	簡單	jiǎndān	2.3
since	自从	自從	zìcóng	1.3
sizzling chicken	铁板鸡	鐵板雞	tiěbǎnjī	2.5EYK
slide	幻灯片	幻燈片	huàndēngpiàn	3.4

English	Simplified	Traditional	Pinyin	Lesson
smoke dust	烟尘	煙塵	yānchén	3.1
socialize	社会化	社會化	shèhuìhuà	1.5EYK
solar energy	太阳能	太陽能	tàiyángnéng	3.6
solve	解决		jiějué	2.1
soy milk	豆浆	豆漿	dòujiāng	3.2
special characteristics/feature	特色		tèsè	2.2
special skill, strong point, specialty	特长	特長	tècháng	4.1
spice	香料		xiāngliào	2.5
spicy chicken	辣子鸡	辣子雞	làzijī	2.5EYK
Spring Festival couplets	春联	春聯	chūnlián	3.1
standardization; standardize	标准化	標準化	biāozhǔnhuà	4.3
start a business	创业	創業	chuàngyè	2.2EYK
start writing	动笔	動筆	dòngbǐ	1.4
starting city	出发城市	出發城市	chūfāchéngshì	1.1EYK
starting date	出发日期	出發日期	chūfārìqī	1.1EYK
statement; state	陈述	陳述	chénshù	4.3
stay	呆		dāi	4.2
steamed chicken with onion	葱油鸡	蔥油雞	cōngyóujī	2.5EYK
storage (method)	保存方法		bǎocúnfāngfǎ	2.4EYK
street food, food sold on street	街头食品	街頭食品	jiētóu shípǐn	2.6
string, string together	串		chuàn	2.3
strive for, fight for	争取	爭取	zhēngqǔ	1.4
strong, dense, thick	浓	濃	nóng	2.2
student ID card	学生证	學生証	xuéshēng zhèng	1.2
student who is off the admission list	落榜生		luòbǎngshēng	4.1EYK
study abroad	留学	留學	liúxué	4.3
subject (in a curriculum), course	科目		kēmù	4.1
such, like that, so	如此		rúcǐ	4.3
suit, fit, be appropriate for	适合	適合	shìhé	3.5

English	Simplified	Traditional	Pinyin	Lesson
summary, summarize	总结	總結	zǒngjié	1.4
supplier	供应商	供應商	gòngyìngshāng	3.3EYK
support, feed	养活	養活	yǎnghuó	2.1
sushi	寿司	壽司	shòusī	2.3EYK
sweet and sour chicken	甜酸鸡	甜酸雞	tiánsuānjī	2.5EYK
swipe the card	刷（卡）		shuā (kǎ)	1.2
synchronous education	同步教学	同步教學	tóngbùjiàoxué	1.4EYK
synchronous, synchronization	同步		tóngbù	1.4

T

English	Simplified	Traditional	Pinyin	Lesson
taco, tortilla	玉米饼	玉米餅	yùmǐbǐng	2.3EYK
take up, occupy	占	佔	zhàn	2.1
taste	尝	嘗	cháng	2.2
taste	品尝	品嘗	pǐncháng	2.3
teachers who administer (monitor) the test	监考老师	監考老師	jiānkǎolǎoshī	4.1EYK
tender, delicate	嫩		nèn	2.2
terrible, terrifying	可怕		kěpà	4.4
test taker	考生		kǎoshēng	4.1EYK
test taker ID card	准考证	准考證	zhǔnkǎozhèng	4.1EYK
the earth, the globe	地球		dìqiú	1.6
the first step is difficult	万事开头难	萬事開頭難	wàn shì kāi tóu nán	4.2
the present graduating year	应届	應屆	yìngjiè	4.1
therefore, hence, for this reason	因此		yīncǐ	4.5
think, consider	认为	認為	rènwéi	4.2
throw, toss, cast	扔		rēng	3.4
topography, landform	地形		dìxíng	3.5
tour	游	遊	yóu	1.1
tour guide services	导游服务	導遊服務	dǎoyóufúwù	1.1EYK
tour guide throughout the trip	全程导游	全程導遊	quánchéngdǎoyóu	1.1EYK
tour route	旅游线路	旅遊線路	lǚyóuxiànlù	1.1EYK

English	Simplified	Traditional	Pinyin	Lesson
tour special	特价游	特價游	tèjiàyóu	1.1EYK
tourism website	旅游网	旅遊網	lǚyóuwǎng	1.1EYK
trash, rubbish	垃圾		lājī	3.1

U

unconsciously, unknowingly	不知不觉	不知不覺	bù zhī bù jué	3.3
underground water	地下水		dìxiàshuǐ	3.4EYK
unshakable in one's determination	铁了心	鐵了心	tiě le xīn	4.1
urbanize	城市化		chéngshìhuà	1.5EYK
use	使用		shǐyòng	3.4
utilities included	包水电	包水電	bāoshuǐdiàn	4.4EYK

V

vending machine	售货机	售貨機	shòuhuòjī	1.3
village	村子		cūnzi	1.1
visa; issue a visa	签证	簽證	qiānzhèng	4.3
visit relatives and friends	走亲访友	走親訪友	zǒuqīnfángyǒu	3.1EYK

W

wallet	钱包	錢包	qiánbāo	1.2
waste	浪费	浪費	làngfèi	3.3
wastewater	污水		wūshuǐ	3.4EYK
watch entertainment shows	看文娱表演		kànwényùbiǎoyǎn	3.1EYK
watch fireworks	看焰火		kànyànhuǒ	3.1EYK
watch sports competition	看体育比赛	看體育比賽	kàntǐyùbǐsài	3.1EYK
water bill	水费	水費	shuǐfèi	4.4EYK
water resource	水源		shuǐyuán	3.4EYK
water supply system	供水系统	供水系統	gòngshuǐxìtǒng	1.3EYK
weekly journal	周记	週記	zhōujì	1.4
well-known saying	名言		míngyán	2.5
Westernization, Westernize	西方化		Xīfānghuà	3.2

English	Simplified	Traditional	Pinyin	Lesson
wet	湿		shī	2.6
wheat	小麦	小麥	xiǎomài	2.1
when in Rome, do as the Romans do	入乡随俗	入鄉隨俗	rù xiāng suí sú	3.2
wild	野生		yěshēng	3.1
wind energy	风能	風能	fēngnéng	3.6
wireless	无线	無線	wúxiàn	1.3
wireless card	无线上网卡	無線上網卡	wúxiànshàngwǎngkǎ	1.2EYK
wish, aspiration, ideal	志愿	志願	zhìyuàn	4.1
withdraw money	取款		qǔkuǎn	1.2
wood	木头	木頭	mùtóu	3.6
work (experience)	工作经历	工作經歷	gōngzuòjīnglì	4.2EYK
work with hands	动手	動手	dòngshǒu	4.2
work with mind	动脑	動腦	dòngnǎo	4.2
worthwhile	值得	值得	zhídé	2.1

Y

English	Simplified	Traditional	Pinyin	Lesson
yield, output	产量	產量	chǎnliàng	2.1EYK

专有名词索引
Proper Nouns Index

This list contains proper nouns from each lesson's New Words and Extend Your Knowledge sections.

Simplified	Traditional	Pinyin	English	Lesson
M				
蒙古族		Ménggǔ zú	Mongolian, the Mongolian ethnic group	2.2
N				
南美洲		Nán Měizhōu	South America	2.3
南大		Nándà	Nanjing University	4.4
内蒙古高原		Nèiménggǔ gāoyuán	Inner Mongolia Plateau	3.5EYK
Q				
青藏高原		Qīng Zàng gāoyuán	Qinghai-Tibet Plateau	3.5EYK
S				
十二味香茶		shíèrwèi xiāngchá	tea with 12 flavors	2.2
T				
台湾海峡	台灣海峽	Táiwān hǎixiá	The Taiwan Straits	3.5EYK
唐朝		Tángcháo	the Tang Dynasty (618-907)	2.2
Y				
伊斯兰教	伊斯蘭教	Yīsīlánjiào	Islam	2.2
元朝		Yuáncháo	the Yuan Dynasty (1271-1368)	2.2
云贵高原	雲貴高原	Yún Guì gāoyuán	Yunnan-Guizhou Plateau	3.5EYK
Z				
中亚	中亞	Zhōng Yà	Central Asia	2.2

语言注释索引
Language Notes Index

Credits

Murray R. Thomas contributed the following images:

1.1 horse cart
1.1 ship
1.3 houses
1.4 computer
1.4 diary and pen
1.4 geometry
2.1 rice
2.1 tractor
2.2 fish
2.4 green food label
2.2 red pepper
3.3 rabbit
3.3 boar
3.3 hippo
3.3 elephant
3.5 map of China
4.6 dog
4.6 cat
4.6 bird
4.6 rabbit

Chuan Zhuang contributed the following images:

1.1 train
1.1 Shanghai railway station
1.1 boat
1.1 plane
1.1 plane 2
1.1 railroad
1.2 foodstand
1.2 on the bus
1.2 shopping street
1.3 Shanghai
1.3 ferry
1.3 subway station
1.4 university
1.5 library
1.6 a Chinese garden
1.6 small town in China
1.6 buildings
2.1 steamed bread
2.1 restaurant
2.2 food 1
2.2 food 2
2.2 food 3
2.2 dried fruits
2.2 Muslim restaurant
2.4 meat
2.4 inside a supermarket
2.5 variety of food
2.5 a dish
3.1 lights
3.1 God of Fortune
3.2 cruise ship
3.2 store 2
3.2 store 3
3.2 store 1
3.3 ads
3.3 ad on bus
3.3 buy, buy
3.4 bus stop
3.5 Huangpu River
3.6 traffic
3.6 construction
4.1 campus
4.2 tour bus
4.4 food stand
4.5 hotel
4.5 park

Jiaying Howard contributed the following images:

1.1 Great Wall
1.1 San Francisco
1.5 reading room
1.1 Yosemite
1.2 card ad
1.3 Dali
2.1 countryside
2.1 green area
2.2 Muslim
2.3 fruits and vegs
2.4 scenery
2.4 tea
2.6 HK street
2.6 Bai people
3.1 poster
3.1 Spring Festival
3.1 spring couplets
3.2 fast food
3.4 trash cans
3.4 environment ad 2
3.5 Sichuan
3.5 Gobi Desert
4.1 university
4.1 campus map
4.4 food store
4.5 Nanjing University

Lanting Xu contributed the following images:

1.2 entry card
1.3 vending machine
2.2 small restaurants
2.3 a western restaurant
3.2 goods
3.4 recycle
3.4 environmental ad
4.2 help wanted
4.2 help wanted 2
4.3 sports
4.4 real estate agency

Peizhi Bai contributed the following images:

2.1 mountains
3.5 village
3.5 fields on a hill
4.6 minority